T0259839

Java 13 Revealed

For Early Adoption and Migration

Second Edition

Kishori Sharan

Apress®

Java 13 Revealed: For Early Adoption and Migration

Kishori Sharan
Montgomery, AL, USA

ISBN-13 (pbk): 978-1-4842-5406-6   ISBN-13 (electronic): 978-1-4842-5407-3
https://doi.org/10.1007/978-1-4842-5407-3

Managing Director, Apress Media LLC: Welmoed Spahr
Acquisitions Editor: Steve Anglin
Development Editor: Matthew Moodie
Coordinating Editor: Mark Powers

Cover designed by eStudioCalamar

Cover image designed by Raw Pixel (www.rawpixel.com)

Distributed to the book trade worldwide by Springer Science+Business Media New York, 233 Spring Street, 6th Floor, New York, NY 10013. Phone 1-800-SPRINGER, fax (201) 348-4505, e-mail orders-ny@springer-sbm.com, or visit www.springeronline.com. Apress Media, LLC is a California LLC and the sole member (owner) is Springer Science + Business Media Finance Inc (SSBM Finance Inc). SSBM Finance Inc is a Delaware corporation.

For information on translations, please e-mail editorial@apress.com; for reprint, paperback, or audio rights, please email bookpermissions@springernature.com.

Apress titles may be purchased in bulk for academic, corporate, or promotional use. eBook versions and licenses are also available for most titles. For more information, reference our Print and eBook Bulk Sales web page at http://www.apress.com/bulk-sales.

Any source code or other supplementary material referenced by the author in this book is available to readers on GitHub via the book's product page, located at www.apress.com/9781484254066. For more detailed information, please visit http://www.apress.com/source-code.

Printed on acid-free paper

*To my friend Richard Castillo, who has been incredible
in helping me in my journey of writing books. Without his help,
I could not have published my three-book "Harnessing Java 7" series.
Thank you, my friend, for all your help.*

Table of Contents

About the Author

 **Kishori Sharan** is a Senior Software Engineer Lead at IndraSoft, Inc. He has 22 years of software development experience. At Indrasoft, he provides technical support to multiple projects ranging from migrating applications to AWS, data migration, coding, prototyping, and configuring AWS services to debugging and troubleshooting applications. He specializes in software development in Java, Spring, and AngularJS and using Amazon Web Services. He has published 12 books on the Java programming language and its related technologies such as JavaFX and Scripting in Java. He holds certifications in different programming languages and development platforms – Java, PowerBuilder, AWS Cloud Practitioner, AWS Solutions Architect Associate, and AWS Developer Associate. He has earned a Master of Science in Computer Information Systems from Troy University, Alabama. Having the opportunity to help multiple teams with different technologies is the best thing he likes to do. He maintains a personal web site: `www.jdojo.com`.

About the Technical Reviewer

Manuel Jordan Elera is an autodidactic developer and researcher who enjoys learning new technologies for his own experiments and creating new integrations. He won the Springy Award – Community Champion and Spring Champion 2013. In his little free time, he reads the Bible and composes music on his guitar. Manuel is known as dr_pompeii. He has tech-reviewed numerous books for Apress, including *Pro Spring Boot 2* (2019), *Rapid Java Persistence and Microservices* (2019), *Java Language Features* (2018), *Spring Boot 2 Recipes* (2018), and *Java APIs, Extensions and Libraries* (2018). Read his 13 detailed tutorials about many Spring technologies, contact him through his blog at www.manueljordanelera.blogspot.com, and follow him on his Twitter account @dr_pompeii.

Acknowledgments

My wife Ellen was patient when I spent long hours at my computer working on this book. I want to thank her for all of her support.

I want to thank my family members and friends for their encouragement and support: my mother, Pratima Devi; my elder brothers, Janki Sharan and Dr. Sita Sharan; my nephews, Babalu, Dablu, Gaurav, and Saurav; my sister, Ratna; my friends, Karthikeya Venkatesan, Preethi Vasudev, Rahul Nagpal, Ravi Datla, Vishwa Mohan, and many more not mentioned here.

My sincere thanks are due to the wonderful team at Apress for their support during the publication of this book. Thanks to Mark Powers, the Editorial Operations Manager, for providing excellent support and for being exceptionally patient with me. My special thanks to Manuel Jordan Elera, the technical reviewer, whose thorough approach to reviewing the book helped weed out many technical errors.

Last but not least, my sincere thanks to Steve Anglin, the Lead Editor at Apress, for taking the initiative for the publication of this book.

Introduction

Introduction to the First Edition

The Java community is excited to see the module system and Java shell finally added to the Java platform in JDK 9, and so am I. After all, we had to wait over 10 years to see this module system in action. Several previous JDK releases saw prototypes of the module system, which were later dropped. The introduction of the module system in JDK 9 has also been a bumpy ride. It went through several iterations of proposals and prototypes. I started writing this book in early 2016. I have to admit that this was a difficult book to write. I had to race against the JDK release date and the changes the Java team was making to the module system. I would write about a topic to find a few months later that the final release date for JDK 9 had moved and whatever I had written was no longer valid. Today is the last day of February 2016 and it seems that the dust has finally settled – the Java team and the Java community are happy with the module system – and you are going to get this book as it exists today. JDK 9 is scheduled to be released in late July 2017. JDK 9 is feature complete at the time of this writing. It is very unlikely that you will see many instances where something covered in this book does not work. However, five months is a long time in terms of software releases, so don't be surprised if a piece of code does not work and you have to tweak it a bit to make it work when you read this book.

In the beginning, this book was supposed to be 140 pages. As my writing progressed, I thought it would be a disservice to readers to write a book so short covering one of the biggest additions to the Java platform. I thank my publisher who never complained about me adding hundreds of pages to the book. I devoted nine chapters (Chapter 2 to Chapter 10) solely to describing the new module system. Chapter 11 covers the Java shell (JShell) with unmatched details.

I spent countless hours researching this topic. I was writing on topics that were under development. There were no materials on the Internet or in books that I could find to learn about these topics. One of the biggest challenges was the fast-changing JDK implementation during the development phase. My main sources of research were the Java source code, Java Enhancement Processes (JEPs), and Java Specification Requests (JSRs).

I also spent quite a bit of time reading the Java source code to learn more about some of the new topics in JDK 9. It was always fun to play with Java programs, sometimes for hours, and then add them to the book. Sometimes, it was frustrating to see that the code worked a week ago and then did not work anymore. Subscribing to the mailing lists for all JDK 9 projects helped me to stay in sync with the JDK development team. A few times I had to go through all the bugs on a JDK topic to verify that there was a bug that had not been fixed yet.

All's well that ends well. Finally, I am happy that I was able to include everything that matters to readers interested in learning Java SE 9. I hope you enjoy reading the book and benefit from it.

Introduction to the Second Edition

I am pleased to present the second edition of this book titled *Java 13 Revealed*. It has been about two and a half years when the first edition of this book titled *Java 9 Revealed* was published. Three Java versions 10, 11, and 12 have already been released; Java 13 is scheduled to be released in about 2 weeks on September 17, 2019. This edition of the book covers all new topics in Java from version 10 to 13 that are relevant to Java developers. If you are interested in learning only JDK9-specific topics, I suggest you to read my *Java 9 Revealed* book (ISBN: 978-1484225912), which contains only JDK9-specific topics.

It is my sincere hope that this edition of the book will help you learn new Java features added in version 10 through 13.

Structure of the Book

This book contains eight chapters, which can be read in any order. If you want to just learn a few new Java features, you need to read only chapters covering those features.

Chapter 1 explains the local variable type inference using the restricted type name var, which was added to Java 10.

Java has adopted a new time-based release model in which it will have a feature release every 6 months, an update release every 3 months, and a long-term support (LTS) release every 3 years. Chapter 2 explains the new Java versioning scheme, which was introduced in Java 9 and updated in Java 10.

Chapter 3 explains the HTTP Client API added in Java 11 as a standard feature that lets you work with HTTP requests and responses in Java applications. The API provides classes and interfaces to develop WebSocket client endpoints with authentication.

Chapter 4 explains the source-file mode for the `java` command, which was added in Java 11. The source-file mode lets you run a single Java source file using the `java` command without first compiling the source file.

Chapter 5 explains the new syntax and semantics for `switch`. It was added as a preview feature in Java 12 and continues as a preview feature in Java 13. This feature lets you use `switch` as statements as well as expressions.

Chapter 6 explains text blocks, which are multiline string literals with automatic transformations performed by the compiler. This is a preview feature added in Java 13. This chapter also explains methods added to the `String` class to support text blocks.

Chapter 7 explains class data sharing (CDS) for JDK classes and application classes, which can speed up the launch time for Java application and reduce runtime footprint. This chapter covers updates in CDS from Java 10 to Java 13.

Chapter 8 explains deprecation and removal of tools. It also covers APIs changes from Java 10 to Java 13. This chapter does not cover all tools and APIs – only those that are relevant to the Java application developers.

Audience

This book is designed to be useful for Java developers who have intermediate-level understanding of Java SE 9 and want to learn new features added to Java 10 through Java 13.

How to Use This Book

Each chapter covers a new Java feature, except Chapter 8, which covers changes to all important tools and APIs. You can read chapters in any order.

Source Code and Errata

Source code and errata for this book can be accessed via the **Download Source Code** button located at www.apress.com/us/book/9781484254066.

The source code contains an Apache NetBeans 11.1 project. The `src` directory contains all the source code for examples in this book. You can download Apache NetBeans from `https://netbeans.apache.org/`. If you prefer to use an IDE other than Apache NetBeans, you can create a Java project in your IDE and copy the source code files in the `src` directory from the supplied source code to the corresponding source code directory of your IDE. Many example programs use preview features. You will need to enable the preview features in your IDE before you can compile those programs. The preview feature is enabled in the Apache NetBeans project supplied with the source code.

Questions and Comments

Please direct all your questions and comments to the author at `ksharan@jdojo.com`.

CHAPTER 1

Local Variable Type Inference

In this chapter, you will learn

- What type inference is

- What local variable type inference is

- What the restricted type name var is

- The rules to use var to declare local variables, indexes of for-each loop and for loop, and formal parameters for implicitly typed lambda expressions

What Is Type Inference?

Suppose you want to store a person ID, say, 10, in a variable. You would declare the variable like

```
int personId = 10;
```

To store a list of person IDs, you would declare a variable like

```
ArrayList<Integer> personIdList = new ArrayList<Integer>();
```

How about rewriting these variable declarations as follows?

```
var personId = 10;
var personIdList = new ArrayList<Integer>();
```

You may say that this looks like JavaScript code, not Java code. That was correct until Java 10. Now you can use var to declare *local variables with an initializer*. The compiler

© Kishori Sharan 2019
K. Sharan, *Java 13 Revealed*, https://doi.org/10.1007/978-1-4842-5407-3_1

1

will take care of inferring the correct type – sometimes, unintended incorrect type – for your variables. In Java 10 and later, the previous snippet of code is the same as follows:

```
int personId = 10;
ArrayList<Integer> personIdList = new ArrayList<Integer>();
```

Does it mean that you do not need to use an explicit type to declare local variables in Java anymore? Does it mean that Java has become dynamically typed like JavaScript? No. None of these is true. Using var to declare local variables has limitations – some are technical, and some are practical. Java is still strongly and statically typed language. The examples you just saw are syntactic sugar added by the compiler. The compiler infers the type of the variables and generates the bytecode, which is the same as it used to generate before Java 10. The Java runtime never sees var! The next few sections will give you a little background of type inference and all the rules and exceptions on how and where to use var to declare local variables.

Everything in Java revolves around types. Either you are declaring types like classes and interfaces or are using them. Every expression and value you use in your program has a type. For example, the value 10 is of int type, 10.67 is of double type, "Hello" is of String type, and the expression new Person() is of Person type.

Deriving type of a variable or an expression from the context of its use is called *type inference.* Java already had type inference long before the introduction of var, for example, in lambda expressions and in object creation expression for a generic type. The following statement uses type inference, which infers the diamond operator (<>) on the right-hand side as <Integer> by reading the ArrayList<Integer> from the left-hand side:

```
ArrayList<Integer> personIdList = new ArrayList<>();
```

The following statement uses an implicitly typed lambda expression in which the types of the formal parameters n1 and n2 are inferred as Integer and Long, respectively:

```
BiFunction<Integer,Long,Double> avg = (n1, n2) -> (n1 + n2)/2.0;
```

What Is var?

Is var a keyword in Java 10? No. It is a *restricted type name* or a *context-sensitive keyword.* It is a type name, which means it denotes a type (primitive type or reference type) like int, double, boolean, String, List, and so on. Because var is a restricted type name, you can still use it as an identifier, except to define another type. That is, you can use var as variable names, method names, and package names. However, you cannot use it as the name of a class or an interface.

Java coding standards recommend that the names of classes and interfaces start with an uppercase letter. If you did not follow the coding standards and used var as a class or interface name, your code will break in Java 10 and later.

You can use var to declare local variables in the following contexts. There are many restrictions to this list. I will cover them one by one:

- Local variables with initializers

- Index in for-each loops

- Indexes in for loops

- Formal parameters in implicitly typed lambda expressions

The following are examples of using var to declare local variables with initializers:

```
// The type of birthYear is inferred as int
var birthYear = 1969;
```

```
// The type of promptMsg is inferred as String
var promptMsg = "Are you sure you want to proceed?";
```

```
// Assuming Person is a class, the type of john is inferred as Person
var john = new Person();
```

The following lambda expression computes the average of an Integer and a Long and returns a Double. The types of n1 and n2 are inferred as Integer and Long, respectively. Here, var is playing no role in type inference. I will explain it later in a separate section.

```
BiFunction<Integer,Long,Double> avg = (var n1, var n2) -> (n1 + n2)/2.0;
```

The compiler infers the type of the variable declared using var. If the compiler cannot infer the type, a compile-time error occurs. The compiler uses the type of the expression used as the initializer to infer the type of the variable being declared. Consider the previous variable declarations. In the first case, the compiler sees 1969, which is an integer literal of type int and infers type of the birthYear variable as int. When the source is compiled, the class file contains the statement

```
int birthYear = 1969;
```

Tip   Type inference using `var` is performed by the compiler. Using `var` has no impact on the existing class file and the runtime.

The same argument goes for the other two statements in which the type of the `promptMsg` and `john` variables are inferred as `String` and `Person`, respectively.

Looking at the previous examples, you may argue that why would you not write these statements using explicit types as the following?

```
int birthYear = 1969;
String promptMsg = "Are you sure you want to proceed?";
Person john = new Person();
```

You have a point. Except for saving a few key strokes, you really made the job of the readers of this code a little harder when you used `var`. When `var` is used, the reader must look at the initializer to know the type of the variable being declared. In simple expressions like these, it may not be very difficult to know the type of the initializer by just looking at it. One of the arguments made by the designer of the `var` type name is that using it to declare multiple variable at the same place makes the variable names easy to read because they all vertically align. Look at the following snippet of code:

```
var birthYear = 1969;
var promptMsg = "Are you sure you want to proceed?";
var john = new Person();
```

Compare the two previous snippets of code declaring the same set of variables. The latter is definably a little easier to read, but still a little harder to understand.

Let us consider the following variable declaration that uses a method call to initialize its value:

```
var personList = persons();
```

In this case, the compiler will infer the type of the `personList` variable based on the return type of the `persons()` method. For the readers of this statement, there is no way to tell the inferred type unless he looks at the declaration of the `persons()` method. I gave the variable a good name, `personList`, to indicate its type. However, it is still not clear whether it is a `List<Person>`, a `Person[]`, or some other type.

Consider another example of a variable declaration:

```
Map<Integer,List<String>> personListByBirthMonth = new HashMap<Integer,List
<String>>();
```

You can rewrite this statement as follows:

```
var personListByBirthMonth = new HashMap<Integer,List<String>>();
```

This time, the declaration looks much simpler and you may benefit from type inference offered by var, provided you keep the variable name intuitive enough to give a clue about its type.

You can mix var and explicit type names in the same section of the code – methods, constructors, static initializers, and instance initializers. Use var to declare variables whenever the types of the variables are clear to the readers, not just clear to you. If the reader of your code cannot figure out the variable types easily, use the explicit type names. Always prefer clarity over brevity. It is very important that you use intuitive variable names when you use var. Consider the following variable declaration:

```
var x = 156.50;
```

The variable name x is terrible. If your method is a few lines long, using x as the variable name may be excused. However, if your method is big, the reader will have to scroll and look at the variable declaration to find what x means whenever it appears in the method's body. So, it is important to keep the variable name intuitive. Consider replacing the previous variable declaration as follows:

```
var myWeightInPounds = 156.50;
```

No one reading the code that uses myWeightInPounds will have any doubts about its type.

A Quick Example

All programs in this chapter are in the jdojo.typeinference module as shown in Listing 1-1.

Listing 1-1. The Declaration of A Module Named jdojo.typeinference

```
// module-info.java
module jdojo.typeinference {
    exports com.jdojo.typeinference;
}
```

Listing 1-2 contains a test class to show you how to use the var restricted type name to declare local variables. I cover many more examples shortly. The comments in the code and the output make it obvious as to what is going on during the type inference. I do not explain the code any further.

Listing 1-2. Using the var Restricted Type Name to Declare Local Variables

```
// VarTest.java
package com.jdojo.typeinference;

import java.util.List;
import java.util.Arrays;
import java.util.function.BiFunction;

public class VarTest {
    public static void main(String[] args) {
        // The inferred type of personId is int
        var personId = 1001;
        System.out.println("personID = " + personId);

        // The inferred type of prompt is String
        var prompt = "Enter a message:";
        System.out.println("prompt = " + prompt);

        // You can use methods of the String class on prompt as you did
        // when you declared it as "String prompt = ..."
        System.out.println("prompt.length() = " + prompt.length());
        System.out.println("prompt.substring(0, 5) = "
                + prompt.substring(0, 5));

        // Use an explicit type name, double
        double salary = 1878.89;
        System.out.println("salary = " + salary);
```

```java
        // The inferred type of luckyNumbers is List<Integer>
        var luckyNumbers = List.of(9, 19, 1969);
        System.out.println("luckyNumbers = " + luckyNumbers);

        // The inferred type of cities is String[]
        var cities = new String[]{"Atlanta", "Patna", "Paris", "Gaya"};
        System.out.println("cities = " + Arrays.toString(cities));
        System.out.println("cities.getClass() = " + cities.getClass());

        System.out.println("\nList of cities using a for loop:");

        // The inferred type of the index, i, is int
        for (var i = 0; i < cities.length; i++) {
            System.out.println(cities[i]);
        }

        System.out.println("\nList of cities using a for-each loop:");

        // The inferred type of the index, city, is String
        for (var city : cities) {
            System.out.println(city);
        }

        BiFunction<Integer, Long, Double> avg
                = (var n1, var n2) -> (n1 + n2) / 2.0;
        System.out.println("\nAverage of 10 and 20 is "
                + avg.apply(10, 20L));
    }
}
```

```
personID = 1001
prompt = Enter a message:
prompt.length() = 16
prompt.substring(0, 5) = Enter
salary = 1878.89
luckyNumbers = [9, 19, 1969]
cities = [Atlanta, Patna, Paris, Gaya]
cities.getClass() = class [Ljava.lang.String;
```

```
List of cities using a for loop:
Atlanta
Patna
Paris
Gaya

List of cities using a for-each loop:
Atlanta
Patna
Paris
Gaya

Average of 10 and 20 is 15.0
```

I am sure you have many questions about local variable type inference covering different use cases. I attempt to cover most use cases in the next section with examples. I found the JShell tool, which is a command-line tool shipped with JDK 9, invaluable to experiment with var. If you are not familiar with the JShell tool, refer to Chapter 23 of my book titled *Beginning Java 9 Fundamentals* (ISBN: 978-1484228432). I use JShell many times to show code snippets and results in next sections. Make sure to set the feedback mode to the JShell session to verbose, so JShell prints the variable declarations with inferred types when you use var. The following JShell session shows a few of the variable declarations used in the previous examples:

```
C:\Java13Revealed>jshell
|  Welcome to JShell -- Version 13-ea
|  For an introduction type: /help intro

jshell> /set feedback verbose
|  Feedback mode: verbose

jshell> var personId = 1001;
personId ==> 1001
|  created variable personId : int

jshell> var prompt = "Enter a message:";
prompt ==> "Enter a message:"
|  created variable prompt : String
```

```
jshell> var luckNumbers = List.of(9, 19, 1969);
luckNumbers ==> [9, 19, 1969]
|  created variable luckNumbers : List<Integer>

jshell> var cities = new String[]{"Atlanta", "Patna", "Paris", "Gaya"}
cities ==> String[4] { "Atlanta", "Patna", "Paris", "Gaya" }
|  created variable cities : String[]

jshell> /exit
|  Goodbye

C:\Java13Revealed>
```

Rules of Using var

The previous sections covered the basic rules of using var. In this section, I cover more detailed rules with examples. While reading these rules, keep in mind that there was only one objective in introducing var in Java 10 – making developers' life easier by keeping the rules of using var simple. I use JShell sessions in examples. I explain the following rules of using var to declare local variables:

- Variable declarations without initializers are not supported.

- The initializer cannot be of the null type.

- Multiple variables in a single declaration are not supported.

- The initializer cannot reference the variable being declared.

- Array initializers by themselves are not supported.

- No array dimensions can be specified while declaring arrays.

- No poly expressions such as lambda expressions and method references are allowed as initializers.

- Instance and static fields are not supported.

- var is not supported as the return type of a method. You cannot use it to declare method's arguments either.

If you need to declare a variable that needs to use features not allowed according to these rules, use an explicit type instead of var.

No Uninitialized Variables

You cannot use var to declare uninitialized variables. In such cases, the compiler has no expression to use to infer the type of the variable.

```
jshell> var personId;
```

```
|  Error:
|  cannot infer type for local variable personId
|    (cannot use 'var' on variable without initializer)
|  var personId;
|  ^-----------^
```

This rule makes using var simple in your code and easy to diagnose errors. Assume that declaring uninitialized variables using var is allowed. You can declare a variable and assign it a value for the first time several lines later in your program, which would make the compiler infer the variable's type. If you get a compile-time error in another part, which tells you that you have assigned a value to your variable wrong type, you will need to look at the first assignment to the variable that decided the variable's type. This is called "action at a distance" inference error in which an action at one point may cause an error in another part later – making the developer's job harder to locate the error.

No null Type Initializers

You can assign null to any reference type variable. The compiler cannot infer the type of the variable if null is used as the initializer with var.

```
jshell> var personId = null;
|  Error:
|  cannot infer type for local variable personId
|    (variable initializer is 'null')
|  var personId = null;
|  ^------------------^
```

No Multiple Variable Declarations

You cannot declare multiple variables in a single declaration using var.

```
jshell> var personId = 1001, days = 9;
|  Error:
|  'var' is not allowed in a compound declaration
|  var personId = 1001, days = 9;
|        ^
```

Cannot Reference the Variable in the Initializer

When you use var, you cannot reference the variable being declared in the initializer. For example, the following declaration is invalid:

```
jshell> var x = (x = 1001);
|  Error:
|  cannot infer type for local variable x
|    (cannot use 'var' on self-referencing variable)
|  var x = (x = 1001);
|        ^
```

However, the following declaration is valid when you use an explicit type:

```
// Declares x as an int and initializes it with 1001
int x = (x = 1001);
```

No Array Initializers by Themselves

Array initializer such as {10, 20} is a poly expression, and its type depends on the left-hand side of the assignment. You cannot use an array initializer with var. You must use an array creation expression with or without an array initializer such as new int[]{10, 20) or new int[2]. In such cases, the compiler infers the type of the variable the same as the type used in array creation expression. The following JShell session shows a few examples:

```
jshell> var evens = {2, 4, 6};
|  Error:
|  cannot infer type for local variable evens
```

```
|    (array initializer needs an explicit target-type)
|  var evens = {2, 4, 6};
|  ^--------------------^

jshell> var evens = new int[]{2, 4, 6};
evens ==> int[3] { 2, 4, 6 }
|  created variable evens : int[]

jshell> var odds = new int[3];
odds ==> int[3] { 0, 0, 0 }
|  created variable odds : int[]
```

No Array Dimensions

While using var to declare a variable, you cannot use brackets ([]) after var or variable's name to specify the dimension of the array. The dimension of the array is inferred from the initializer.

```
jshell> var[] cities = new String[3];
|  Error:
|  'var' is not allowed as an element type of an array
|  var[] cities = new String[3];
|        ^

jshell> var cities = new String[3];
cities ==> String[3] { null, null, null }
|  created variable cities : String[]

jshell> var points3D = new int[3][][];
points3D ==> int[3][][] { null, null, null }
|  created variable points3D : int[][][]
```

No Poly Expressions As Initializers

Poly expressions need a target type to infer their types. No poly expressions such as lambda expression and method references are allowed in initializers for variable declaration using var. Array initializers are poly expressions, which are also not allowed. You need to use explicit types with poly expressions. The following JShell session shows a few examples in which I use var to declare variables with poly expression initializers, which generates errors. I also show using explicit types instead of var that does not generate errors.

```
jshell> var increment = x -> x + 1;
|  Error:
|  cannot infer type for local variable increment
|    (lambda expression needs an explicit target-type)
|  var increment = x -> x + 1;
|  ^-------------------------^

jshell> Function<Integer,Integer> increment = x -> x + 1;
increment ==> $Lambda$17/0x0000000800bb2c40@7823a2f9
|  created variable increment : Function<Integer, Integer>

jshell> var next = increment.apply(10);
next ==> 11
|  created variable next : Integer

jshell> var intGenerator = new Random()::nextInt;
|  Error:
|  cannot infer type for local variable intGenerator
|    (method reference needs an explicit target-type)
|  var intGenerator = new Random()::nextInt;
|  ^---------------------------------------^

jshell> Supplier<Integer> intGenerator = new Random()::nextInt;
intGenerator ==> $Lambda$18/0x0000000800bb3c40@4678c730
|  created variable intGenerator : Supplier<Integer>

jshell> int nextInteger = intGenerator.get();
nextInteger ==> -1522642581
|  created variable nextInteger : int
```

Inferring Types on Both Sides

In most cases, you get an error when the compiler cannot infer the type of the initializer and the variable. In some cases, Object is inferred as the type. Consider the following:

```
var list = new ArrayList<>();
```

The initializer uses a diamond operator, which makes the compiler infer the type for ArrayList<>, whereas using var on the left-hand side makes the compiler infer the type in ArrayList<>. You might expect an error in this case. However, the compiler replaces the previous declaration with the following:

```
ArrayList<Object> list = new ArrayList<>();
```

Consider the following snippet of code, which requires type inference on both sides:

```
public class NumberWrapper<E extends Number> {
    // More code goes here
}
```

```
var wrapper = new NumberWrapper<>();
```

In this case, the inferred type is the upper bound of the type parameter "E extends Number", which is Number. The compiler will replace the previous variable declaration with the following:

```
NumberWrapper<Number> wrapper = new NumberWrapper<>();
```

Inferring Non-denotable Types

Using var to declare variables may lead the compiler to infer non-denotable types such as capture variable types, intersection types, and anonymous class types. Consider the following snippet of code, which uses an anonymous class. Note that an anonymous class does not have a name, so it is non-denotable.

```
class Template implements Serializable, Comparable {
    @Override
    public int compareTo(Object o) {
        throw new UnsupportedOperationException("Not supported yet.");
    }
```

```
    // More code goes here
}

var myTemplate = new Template() {
    // More code goes here
};
```

What would be the inferred type of the variable myTemplate? If you specified an explicit type for the myTemplate variable, you had the following four choices:

- Template myTemplate = ...

- Serializable myTemplate = ...

- Comparable myTemplate = ...

- Object myTemplate = ...

The compiler has a fifth choice, which is the non-denotable type of the anonymous class. In this case, compiler infers the non-denotable type of the anonymous class. When you add a new method to the anonymous class, which does not override any method in its superclass or superinterface, you cannot call that method statically. That is, you cannot call that method in your source code – the compiler won't compile it. However, using var in anonymous class declaration allows you to do so, because your inferred variable type is compiler-generated non-denotable type of the anonymous class. The following JShell session demonstrates this:

```
jshell> var runnable = new Runnable() {
   ...>        public void run() {
   ...>            System.out.println("Inside run()...");
   ...>        }
   ...>
   ...>        public void test() {
   ...>            System.out.println(
   ...>                "Calling this method is possible because of var...");
   ...>        }
   ...> };
runnable ==> $0@7823a2f9
```

```
jshell> runnable.run();
Inside run()...
```

```
jshell> runnable.test();
Calling this method is possible because of var...
```

Consider the following statement, where the return type of the getClass() method in the Object class is Class<?>:

```
// The inferred type of name is String
var name = "John";
```

```
// The inferred type of cls is Class<? extends String>
var cls = name.getClass();
```

In this case, the capture variable type in Class<?> has been projected upward to the supertype of the class of the name variable and the inferred type of cls is Class<? extends String> rather than Class<?>.

Here is the last example of the inferred non-denotable types:

```
var list = List.of(10, 20, 45.89);
```

What would be the inferred type of the list variable? This is a harder case to understand. The arguments to the List.of() method are of Integer and Double types. The Integer and Double classes are declared as follows:

- public final class Integer extends Number implements
  Comparable<Integer>, Constable, ConstantDesc

- public final class Double extends Number implements
  Comparable<Double>, Constable, ConstantDesc

Both Integer and Double types implement three interfaces: Comparable, Constable, and ConstantDesc. The Constable and ConstantDesc interfaces were added in Java 12, and they are in the java.lang.constant package. In this case, the compiler projects the Integer and Double to their common supertype Number and uses an intersection of the Number and the three interface types as the inferred type.

The previous variable declaration (var list = List.of(10, 20, 45.89);) is equivalent to the following. Note that an intersection type is non-denotable, so you cannot use the following statement in your source code. I am showing it here just to show you the actual type being inferred. You can also use JShell to enter the previous statement to see the following as its inferred type:

```
List<Number&Comparable<? extends Number&Comparable<?>>&java.lang.
constant.Constable&java.lang.constant.ConstantDesc>&java.lang.constant.
Constable&java.lang.constant.ConstantDesc> list = List.of(10, 20, 45.89);
```

Using var to declare variables may become complex at the compiler level. Use explicit types in such situations to make your intention clear. Remember, clarity is more important than brevity. You could rewrite the previous statement as follows:

```
List<Number> list = List.of(10, 20, 45.89);
```

Not Allowed in Fields and Methods Declarations

Using var to declare fields (instance and static), method's parameters, and method's return type is not allowed. Public fields and methods define the interface for a class. They are referenced in other classes. Making a subtle change in their declaration may need other classes to be recompiled. Using var in local variables has only local effects. This is the reason that fields and methods are not supported by var. Private fields and methods were considered during the design, but not supported, to keep the implementation of var simple.

Using final with var

You can use var to declare a final variable. The final modifier behaves the same as it did before the introduction of var. The following local variable declaration is valid:

```
// The inferred type of personId is int.
// personId is final. You cannot assign another value to it.
final var personId = 1001;
```

Formal Parameters in Lambda Expressions

Java 10 did not support var to declare formal parameters of implicitly typed lambda expressions. Consider the following statement, which uses an implicitly typed lambda expression:

```
BiFunction<Integer,Integer,Long> adder = (x, y) -> (long)(x + y);
```

In this case, the types of both x and y parameters are inferred as Integer. In JDK 10, you cannot write like

```
// A compile-time error in Java 10, but allowed in Java 11 and later
BiFunction<Integer,Integer,Long> adder = (var x, var y) -> (long)(x + y);
```

The previous statement is possible in Java 11, which introduced support for var in formal parameters in implicitly typed lambda expressions. Using var in formal parameters for implicitly typed lambda expressions plays no role in type inference. An implicitly typed lambda expression infers the type of its formal parameters from the context of its use. Both of the following statements are the same to the compiler:

```
BiFunction<Integer,Integer,Long> adder = (x, y) -> (long)(x + y);
BiFunction<Integer,Integer,Long> adder = (var x, var y) -> (long)(x + y);
```

In both cases, it is inferring the type for x and y by looking at the variable declaration on the left. You might wonder why you would even use var in this case. There are two simple reasons:

- For consistency in using the local variable type inference syntax

- For allowing modifiers and annotations to be used on the formal parameters of implicitly typed lambda expressions

Because var was allowed for local variable in other contexts, its designer allowed it on the formal parameters of implicitly typed lambda expressions just for the sake of consistency in its use. Remember that just using var with formal parameters in implicitly typed lambda expressions has no actual effect, except for consistency.

Before Java 11, you could not use modifiers or annotations on the formal parameters of an implicitly typed lambda expression. Suppose, in our example, you wanted to declare n1 and n2 as final. You cannot achieve it like so:

```
// A compile-time error
BiFunction<Integer,Long,Double> avg = (final n1, final n2) -> (n1 + n2)/2.0;
```

You can see the actual compile-time error in the following JShell session:

```
jshell> BiFunction<Integer,Long,Double> avg = (final n1, final n2) ->
(n1 + n2)/2.0;
|  Error:
|  <identifier> expected
|  BiFunction<Integer,Long,Double> avg = (final n1, final n2) ->
   (n1 + n2)/2.0;
|                                                   ^
|  Error:
|  <identifier> expected
|  BiFunction<Integer,Long,Double> avg = (final n1, final n2) ->
   (n1 + n2)/2.0;
|                                                         ^
```

If you wanted to use the final modifier on n1 and n2 before Java 11, you could do so by using an explicitly typed lambda expression:

```
BiFunction<Integer,Long,Double> avg = (final Integer n1, final Long n2) ->
(n1 + n2)/2.0;
```

From Java 11, you can declare the formal parameters of an implicitly typed lambda expression final by using var as follows:

```
BiFunction<Integer,Long,Double> avg = (final var n1, final var n2) ->
(n1 + n2)/2.0;
```

You can also use annotations on formal parameters for implicitly typed lambda expressions as follows:

```
BiFunction<Integer,Long,Double> avg = (@NonNull var n1, @NonNull var n2) ->
(n1 + n2)/2.0;
```

There are a few restrictions on using var with formal parameters in implicitly typed lambda expressions. They are described as follows:

An implicitly typed lambda expression must use var for all its formal parameters or for none.

```
// A compile-time error. Uses var only on one parameter n1, and not on both
BiFunction<Integer,Long,Double> avg = (var n1, n2) -> (n1 + n2)/2.0;
```

You can use var only on the formal parameters for implicitly typed lambda expression, not on explicitly typed lambda expressions. That is, you cannot specify the explicit type for some formal parameters and use var on others.

```
// A compile-time error. Mixes var and explicit type Long
BiFunction<Integer,Long,Double> avg = (var n1, Long n2) -> (n1 + n2)/2.0;
```

It might seem counterintuitive not to allow var in semi-implicitly typed lambda expressions as the previous one. In this case, the compiler has to infer type partially – only for the formal parameter n1. It is simply not allowed because the type inference and overload resolution become very complex in these cases. Mixing of var with explicit type for formal parameters may be allowed in the future.

For brevity, implicitly typed lambda expressions allow you to drop the parenthesis when you have only one formal parameter:

```
Function<Integer,Integer> twice = x -> x * 2;
```

If you use var to declare the formal parameter in the previous lambda expression, you must use parentheses:

```
Function<Integer,Integer> twice = var x -> x * 2; // A compile-time error
Function<Integer,Integer> twice = (var x) -> x * 2; // OK
```

Backward Compatibility

If your existing code uses var as a class or interface name, your code will break in Java 10 and later. Using it as method, package, and variable names is fine. It is very unlikely that you have named a class or interface as var because that would have been against the Java naming convention.

Summary

Deriving type of a variable or an expression from the context of its use is called type inference. Java 10 introduced a restricted type name called var that can be used to declare local variables with initializers and indexes for for-each and for loops. Java 11 extended the support for var in declaring the formal parameters of implicitly typed lambda expressions. The type of the variable declared using var is inferred from the expression in the initializer. var is not a keyword; rather, it is a restricted type name, which means you cannot have a type such as a class or interface named as var. If you have a type named var in your existing code, your code will break when compiled in JDK 10 and later.

It is not always possible to infer the type of local variables from initializers. For example, if the initializer is null, it is not possible to infer the type. There are few limitations for using var to declare variables:

- Variable declarations without initializers are not supported.

- The initializer cannot be of the null type.

- Multiple variables in a single declaration are not supported.

- The initializer cannot reference the variable being declared.

- Array initializers by themselves are not supported.

- No array dimensions can be specified while declaring arrays.

- No poly expressions such as lambda expressions and method references are allowed in initializer.

- Instance and static fields are not supported.

- Using var on some but not on all formal parameters in implicitly typed lambda expressions is not allowed.

- You cannot mix var and explicitly typed formal parameters in a lambda expression.

- If you use var to declare a formal parameter for an implicitly typed lambda expression, you must enclose the formal parameter declaration in parentheses even if there is only one formal parameter.

CHAPTER 2

Java Versioning Scheme

In this chapter, you will learn

- About the old and new Java release models

- What the JDK versioning scheme had been before JDK 9

- About the new JDK versioning scheme in JDK 9 and its updates in JDK 10

- How to parse a JDK version string using the `Runtime.Version` class

- About the formats used to print the Java version string using different options with the `java` command

Java Release Models

Up to Java 9, which was released in September 2017, Java used a feature-driven release model with a new feature release every 2 years. In this model, every feature release contained one or more major features. Several times, a new feature release, for example, Java 8 and Java 9, was delayed by several months –sometimes over a year – because the development of the major features was not complete. This release model had a major drawback that small features had to wait for a long time to be available to developers.

Java has switched to a new time-based release model in which it will have

- A feature release every 6 months

- An update release every 3 months

- A long-term support (LTS) release every 3 years

In the new time-based release model, you will get a new feature release every 6 months, starting from March 2018, for example, Java 10 in March 2018, Java 11 in September 2018, Java 12 in March 2019, Java 13 in September 2019, and so on. A feature

© Kishori Sharan 2019
K. Sharan, *Java 13 Revealed*, https://doi.org/10.1007/978-1-4842-5407-3_2

release may contain small and/or big additions to the Java language, JVM, or APIs. Development of a new feature is a continuous process, which is not linked to any future feature release until the feature is completely developed. Once a new feature is completely developed, it is merged to the upcoming feature release. This way, a new feature will not delay any upcoming release.

Starting from April 2018, you will get a new update release every 3 months in April, July, October, and January. An update release will contain only security fixes and bug fixes for newer releases.

Starting from September 2018, you will get an LTS feature release, which will be supported through updates for at least 3 years.

What Is a Version String?

Each release of Java is identified by a unique string, which is known as the *version string*. For example, the version strings "1.8", "9", and "10" identify three different Java releases. The Java version string is important for several reasons. If you are developing a Java application, you want to use a Java version based on features supported by Java, support available in your organization, and how long the Java version will be supported by your vendor. Until Java 9, Java used version strings, which were like "1.7", "1.8.0_162", and so on. Java 9 introduced a new version string scheme, and Java 10 extended the version string scheme introduced in Java 9. The subsequent sections will give you an overview of all the version string schemes and how to print them on command line and use them in programs.

Old Version String Scheme

Before JDK 9, the version string used to be of the following form:

```
$n.$feature.$maintenance_$update-$identifier
```

Here,

- $n is always 1.

- $feature is an integer incremented sequentially starting from 1, and it indicates a feature release that contains new functionalities.

- $maintenance is an integer to indicate a maintenance release, which contains engineering focused bug fixes. It is always zero for a feature release.

- $update is a two-digit integer with a leading zero if needed. It indicates a customer focused bug fixes. $update is not numbered sequentially.

- $identifier is used to identify a milestone before general availability (GA) of a product such as "ea" for early access build, beta for beta release, build number, and so on. Identifier is not part of the version string for GA releases.

The following are a few examples of the JDK version strings before JDK 9:

- "1.8.0" is a GA feature release.

- "1.8.0_162" is an update release (with an update number 162) for the feature release "1.8.0".

- "1.8.0_162-b12" is an update release (with an update number 162) for the feature release "1.8.0" with a build identifier of "b12".

Before JDK 9, the JDK versioning scheme was not intuitive to developer and not easy for programs to parse. Looking at two JDK versions, you could not tell the subtle differences between them. It was hard to answer a simple question: Which release contains the most recent all security fixes "1.7.0_55" or "1.7.0_60"? The answer is not the obvious one, which you would have guessed – "1.7.0_60". Both releases contain the same security fixes. What is the difference between releases named *JDK 8 Update 66*, *1.8.0_66*, and *JDK 8u66*? They represent the same release. It was necessary to understand the versioning scheme in detail before you could tell the details contained in a version string. For example, after the initial release of JDK 1.5.0, the update release numbers in multiple of 20 meant different types of updates than the odd update numbers. The text in this section has not given you enough information to understand the JDK version string scheme completely. Refer to the following web pages for more details on the JDK version string schemes before JDK 9:

- www.oracle.com/technetwork/java/javase/versioning-naming-139433.html

- www.oracle.com/technetwork/java/javase/overview/jdk-version-number-scheme-1918258.html

New Version String Scheme

JDK 9 attempted to standardize the JDK versioning scheme, so it could be easily understood by humans, be easily parsed by programs, and follow the industry-standard versioning scheme.

JDK 9 added a static nested class named `Runtime.Version`, which represents a version string for an implementation of the Java SE Platform. The class can be used to represent, parse, validate, and compare version strings.

A *version string* consists of the following four elements in order. Only the first element is mandatory:

- Version number (`$vnum`)

- Pre-release information (`$pre`)

- Build information (`$build`)

- Additional information (`$opt`)

The following regular expression defines the format for a version string:

```
$vnum(-$pre)?(\+($build)?(-$opt)?)?
```

A *short version string* consists of a version number optionally followed by pre-release information:

```
$vnum(-$pre)?
```

You can have a version string as short as "9" and "10", which contains only the feature release number, and as big as "10.0.1.2-ea+40-20180201.07.36am", which contains all parts of a version string. I have made this big version string up to show you all elements of a version string. Typically, a pre-release (with -ea in the version string) does not have update and patch releases. The subsequent sections explain all parts and their sub-parts of the version string in details.

Version Number

A version number is a sequence of elements separated by a period. It can be of an arbitrary length. Its format is as follows:

```
^[1-9][0-9]*(((\.0)*\.[1-9][0-9]*)*)*$
```

A version number may consist of one to four elements or more, which are as follows. The fifth and subsequent elements do not have any specific meanings; JDK vendors can use them to identify vendor-specific patches. The format of a version number is as follows:

`$feature.$interim.$update.$patch(.$addtionalInfo)`

The `$feature` element was called `$major` in JDK 9. It is a feature release counter, which is increased by 1 for every feature release. A feature release represents a major version of a JDK release and contains new features. For example, the feature release for JDK 10 is 10 and for JDK 11 is 11. When the feature number is incremented, all other parts in the version number are removed. For example, if you have a version number 10.0.2.1, the new version number will be 11 when the feature counter is incremented from 10 to 11. With a 6-month release model, `$feature` will be incremented by 1 in March and September every year, starting from March 2018. Therefore, the March 2018 release is JDK 10, the September 2018 release is JDK 11, the March 2019 release is JDK 12, and so on.

The `$interim` element was called `$minor` in JDK 9. It represents a non-feature release that contains compatible bug fixes and enhancements. An interim release will not contain any incompatible changes, feature removals, or any changes to standard APIs. The value for `$interim`, if present, is always zero because in a 6-month release model there will be no interim releases. In the future, the release model may change to start including interim releases and, in that case, `$interim` will be used.

The `$update` element was called `$security` in JDK 9. It is incremented for compatible update releases that fix security issues, regressions, and bugs in newer features.

The `$patch` element represents an emergency patch release containing fixes for critical issues.

The following rules apply to a version number:

- All elements must be an unsigned integer.

- Only `$feature` is mandatory.

- Elements of a version number cannot contain leading zeros. For example, the second update version of the JDK 10 is 10.0.2, not 10.0.02.

- Trailing elements cannot be zero. That is, you cannot have a version number as 10.0.0.0. It can be 10, 10.0.1, 10.0.0.1, and so on.

- When an element is incremented, all subsequent elements are removed. Suppose the current JDK version is 10.0.1.4. If the update counter is incremented from 1 to 2, the patch counter 4 will be reset to zero and hence removed making the version number as 10.0.2. If the feature counter is incremented to 11, all other counters will be removed and the version number will change from 10.0.1.4 to 11.

- Two version numbers are compared using their respective counters from left to right. For example, 10.0.4.1 is greater than 10.0.3.5, but less than 10.0.4.2.

Pre-release Information

The $pre element in a version string is a pre-release identifier such as ea for an early access release, snapshot for a pre-release snapshot, and internal for a developer internal build. It is optional. If it is present, it is prefixed with a hyphen (-) and it must be alphanumeric matching the regular expression ([a-zA-Z0-9]+). The version string "10-ea" contains 10 as a version number and ea as a pre-release identifier.

Build Information

The $build element in a version string is a build number incremented for each promoted build. It is optional. It is reset to 1 when any part of the version number is incremented. If it is present, it is prefixed with a plus sign (+) and it must match the regular expression (0|[1-9][0-9]*). The version string "10-ea+40" contains 40 as the build number.

Additional Information

The $opt element in a version string contains additional build information such as date and time of an internal build. It is optional. It is alphanumeric and can contain hyphens and periods. If it is present, it is prefixed with a hyphen (-) and it must match the regular expression ([-a-zA-Z0-9\.]+). If $build is absent, you need to prefix $opt with a plus sign followed by a hyphen (+-). For example, in "10-ea+40-2018-02-19", $build is 40 and $opt is "2018-02-19"; in "9+-123", $pre and $build are absent and $opt is 123. The version string "10-ea+40-20180219.07.36am" embeds the date and time of the release in its additional information element.

Parsing Old and New Version Strings

Before JDK 9, JDK releases had either been Limited Update releases that include new functionality and non-security fixes or Critical Patch Updates that only include fixes for security vulnerabilities. The version string included the version number including the update number and the build number. Limited Update releases were numbered in multiples of 20. Critical Patch Updates used odd numbers, which were calculated by adding multiples of 5 to the prior Limited Update and, when needed, adding 1 to keep the resulting number odd. An example is 1.8.0_31-b13, which is update 31 of the major version 8 of the JDK. Its build number is 13. Note that prior to JDK 9, the version string always started with 1.

Your existing code that parses the version string to get the feature version of a JDK release may fail in JDK 9 and later, depending on the logic it used. For example, if the logic looked for the feature version at the second element by skipping the first, which used to be always 1 before JDK 9, the logic will fail. For example, if it returned 8 from 1.8.0, now it will return 0 from 10.0.1.0 where you would expect 10.

Changes to System Properties

In JDK 9, the values returned for the system properties that contain the JDK version string have changed. Table 2-1 contains the list of those system properties and the format of their values. $vstr, $vnum, and $pre in the table mean version string, version number, and pre-release information, respectively.

Table 2-1. *System Properties and Their Changed Values in JDK 9*

System Property Name	Value
java.version	$vnum(\-$pre)?
java.runtime.version	$vstr
java.vm.version	$vstr
java.specification.version	$vnum
java.vm.specification.version	$vnum

JDK 10 added two new system properties:

- `java.version.date`
- `java.vendor.version`

The `java.version.date` system property contains the GA date of the current JDK release in ISO-8601 YYYY-MM-DD format. For early access releases, this is the planned GA date for the release. This system property lets you figure out how old your JDK is. Its value is also printed when you print the JDK version using "`java --version`" and other commands.

The `java.vendor.version` system property is a vendor-specific product version string. It is optional and assigned by the JDK vendor. Its value, if set, must match the regular expression \p{Graph}+ which allows one or more alphanumeric and punctuation characters. In the open JDK, it is set to the $year.$month, which indicates the year and month of the JDK release. For example, in JDK 10, it is set to 18.3, which means March 2018 release of the JDK. Its value is also printed when you print the JDK version using "`java --version`" and other commands.

Using the Runtime.Version Class

JDK 9 added a static nested class called `Runtime.Version` whose instances represent version strings. The class does not have a public constructor. You can obtain an instance of this class in the following two ways:

- Using the static `version()` method of the `Runtime` class
- Using the static `parse(String vstr)` method of the `Runtime.Version` class

The static `version()` method of the `Runtime` class returns a `Runtime.Version`, which represents the version of the JRE. The following snippet of code prints the current version of the JRE, which indicates that my JRE is an early access build 29 of the feature release 13:

```
Runtime.Version version = Runtime.version();
System.out.println(version);
```

13-ea+29

You can use the parse() method of the Runtime.Version class to parse a version string and obtain a Runtime.Version. The parse() method throws an IllegalArgumentException if the specified string is not a valid version string:

```
// Parse a version string "12.0.1+12"
Runtime.Version version = Runtime.Version.parse("12.0.1+12");
System.out.println(version);
```

```
12.0.1+12
```

The following methods in the Runtime.Version class return elements of a version string. Method names are intuitive enough to guess the type of element they return:

- int feature()

- int interim()

- int update()

- int patch()

- Optional<String> pre()

- Optional<Integer> build()

- Optional<String> optional()

Tip   The major(), minor(), and security() methods in the Runtime. Version class were deprecated in JDK 10. Use the feature(), interim(), and update() methods of the class instead.

Notice that for the optional elements, $pre, $build, and $opt, the return type is Optional. For the optional $interim, $update, and $patch elements, the return type is int, not Optional, which will return zero if they are absent in the version string.

The version number in a version string may contain additional information after the fourth element. The Runtime.Version class does not contain a method to get the additional information directly. It contains a version() method that returns a List<Integer> where the list contains all elements of the version number. The first four elements in the list are $feature, $interim, $update, and $patch in order. The

31

remaining elements are the additional version number information. The list contains at least one element, which is the feature version number (`$feature`).

The `Runtime.Version` class contains methods to compare two version strings for order and equality. You can compare them with or without the optional build information (`$opt`). Those comparison methods are as follows:

- `int compareTo(Runtime.Version v)`

- `int compareToIgnoreOptional(Runtime.Version v)`

- `boolean equals(Object v)`

- `boolean equalsIgnoreOptional(Object v)`

The expression `v1.compareTo(v2)` will return a negative integer, zero, or a positive integer if `v1` is less than, equal to, or greater than `v2`. The `compareToIgnoreOptional()` method works the same way as the `compareTo()` method, except that it ignores the optional build information while comparing. The `equals()` and `equalsIgnoreOptional()` methods compare two version strings for equality with and without the optional build information.

Which version string represents the latest build, `10.0.1.1` or `10.0.1.1-ea`? The first one does not contain the pre-release element, whereas the second one does, so the first one is the latest build. Which version string represents the latest build, `10.0.1.1` or `10.0.1.2-ea`? This time, the second one represents the latest build because the version number `10.0.1.1` is considered less than `10.0.1.2`. When the version number is greater, other elements in the version string are not compared. Here are the detailed rules for comparing two version strings:

- Comparison occurs in the following sequence: `$vnum`, `$pre`, `$build`, and `$opt`.

- Comparison begins by comparing each element of the version number. A zero is assumed if any part in the version number is missing. In the string from the feature version number, if any element in first version string is greater than the corresponding element in the second version string, the first version string is greater. For example, 10.0.1.1 is less than 11.

- If two version strings are the same based on their version numbers, the pre-release elements are compared. A version string with a pre-release element is always less than a version string without one. If pre-release elements consist only of digits, numerical comparison is made; otherwise, they are compared lexicographically. A numeric pre-release element is considered less than a non-numeric one.

- A version without a build number is always less than the one with a build number. If both version strings have a build number, they are compared numerically.

- A version with additional information element ($opt) is considered greater than the one without a $opt. Otherwise, the values of $opt are compared lexicographically.

Programs in this chapter are in the `jdojo.version.scheme` module as shown in Listing 2-1.

Listing 2-1. A Module Named jdojo.version.scheme

```
// module-info.java
module jdojo.version.scheme {
    exports com.jdojo.version.scheme;
}
```

Listing 2-2 contains a complete program to show how to extract all parts of version string using the `Runtime.Version` class. You may get a different output in the first section where the details of the current JRE version are printed.

Listing 2-2. A VersionTest Class That Shows How to Use the Runtime.Version Class to Work with Version Strings

```
// VersionTest.java
package com.jdojo.version.scheme;

import java.lang.Runtime.Version;
import java.util.stream.Collectors;
import static java.lang.System.out;

public class VersionTest {
```

```java
public static void main(String[] args) {
    // Print the version string details of the current JRE
    Version jreVersion = Runtime.version();
    out.println("Current JRE Version: " + jreVersion);
    printVersionDetails(jreVersion.toString());

    // Have some version strings
    String[] versionStrings = {
        "10", "10.1", "10.0.1.2", "10.0.2.3.4", "10.0.0",
        "10.1.2-ea+153", "10+132", "10-ea+24-2018-01-23", "10+-123",
        "10.0.1-ea+132-2018-01-28.10.56.45am"};

    // Parse each version string and display their components
    for (String vstr : versionStrings) {
        printVersionDetails(vstr);
    }
}

public static void printVersionDetails(String vstr) {
    try {
        Version version = Version.parse(vstr);

        // Get the additional version number elements which starts
        // at the 5th element in the version number part
        String vnumAdditionalInfo = version.version()
                .stream()
                .skip(4)
                .map(n -> n.toString())
                .collect(Collectors.joining("."));

        out.printf("Version String=%s%n", vstr);
        out.printf("feature=%d, interim=%d, update=%d, patch=%d,"
                + " additional info=%s,"
                + " pre=%s, build=%s, optional=%s %n%n",
                version.feature(),
                version.interim(),
                version.update(),
                version.patch(),
```

```
                vnumAdditionalInfo,
                version.pre().orElse(""),
                version.build().isPresent()
                ? version.build().get().toString()
                : "",
                version.optional().orElse(""));
        } catch (Exception e) {
            out.printf("%s%n%n", e.getMessage());
        }
    }
}
```

```
Current JRE Version: 13-ea+29
Version String=13-ea+29
feature=13, interim=0, update=0, patch=0, additional info=, pre=ea,
build=29, optional=

Version String=10
feature=10, interim=0, update=0, patch=0, additional info=, pre=, build=,
optional=

Version String=10.1
feature=10, interim=1, update=0, patch=0, additional info=, pre=, build=,
optional=

Version String=10.0.1.2
feature=10, interim=0, update=1, patch=2, additional info=, pre=, build=,
optional=

Version String=10.0.2.3.4
feature=10, interim=0, update=2, patch=3, additional info=4, pre=, build=,
optional=

Invalid version string: '10.0.0'

Version String=10.1.2-ea+153
feature=10, interim=1, update=2, patch=0, additional info=, pre=ea,
build=153, optional=
```

```
Version String=10+132
feature=10, interim=0, update=0, patch=0, additional info=, pre=,
build=132, optional=

Version String=10-ea+24-2018-01-23
feature=10, interim=0, update=0, patch=0, additional info=, pre=ea,
build=24, optional=2018-01-23

Version String=10+-123
feature=10, interim=0, update=0, patch=0, additional info=, pre=, build=,
optional=123

Version String=10.0.1-ea+132-2018-01-28.10.56.45am
feature=10, interim=0, update=1, patch=0, additional info=, pre=ea,
build=132, optional=2018-01-28.10.56.45am
```

Printing Java Version Strings

You can use one of the options in Table 2-2 with the java command to print the Java product version string. The output is printed to the standard output or standard error.

Table 2-2. *Options for the java Command to Print the Product Version*

Option	Description
-version	Prints the product version to the error stream and exits.
--version	Prints the product version to the output stream and exits.
-showversion	Prints the product version to the error stream and continues.
--show-version	Prints the product version to the output stream and continues.
-fullversion	Prints the product version to the error stream and exits.
--full-version	Prints the product version to the output stream and exits.

These options differ in three ways: the output format, the destination of the output, and the post-output behavior. I will show their output format shortly. If an option continues, it means it prints the output to its destination and continues to execute other parts of the command, if any. For example, you can use the -showversion and --show-version options to print the product version and run a class:

```
java --show-version --module-path dist --module test/com.jdojo.Test
```

The following is the list of the output formats of each of the options where \u0020 stands for the Unicode value for the space character. In the format specifier,

- The free-form text such as "openjdk version" will be printed as is for open JDK. When you use Oracle JDK, "openjdk version" is replaced with "java version".

- ${LTS} expands to "\u0020LTS" if the first three characters in the $opt part of the version string are "LTS".

- ${JVV} expands to "\u0020${java.vendor.version}" if the java.vendor.version system property is defined.

```
C:\> java -version
openjdk version \"${java.version}\" ${java.version.date}${LTS}
${java.runtime.name}${JVV} (build ${java.runtime.version})
${java.vm.name}${JVV} (build ${java.vm.version}, ${java.vm.info})

C:\> java --version
openjdk ${java.version} ${java.version.date}${LTS}
${java.runtime.name}${JVV} (build ${java.runtime.version})
${java.vm.name}${JVV} (build ${java.vm.version}, ${java.vm.info})

C:\> java -showversion <other-options-if-any>
openjdk version \"${java.version}\" ${java.version.date}${LTS}
${java.runtime.name}${JVV} (build ${java.runtime.version})
${java.vm.name}${JVV} (build ${java.vm.version}, ${java.vm.info})
[Output of other options, if used...]

C:\> java --show-version <other-options-if-any>
openjdk ${java.version} ${java.version.date}${LTS}
${java.runtime.name}${JVV} (build ${java.runtime.version})
${java.vm.name}${JVV} (build ${java.vm.version}, ${java.vm.info})
[Output of other options, if used...]
```

```
C:\> java -fullversion
openjdk full version \"${java.runtime.version}\"
```

```
C:\> java --full-version
openjdk ${java.runtime.version}
```

The following is the output of using the `--version` option with the `java` command in Java 13 early access build 29. You may get a different output, which depends on the JRE version you are using.

```
C:\>java --version
openjdk 13-ea 2019-09-17
OpenJDK Runtime Environment (build 13-ea+29)
OpenJDK 64-Bit Server VM (build 13-ea+29, mixed mode, sharing)
```

Summary

Java has adopted a new time-based release model in which it will have a feature release every 6 months, an update release every 3 months, and a long-term support (LTS) release every 3 years. New feature releases will happen in March and September, starting from March 2018 with Java 10. Update releases will happen in January, April, July, and October. LTS releases will happen every 3 years starting from September 2018.

The non-intuitive versioning scheme for the JDK was revamped in JDK 9. A JDK version string consists of the following four elements in order, of which only the first one is mandatory: a version number, pre-release information, build information, and additional information. The regular expression "$vnum(-$pre)?(\+($build)?(-$opt)?)?" defines the format of a version string. In JDK 9, $vum consisted of four parts: $major.$minor.$security(.$additionalInfo). From JDK 10, $vnum consists of five parts: $feature.$interim.$update.$patch(.$addtionalInfo). The $feature, $interim, $update elements in $vnum in JDK 10 were called $major, $minor, and $security in JDK 9.

A short version string consists of only the first two elements – a version number optionally followed by pre-release information. You can have a version string as short as "10", which contains only the major version number, and as big as "10.0.1.1-ea+54-20180210.07.36am", which contains all elements.

JDK 9 added a static nested class called `Runtime.Version` whose instances represent JDK version strings. The class does not have a public constructor. You can get the current version of the JRE using the `version()` static method of the `Runtime` class. The method returns a `Runtime.Version`. You can use the `parse(String vstr)` static method of the `Runtime.Version` class to parse a version string to obtain a `Runtime.Version`. The `parse()` method may throw a runtime exception if the version string is `null` or invalid. The class contains several methods to get different parts of a version string.

JDK 10 has added two new system properties named `java.version.date` and `java.vendor.version`. The `java.version.date` system property contains the general availability (GA) date of the current JDK release in ISO-8601 YYYY-MM-DD format. The `java.vendor.version` system property is a vendor-specific product version string, which is optional and assigned by the JDK vendor.

The `Runtime.Version` class contains several methods to compare and retrieve different parts of a version string. For example, you can use the `feature()` method to get the $feature element for a version string. The `major()`, `minor()`, and `security()` methods in the `Runtime.Version` class have been deprecated in JDK 10; use the `feature()`, `interim()`, and `update()` methods of the class instead.

CHAPTER 3

The HTTP Client API

In this chapter, you will learn

- What the HTTP Client API is

- How to create HTTP clients

- How to make HTTP requests

- How to receive and process HTTP responses

- How to push unsolicited data from server to client using server push

- How to use HTTP basic authentication to authenticate access to resources on the server

- How to create WebSocket client endpoints

JDK 9 and 10 delivered the HTTP Client API as an incubator module. JDK 11 included it as a standard module named `java.net.http`. The types are in the `java.net.http` package.

What Is the HTTP Client API?

Java has supported HTTP Client API from very early releases. The legacy API supported HTTP/1.1, and it consisted of several classes and interfaces in the `java.net` package. The `URLConnection` was the base class to represent a communication, and the `HttpURLConnection` was the class to represent an HTTP communication. The legacy API had the following issues:

- It was designed to support multiple protocols such as http, ftp, gopher, and so on, many of which are not used anymore.

- It was too abstract and hard to use.

41

© Kishori Sharan 2019
K. Sharan, *Java 13 Revealed*, https://doi.org/10.1007/978-1-4842-5407-3_3

- It contained many undocumented behaviors.

- It supported only one mode, blocking mode, which required you to have one thread per request/response.

- It did not support HTTP/2.

In May 2015, the Internet Engineering Task Force (IETF) published a specification for HTTP/2. Refer to the web page at `https://tools.ietf.org/html/rfc7540` for the complete text of the HTTP/2 specification. HTTP/2 does not modify the application-level semantics. That is, what you know about and have been using about the HTTP protocol in your application have not changed. It has a more efficient way of preparing the data packets and sending them over to the wire between the client and the server. All you knew about HTTP before, such as HTTP headers, methods, status codes, URLs, and so on, remain the same. HTTP/2 attempts to solve many problems related to performance faced by HTTP/1.1 connections:

- HTTP/2 supports binary data exchange instead of textual data supported by HTTP/1.1.

- HTTP/2 supports multiplexing and concurrency, which means that multiple data exchanges can occur concurrently in both directions of a TCP connection and responses to requests can be received out of order. This eliminates the overhead of having multiple connections between peers, which was typically the case while using HTTP/1.1. In HTTP/1.1, responses must be received in the same order as the requests were sent, which is called *head-of-line* blocking. HTTP/2 has solved the head-of-line blocking problem by enabling multiplexing over the same TCP connection.

- The client can suggest the priority of a request, which may be honored by the server in prioritizing responses.

- HTTP headers are compressed, which reduces the header size significantly, thus lowering latency.

- It allows for unsolicited push of resources from server to clients, which is called server push.

Instead of updating the existing API for HTTP/1.1, the HTTP Client API in JDK 11 provides a new API that supports both HTTP/1.1 and HTTP/2. It is intended that the HTTP Client API will eventually replace the old API provided by the `URLConnection` class. The new API also contains classes and interfaces to develop client applications using the WebSocket protocol. Refer to the web page at `https://tools.ietf.org/html/rfc6455` for the complete WebSocket protocol specification. The new HTTP Client API has several benefits over the legacy API:

- It is simple. It is easy to learn and use for most common cases.

- It processes request and response bodies using reactive stream using the Flow API introduced in Java 9.

- It supports server push, which allows the server to push resources to the client without the client making an explicit request for those resources. It makes setting up WebSocket communication with servers simple.

- It supports HTTP/2 and HTTPS/TLS protocols.

- It works in both synchronous (blocking) and asynchronous (non-blocking) modes.

Components of the HTTP Client API

A typical HTTP communication consists of a request and a response. The client creates a request, which consists of a URL, headers, and a body. The request is sent to a server, which is indicated by the URL. The server responds with a response, which consists of a status code, headers, and a body. The HTTP Client API provides classes representing HTTP requests and responses.

The HTTP Client API is small. It consists of fewer than 20 types, four of which are the main types. Others are used while you are using one of these four. The new API also uses a few types from the legacy HTTP API. The new API is in the `java.net.http` package in the `java.net.http` module. If you want to use the HTTP Client API in your module, your module needs to read the `java.net.http` module.

The main four types in the HTTP Client API are as follows:

- The HttpClient class

- The HttpRequest class

- The HttpResponse<T> interface

- The WebSocket interface

An HttpClient acts as a container for storing configurations that can be used for multiple HTTP requests instead of setting them separately for each request.

An HttpRequest represents an HTTP request that can be sent to a server. Once you create an HttpRequest, it is immutable and can be reused to send the same request multiple times.

An HttpResponse represents an HTTP response. You do not create an HttpResponse; rather, you receive it as a response from a server to an HttpRequest.

A WebSocket represents a WebSocket client. You can create a WebSocket server using the Java EE 7 WebSocket API or using several other programming languages such as Python, NodeJS, and so on. This chapter does not show you how to create a WebSocket server.

Tip   An HttpClient is immutable. A few of the configurations stored in an HttpClient may be overridden for HTTP requests when such requests are built. You do not create an HttpResponse; it is returned to you as part of an HTTP request that you send to the server.

Instances of HttpClient, HttpRequest, and WebSocket are created using builders. Each of them contains a nested interface named Builder that is used to build an instance of that type.

The HTTP Client API is so simple to use that you can read an HTTP resource in just one statement! The following statement reads the contents at the URL http://httpbin.org/ip as a string using a GET HTTP request and prints the response body to the standard output:

```
HttpClient.newHttpClient()
        .sendAsync(HttpRequest.newBuilder()
                    .uri(URI.create("http://httpbin.org/ip"))
```

```
                    .build(), BodyHandlers.ofString())
        .thenApply(HttpResponse::body)
        .thenAccept(System.out::println)
        .join();
```

Do not worry if this statement looks intimidating. I will explain each of its parts after breaking them down into separate statements and then re-assembling them into one. At this point, all you need to know is that the new HTTP Client API is so simple and easy to use that you can read an HTTP resource by writing just one statement.

Setting Up Examples

Many examples in this chapter involve interacting with a web server. Instead of creating a web application for all examples, I use `httpbin.org`, which supports many types of HTTP and HTTPS communications for demonstration purposes. If you want to try the examples on any other web server, feel free to replace the URIs in the examples with yours. Note that `httpbin.org` web site is not mine. It is maintained by Kenneth Reitz. I am just using this web site in examples for this chapter. There is another web site `http://postman-echo.com` that provides functionalities similar to `httpbin.org`.

The code for examples of all HTTP client programs are in the `jdojo.http.client` module whose declaration is shown in Listing 3-1.

Listing 3-1. A Module Named jdojo.http.client

```
// module-info.java
module jdojo.http.client {
    requires java.net.http;
    exports com.jdojo.http.client;
}
```

A Quick Example

Let us have a quick, but complete, example in which you will send an HTTP request to a web server and print the status code and body of the response. Typical steps in an HTTP communication are as follows:

- Create an HttpClient to store HTTP configuration information.

- Create an HttpRequest and populate it with information to be sent to the server such as URI, header, HTTP method, request body, and so on.

- Send the request to the server using the HttpClient.

- Receive a response from the server as an HttpResponse<T>.

- Process the HTTP response such as print the status code and body.

You can create an HttpClient with default configurations using the newHttpClient() static method of the HttpClient class:

```
// Create an HttpClient
HttpClient client = HttpClient.newHttpClient();
```

The newBuilder() static method of the HttpRequest class returns a builder to create an HttpRequest. You need to call builder's methods to set parts of the request. Finally, you need to call the build() method that returns an HttpRequest:

```
// Create an HttpRequest
HttpRequest request = HttpRequest.newBuilder()
                        .uri(URI.create("http://httpbin.org/ip"))
                        .build();
```

The default request HTTP method used by the HttpRequest.Builder is GET. You can also set it explicitly by calling the GET() method on the builder:

```
// Create an HttpRequest
HttpRequest request = HttpRequest.newBuilder()
                        .uri(URI.create("http://httpbin.org/ip"))
                        .GET()
                        .build();
```

Call the send() method of the HttpClient to send the request to the server, which sends the request synchronously – it blocks until the response is received. While sending a request, you need to specify a body handler to process the response body. Several built-in body handlers are available from the factory methods of the HttpResponse. BodyHandlers class. For example, BodyHandlers.ofString() static method returns a body handler to process the response body as a String. The send() method returns an HttpResponse<T>, where the type parameter T is the type of the body handler. If the body handler if of type String, the send() method returns HttpResponse<String>. The statusCode() method of the HttpResponse returns the HTTP status code as an int and its body() method returns the response body. The send() method throws checked exceptions IOException and InterruptedExceptionIOException, so you need to handle the exceptions in your code. The following snippet of code shows how to send the request to the server and process its body as a String:

```
// Send the request to the server handling the response body as a String
HttpResponse<String> response
        = client.send(request, BodyHandlers.ofString());

// Get the response status and body
int statusCode = response.statusCode();
String body = response.body();
```

Listing 3-2 contains the complete program to send a request to the server and process the response. The URL http://httpbin/ip returns the IP address of the requestor in JSON format. The program reads the JSON data as String and prints it to the standard output. The response status code of 200 indicates success. You may get a different output.

Listing 3-2. Sending an HTTP Request to a Server and Processing the Response

```
// PrintMyIP.java
package com.jdojo.http.client;

import java.io.IOException;
import java.net.URI;
import java.net.http.HttpClient;
import java.net.http.HttpRequest;
import java.net.http.HttpResponse;
```

```java
import java.net.http.HttpResponse.BodyHandlers;

public class PrintMyIP {
    public static void main(String[] args) {
        // Create an HttpClient with default configurations
        HttpClient client = HttpClient.newHttpClient();

        // Create an HttpRequest
        HttpRequest request = HttpRequest.newBuilder()
                .uri(URI.create("http://httpbin.org/ip"))
                .build();

        try {
            // Send the request to the server
            HttpResponse<String> response
                    = client.send(request, BodyHandlers.ofString());

            // Get the response status and body
            int statusCode = response.statusCode();
            String body = response.body();

            // Print the response status and body
            System.out.println("Response Status: " + statusCode);
            System.out.println("Response body:\n" + body);
        } catch (IOException | InterruptedException e) {
            e.printStackTrace();
        }
    }
}
```

```
Response Status: 200
Response body:
{
  "origin": "75.76.172.37, 75.76.172.37"
}
```

Creating HTTP Clients

An HTTP request that is sent to a server needs to be configured so that the server knows which authenticator to use, the SSL configuration details, the cookie manager to be used, proxy information, the redirect policy if the server redirects the request, and so on. An instance of the `HttpClient` class stores these request-specific configurations, and they can be reused for multiple requests. You can override a few of these configurations on a per request basis. You need to use an `HttpClient` to send an HTTP request to a server. An `HttpClient` holds the following pieces of information that are used for all HTTP requests: an authenticator, a connection timeout, a cookie manager, an executor, a redirect policy, a request priority, a proxy selector, an SSL context, SSL parameters, and an HTTP version.

An *authenticator* is an instance of the `java.net.Authenticator` class. It is used for HTTP authentication. The default is to use no authenticator. The HTTP Client API has built-in support for HTTP basic authentication.

If the `HttpClient` cannot establish a new connection within the specified connection timeout, its `send()` method throws `HttpConnectTimeoutException` and its `sendAsync()` method completes exceptionally with `HttpConnectTimeoutException`. If a new connection is not needed – in the case of an established connection being reused – the connection timeout value has no effect.

A *cookie handler* is used to handle HTTP cookies. It is an instance of the `java.net.CookieHandler` class. The default is to use no cookie handler.

An *executor* is an instance of the `java.util.concurrent.Executor` interface, which is used to send and receive asynchronous HTTP requests and responses. A default executor is provided if it is not specified.

A *redirect policy* is one of the constants of the `HttpClient.Redirect` enum that specifies how to handle redirects issued by the server. The default is `NEVER`, which means the redirects issued by the server are never followed.

A *request priority* is the default priority for HTTP/2 requests, which can be between 1 and 256 (inclusive). It is a hint for the server to prioritize the request processing. A higher value means a higher priority.

A *proxy selector* is an instance of the `java.net.ProxySelector` class that selects the proxy server to use. The default is not to use a proxy server.

An *SSL context* is an instance of the `javax.net.ssl.SSLContext` class that provides an implementation for the secure socket protocol. A default `SSLContext` is provided, which works when you do not need to specify protocols or do not need client authentication.

SSL parameters are parameters for SSL/TLS/DTLS connections. They are stored in an instance of the javax.net.ssl.SSLParameters class.

An HTTP version is the version of HTTP, which is 1.1 or 2. It is specified as one of the constants of the HttpClient.Version enum: HTTP_1_1 and HTTP_2. It requests a specific HTTP protocol version wherever possible. The default is HTTP_2. That is, if you do not set the HTTP version in the HttpClient, by default, it will try using HTTP/2. If the server does not support HTTP/2, it will downgrade to HTTP/1.1.

Tip   An HttpClient is immutable. A few of the configurations stored in an HttpClient may be overridden for HTTP requests when such requests are built.

The HttpClient class is abstract and you cannot create its instances directly. There are two ways you can create instances of the HttpClient class:

- Using the newHttpClient() static method of the HttpClient class

- Using the build() method of the HttpClient.Builder interface

The following snippet of code gets an HttpClient, which contains default configurations:

```
// Get an HttpClient with default configurations
HttpClient defaultClient = HttpClient.newHttpClient();
```

You can also create an HttpClient using the HttpClient.Builder interface. The HttpClient.newBuilder() static method returns a new instance of the HttpClient.Builder interface. The HttpClient.Builder interface provides a method for setting each configuration value. The value for the configuration is specified as the parameter of the method and the method returns the reference of the builder object itself, so you can chain multiple methods. In the end, call the build() method that returns a configured HttpClient object. The following statement creates an HttpClient with the redirect policy set to ALWAYS, the HTTP version set to 1.1, and connection timeout set to 2 seconds:

```
// Create an HttpClient with custom configurations
HttpClient client = HttpClient.newBuilder()
                        .followRedirects(ALWAYS)
                        .version(HTTP_1_1)
                        .connectTimeout(Duration.ofSeconds(2))
                        .build();
```

The HttpClient class contains a method corresponding to each configuration setting that returns the value for that configuration:

- Optional<Authenticator> authenticator()

- Optional<Duration> connectTimeout()

- Optional<CookieHandler> cookieHandler()

- Optional<Executor> executor()

- HttpClient.Redirect followRedirects()

- Optional<ProxySelector> proxy()

- SSLContext sslContext()

- SSLParameters sslParameters()

- HttpClient.Version version()

There are no setter methods in the HttpClient class because the class is immutable. You cannot use an HttpClient by itself. You need to have an HttpRequest before you use an HttpClient to send a request to a server. I will explain the HttpRequest class in the next section. The HttpClient class contains the following three methods to send a request to a server:

- <T> HttpResponse<T> send(HttpRequest request, HttpResponse. BodyHandler<T> responseBodyHandler)

- <T> CompletableFuture<HttpResponse<T>> sendAsync (HttpRequest request, HttpResponse.BodyHandler<T> responseBodyHandler)

- <T> CompletableFuture<HttpResponse<T>> sendAsync (HttpRequest request, HttpResponse.BodyHandler<T> responseBodyHandler, HttpResponse.PushPromiseHandler<T> pushPromiseHandler)

The send() method sends the request synchronously, whereas the sendAsync() methods send the request asynchronously. The second version of the sendAsync() method lets you send a request asynchronously and process server push responses. I will cover these methods in more detail in subsequent sections.

Processing HTTP Requests

A client application communicates with a web server using HTTP requests. It sends a request to the server and the server sends back a response. An instance of the HttpRequest class represents a request. The following are the steps you need to perform to process a request:

- Obtain an HTTP request builder.

- Set the parameters for the request.

- Create an HTTP request from the builder.

- Send the HTTP request to a server – synchronously or asynchronously.

- Process the response from the server.

Obtaining an HTTP Request Builder

You need to use a builder object, which is an instance of the HttpRequest.Builder interface, to create an HttpRequest. You can get an HttpRequest.Builder using one of the following static methods of the HttpRequest class:

- HttpRequest.Builder newBuilder()

- HttpRequest.Builder newBuilder(URI uri)

The following snippet of code shows you how to use these methods to get an HttpRequest.Builder:

```
// Create an URI for httpbin.org
URI uri = URI.create("http://httpbin.org");

// Get a builder with an URI
HttpRequest.Builder builder1 = HttpRequest.newBuilder(uri);

// Get a builder without specifying a URI at this time
HttpRequest.Builder builder2 = HttpRequest.newBuilder();
```

Setting Up HTTP Request Parameters

Once you have an HTTP request builder, you can set the parameters for the request such as request method, body, and headers using the builder's methods. The following sections show you how to set different types of parameters in an `HttpRequest` with examples.

Setting Up Request Method and Body Publisher

HTTP supports the following types of methods: GET, POST, PUT, DELETE, PATCH, HEAD, OPTIONS, CONNECT, and TRACE. The `HttpRequest.Builder` interface provides four methods to set the similarly named HTTP methods directly:

- `HttpRequest.Builder GET()`

- `HttpRequest.Builder POST(HttpRequest.BodyPublisher bodyPublisher)`

- `HttpRequest.Builder PUT(HttpRequest.BodyPublisher bodyPublisher)`

- `HttpRequest.Builder DELETE()`

Some HTTP methods such as POST and PUT require you to pass data as request body. Some HTTP methods such as GET and DELETE do not support request body. This is reflected in the method's declaration in the previous list.

A request body is represented as an instance of the `HttpRequest.BodyPublisher` interface. The `BodyPublisher` interface extends `Flow.Publisher<ByteBuffer>`, and its job is to convert Java objects passed as the request body into a flow of byte buffers suitable for sending a request body. Do not worry about creating a `BodyPublisher` from scratch. For common use cases, predefined body publishers are provided through the `HttpRequest.BodyPublishers` static class.

Table 3-1 lists the factory methods in the `HttpRequest.BodyPublishers` class. All methods in the table return an `HttpRequest.BodyPublisher`. The class also provides a `fromPublisher()` method that is an adaptor between `Flow.Publisher` and `HttpRequest.BodyPublisher`. The method takes a `Flow.Publisher` and returns an `HttpRequest.BodyPublisher`. You can use this method when you want to use an existing `Flow.Publisher` as an `HttpRequest.BodyPublisher`.

Table 3-1. *List of Factory Methods in the HttpRequest.BodyPublishers Class That Returns an HttpRequest.BodyPublisher Instance*

Method	Description
noBody()	Returns a request body publisher that sends no request body. Use this method to get a body publisher when you do not have a request body to send to the server, but the method you are using to send the request requires you to specify a body publisher.
ofByteArray(byte[] buf)	Returns a request body publisher that sends the specified byte array as the request body.
ofByteArray(byte[] buf, int offset, int length)	Returns a request body publisher that sends length bytes from offset in the specified byte array as the request body.
ofByteArrays(Iterable<byte[]> iterable)	Returns a request body publisher that sends byte arrays in an Iterable as the request body.
ofFile(Path path)	Returns a request body publisher that sends data in a file specified by path as the request body. A FileNotFoundException is thrown if the specified path does not exist.
ofInputStream (Supplier<? extends InputStream> streamSupplier)	Returns a request body publisher that sends the request body by reading from an InputStream. Note the use of a Supplier as an argument instead of an InputStream. Using a supplier allows for reuse if a request is resent. If the Supplier returns null, the request fails.
ofString(String body)	Returns a request body publisher whose request body is the specified String converted to bytes using UTF8 character set.
ofString(String s, Charset charset)	Returns a request body publisher whose request body is the specified String converted to bytes using the specified charset.

The following snippet of code shows how to post form data to a server using the HTTP POST method:

```
// Set the request body in a String
String requestBody = "first_name=Kishori&last_name=Sharan";

// Create an HttpRequest
HttpRequest request = HttpRequest.newBuilder()
        .uri(URI.create("http://httpbin.org/post"))
        .header("Content-Type", "application/x-www-form-urlencoded")
        .POST(BodyPublishers.ofString(requestBody))
        .build();
```

The form contains two fields–first_name and last_name. Intentionally, I have set the simple values for these fields (Kishori and Sharan), which do not require URL encoding. Otherwise, you would need to use the encode() method of the java.net. URLEncoder class to encode the field's values before sending them to the server. Note that you must set the "Content-Type" header in your request to "application/x-www-form-urlencoded" if you are posting form data.

The HttpRequest.Builder interface provides a method named method() that you can use to set any type of HTTP method for a request. It is declared as follows:

```
HttpRequest.Builder method(String method, HttpRequest.BodyPublisher
bodyPublisher)
```

The value for the method argument is the same as the HTTP method names such as "POST", "OPTIONS", "HEAD", and so on. Currently, the HTTP Client API does not support CONNECT HTTP method. The following statement uses the method() method with the HTTP OPTIONS method to create an HttpRequest:

```
// Create an HttpRequest
HttpRequest request = HttpRequest.newBuilder()
        .uri(URI.create("http://httpbin.org/post"))
        .method("OPTIONS", BodyPublishers.noBody())
        .build();
```

Typically, you do not send a request body with the OPTIONS method. Note that we are using BodyPublishers.noBody() factory method to get a HttpRequest. BodyPublisher, which sends no request body. You can rewrite the previous example of creating an HttpRequest to post form data using the method() method as follows:

```
// Set the request body in a String
String requestBody = "first_name=Kishori&last_name=Sharan";

// Create an HttpRequest
HttpRequest request = HttpRequest.newBuilder()
        .uri(URI.create("http://httpbin.org/post"))
        .header("Content-Type", "application/x-www-form-urlencoded")
        .method("POST", BodyPublishers.ofString(requestBody))
        .build();
```

Overriding HTTP Version

An HttpRequest is sent to a server using an HttpClient. When you are building an HttpRequest, you can set the HTTP version value through its HttpRequest.Builder object using the version() method that will override the HTTP version set in the HttpClient when this request is sent. The following snippet of code sets the version to HTTP 1.1 for a request, which overrides the default value of HTTP 2 in the HttpClient. Recall that whether HTTP 2 is used depends on the server. If the server does not support HTTP 2, the HTTP communication is downgraded to use HTTP 1.1.

```
// All requests sent using this HttpClient will use HTTP 2
// unless overridden by the request
HttpClient client = HttpClient.newHttpClient();

// Get an HttpRequest that uses HTTP 1.1
HttpRequest request = HttpRequest.newBuilder()
        .uri(URI.create("http://httpbin.org/ip"))
        .version(HTTP_1_1)
        .build();

// The client object uses HTTP 2 and the request object overrides
// it with HTTP 1.1. The following statement will send the request
```

```
// using HTTP 1.1, which is in the request object.
HttpResponse<String> response =
        client.send(request, BodyHandlers.ofString());
```

Setting Up a Timeout

You can use the timeout(Duration timeout) method of the HttpRequest.Builder
instance to specify a timeout for the request. If a response is not received within the
specified timeout period, an HttpTimeoutException is thrown. If you do not set a
request timeout, the request can block forever. The httpbin.org/delay/{delay} URL
sends a response back after a delay specified in {delay} part of the URL. The following
HttpRequest will always fail with an HttpTimeoutException because the server sends a
response after 5 seconds and we have set the request timeout for 2 seconds:

```
// An HttpRequest that will fails when sent
HttpRequest request = HttpRequest.newBuilder()
        .uri(URI.create("http://httpbin.org/delay/5"))
        .timeout(Duration.ofSeconds(2))
        .build();
```

Setting Expect Continue Header

An HTTP request may contain a header named Expect with its value "100-Continue".
If this header is set, the client sends only headers (without a body) to the server and the
server is expected to send back an error response or a 100-Continue response. Upon
receiving a 100-Continue response, the client sends the request body to the server. A
client uses this technique to check if the server can process the request based on the
request headers before sending the actual request body. Typically, you do this when the
request body is big, and you do not want to send a big request body only to find out that
the request cannot be completed.

The Expect header is not set by default. You need to call the expectContinue(true)
method of the request builder to enable this. The following snippet of code shows you
how to use this:

```
// Enable the Expect=100-Continue header in the request
HttpRequest request = HttpRequest.newBuilder()
        .uri(URI.create("http://httpbin.org/post"))
```

57

```
        .header("Content-Type", "application/x-www-form-urlencoded")
        .POST(BodyPublishers.ofString("name=Kishori"))
        .expectContinue(true)
        .build();
```

When you send this request, internally there will be two exchanges between the
client and the server. The first request will not send the request body. After receiving an
HTTP 100 status code in the response, the request body will be sent as part of the second
exchange. However, you see just one response.

Calling the header("Expect", "100-Continue") method of the request builder does
not enable this feature. You must use the expectContinue(true) method to enable it.

Setting Request Headers

A header in an HTTP request is a name-value pair. You can have multiple headers in
a request. You can use the header(), headers(), and setHeader() methods of the
HttpRequest.Builder class to add headers to a request. The header() and headers()
methods add headers if they are not already present. If headers were already added,
these methods do nothing. The setHeader() method replaces the header if it was
present; otherwise, it adds a new header.

The header() and setHeader() methods let you add/set one header at a time,
whereas the headers() method lets you add multiple headers. The headers() method
takes a var-args argument, which should contain name-value pairs in sequence. The
following snippet of code shows how to set headers for a request using these three
methods. All three requests contain the same headers.

```
// Use the header() method
HttpRequest request1 = HttpRequest.newBuilder()
        .uri(URI.create("http://httpbin.org/post"))
        .header("Content-Type", "application/x-www-form-urlencoded")
        .header("Accept", "text/plain")
        .POST(BodyPublishers.ofString("name=Kishori"))
        .build();

// Use the headers() method
HttpRequest request2 = HttpRequest.newBuilder()
        .uri(URI.create("http://httpbin.org/post"))
```

```
    .headers("Content-Type", "application/x-www-form-urlencoded",
            "Accept", "text/plain")
    .POST(BodyPublishers.ofString("name=Kishori"))
    .build();

// Use the setHeader() method
HttpRequest request3 = HttpRequest.newBuilder()
        .uri(URI.create("http://httpbin.org/post"))
        .setHeader("Content-Type", "application/x-www-form-urlencoded")
        .setHeader("Accept", "text/plain")
        .POST(BodyPublishers.ofString("name=Kishori"))
        .build();
```

Creating HTTP Requests

In previous sections, you learned how to create an HttpRequest.Builder and how to use it to set different properties of an HTTP request. Creating an HttpRequest is simply calling the build() method on the HttpRequest.Builder. The following snippet of code creates an HttpRequest that uses the HTTP GET method:

```
HttpRequest request = HttpRequest.newBuilder()
                            .uri(URI.create("http://httpbin.org/ip"))
                            .GET()
                            .build();
```

Note that creating an HttpRequest object does not send the request to the server. You will need to call the send() or sendAsync() method of an HttpClient to send the request to the server. I will explain how to send requests to a server in the next section.

Processing HTTP Responses

Once you have an HttpRequest, you can send the request to a server and receive the response synchronously or asynchronously. An instance of the HttpResponse<T> interface represents a response received from a server, where the type parameter T indicates the type of the response body such as String, byte[], or Path. You can use one of the following methods of the `HttpClient` class to send an HTTP request and receive an HTTP response:

- `<T> HttpResponse<T> send(HttpRequest request, HttpResponse.BodyHandler<T> responseBodyHandler) throws IOException, InterruptedException`

- `<T> CompletableFuture<HttpResponse<T>> sendAsync (HttpRequest request, HttpResponse.BodyHandler<T> responseBodyHandler)`

- `<T> CompletableFuture<HttpResponse<T>> sendAsync (HttpRequest request, HttpResponse.BodyHandler<T> responseBodyHandler, HttpResponse.PushPromiseHandler<T> pushPromiseHandler)`

The `send()` method is synchronous. That is, it blocks until the response is fully received. The `sendAsync()` method processes the response asynchronously. It returns immediately with a `CompletableFuture<HttpResponse<T>>`, which completes when the response is ready to be processed. You will see examples of both types in subsequent sections.

Processing Response Status and Headers

An `HttpResponse` contains a status code, headers, and a body. Sometimes, an `HttpResponse` is made available to you as soon as the status code and headers are received from the server, but before the body is received. The availability of the response before its body is fully available depends on the body handler that you provide. For example, if you provide a `String` body handler, the `HttpResponse` is available after the entire response body is received and has been converted to a `String`. If you provide a body handler to process the response body as a stream of lines, the `HttpResponse` will be available after the status code and headers are received.

The `statusCode()` method of the `HttpResponse` interface returns the status code of the response as an `int`.

The `headers()` method of the `HttpResponse` interface returns the headers of the response as an instance of the `HttpHeaders` class. The `HttpHeaders` class contains the

following methods to conveniently retrieve header's values by name or all headers as a
Map<String,List<String>>:

- List<String> allValues(String name)

- Optional<String> firstValue(String name)

- OptionalLong firstValueAsLong(String name)

- Map<String,List<String>> map()

Listing 3-3 contains a complete program to send a request to the
URL http://httpbin.org with a HEAD request. It prints the received response's status
code and headers. You may get different output.

Listing 3-3. Processing an HTTP Response's Status Code and Headers

```
// PrintHeaders.java
package com.jdojo.http.client;

import java.io.IOException;
import java.net.URI;
import java.net.http.HttpClient;
import java.net.http.HttpRequest;
import java.net.http.HttpRequest.BodyPublishers;
import java.net.http.HttpResponse;
import java.net.http.HttpResponse.BodyHandlers;

public class PrintHeaders {
    public static void main(String[] args) {
        // Create an HttpClient with default configurations
        HttpClient client = HttpClient.newHttpClient();

        // Create an HttpRequest
        HttpRequest request = HttpRequest.newBuilder()
                .uri(URI.create("http://httpbin.org"))
                .method("HEAD", BodyPublishers.noBody())
                .build();
```

```java
    try {
        // send the request to the server
        HttpResponse<Void> response
                = client.send(request, BodyHandlers.discarding());

        // Print the response status code and headers
        System.out.println("Status Code:" + response.statusCode());

        System.out.println("Response Headers:");
        response.headers()
                .map()
                .entrySet()
                .forEach(System.out::println);
    } catch (IOException | InterruptedException e) {
        e.printStackTrace();
    }

    }
}
```

```
Status Code:200
Response Headers:
access-control-allow-credentials=[true]
access-control-allow-origin=[*]
connection=[keep-alive]
content-length=[9593]
content-type=[text/html; charset=utf-8]
date=[Tue, 23 Jul 2019 18:01:12 GMT]
referrer-policy=[no-referrer-when-downgrade]
server=[nginx]
x-content-type-options=[nosniff]
x-frame-options=[DENY]
x-xss-protection=[1; mode=block]
```

Let us look at the important parts of the request and response. The statement to create an HttpRequest is

```
// Create an HttpRequest
HttpRequest request = HttpRequest.newBuilder()
        .uri(URI.create("http://httpbin.org"))
        .method("HEAD", BodyPublishers.noBody())
        .build();
```

Notice the use of the HEAD HTTP method and the method() method. You are interested in receiving only the headers in the response, so you used HEAD as the HTTP method. You are not sending any request body, so you used a body publisher that publishes no body as indicated in BodyPublishers.noBody().

The following statement sends request to the server:

```
HttpResponse<Void> response
        = client.send(request, BodyHandlers.discarding());
```

Here, you are using body handler for the response body that is returned from the BodyHandlers.discarding(). This body handler simply discards the response body, which you can see as the type parameter Void in the returned value from the send() method in HttpResponse<Void>. The return type for the body() method for the response object is Void, and calling response.body() will return null.

Processing the Response Body

Processing the body of an HTTP response is a two-step process:

- You need to specify a response body handler, which is an instance of the HttpResponse.BodyHandler<T> interface, when you send a request using the send() or sendAsync() method of the HttpClient class.

- When the response status code and headers are received, the apply(HttpResponse.ResponseInfo responseInfo) method of the response body handler is called. The ResponseInfo contains the response status code, headers, and HTTP protocol version. The apply() method returns an instance of the HttpResponse.BodySubscriber<T> interface, which reads the response body and converts the read data into the type T. The HttpResponse.BodySubscriber<T> interface

extends `Flow.Subscriber<List<ByteBuffer>>`, which means a body
subscriber is a subscriber in the Flow API whose job is to consume
response body and make it available to you as a high-level Java object.

Don't worry about these details of processing a response body. Several
implementations of the `HttpResponse.BodyHandler<T>` are provided. You can use one of
the following `static` factory methods of the `HttpResponse.BodyHandlers` class to get its
instance for a different type parameter T:

- `<T> HttpResponse.BodyHandler<T> buffering(HttpResponse.BodyHandler<T> downstreamHandler, int bufferSize)`

- `HttpResponse.BodyHandler<Void> discarding()`

- `HttpResponse.BodyHandler<byte[]> ofByteArray()`

- `HttpResponse.BodyHandler<Void> ofByteArrayConsumer (Consumer<Optional<byte[]>> consumer`

- `HttpResponse.BodyHandler<Path> ofFile(Path file)`

- `HttpResponse.BodyHandler<Path> ofFile(Path file, OpenOption... openOptions)`

- `HttpResponse.BodyHandler<Path> ofFileDownload(Path directory, OpenOption... openOptions)`

- `HttpResponse.BodyHandler<InputStream> ofInputStream()`

- `HttpResponse.BodyHandler<Stream<String>> ofLines()`

- `HttpResponse.BodyHandler<Flow.Publisher<List<ByteBuffer>>> ofPublisher()`

- `HttpResponse.BodyHandler<String> ofString()`

- `HttpResponse.BodyHandler<String> ofString(Charset charset)`

- `<U> HttpResponse.BodyHandler<U> replacing(U value)`

These methods' signatures are intuitive enough to tell you what type of response
body they handle. For example, if you want to get the response body as a `String`, use
the `ofString()` method to get a body handler. The `discarding()` method returns a
body handler, which will discard the response body. The `replacing(U value)` method
returns a body handler that discards the original response body and returns the specified

value as the body. The ofLines() method returns a body handler that returns response body as a stream of lines. The ofFile() methods return a body handler that saves the response body in a specified file represented by the specified Path.

The body() method of the HttpResponse<T> interface returns the response body, which is of type T.

Tip   The HttpResponse.BodyHandlers class contains fromSubscriber() and fromLineSubscriber() methods. They act as an adapter between Flow.Subscriber<T> and HttpResponse.BodyHandler<T>. They let you convert a Flow.Subscriber<T> into an HttpResponse.BodyHandler<T>.

You have already seen examples of handling a response body as a String.

Subsequent sections explore some more options to process a response body such as saving a response body to a file, downloading it to a file as an attachment. Currently, there is no built-in body handler to process response body as a JSON object. You need to use a Java library, for example, Jackson JSON Parser, to process JSON response body. Several of our examples return JSON response body. I simply process them as a String.

Saving a Response Body to a File

In this section, I will show you how to save the response body in a file. You will use the http://httpbin.org/image/jpeg, which returns an image with the content type as image/jpeg. Assume that you want to save the contents of the image, which will be in the response body, in a file named myimage.jpeg in the current directory. You can achieve this by using a body handler returned from the ofFile() method of the HttpResponse. BodyHandlers class. The response body will be a Path to the saved file. The following snippet of code shows this part of the logic:

```
// Create a Path to save the image in a file named myimage.jpeg
// in the current directory
Path filePath = Paths.get("myimage.jpeg");

// Set the request to the server
HttpResponse<Path> response
        = client.send(request, BodyHandlers.ofFile(filePath));
```

```
// Get the response status and body. Here, body is the Path of the
// file location where the response body was saved
int statusCode = response.statusCode();
Path savedFilePath = response.body();
```

Listing 3-4 contains a complete program to save a response body in a file. You may get a different output because it prints the saved file location, which depends on the current directory.

Listing 3-4. Saving a Response Body to a File

```java
// SaveInFile.java
package com.jdojo.http.client;

import java.io.IOException;
import java.net.URI;
import java.net.http.HttpClient;
import java.net.http.HttpRequest;
import java.net.http.HttpResponse;
import java.net.http.HttpResponse.BodyHandlers;
import java.nio.file.Path;
import java.nio.file.Paths;

public class SaveInFile {
    public static void main(String[] args) {
        // Create an HttpClient with default configurations
        HttpClient client = HttpClient.newHttpClient();

        // Use the Get HTTP method
        HttpRequest request = HttpRequest.newBuilder()
                .uri(URI.create("http://httpbin.org/image/jpeg"))
                .build();

        try {
            // Create a Path to save the image in a file named myimage.jpeg
            // in the current directory
            Path filePath = Paths.get("myimage.jpeg");
```

```
        // Set the request to the server
        HttpResponse<Path> response
                = client.send(request, BodyHandlers.ofFile(filePath));

        // Get the response status and body
        int statusCode = response.statusCode();
        Path savedFilePath = response.body();

        // Print the response status and body
        System.out.println("Response Status: " + statusCode);
        System.out.println("Response body was saved at "
                + savedFilePath.toAbsolutePath());
    } catch (IOException | InterruptedException e) {
        e.printStackTrace();
    }
  }
}
```

```
Response Status: 200
Response body was saved at C:\Java13Revealed\myimage.jpeg
```

Downloading a Response Body As an Attachment

In this section, I will show you how to download a response body as an attachment and save it in a file. To download a file as an attachment, the response needs to contain a header named Content-Disposition with two values – the first being attachment and the second filename with the name of a file. The header looks like

Content-Disposition: attachment; filename="myimage.jpeg"

The HttpResponse.BodyHandlers.ofFileDownload() method returns a body handler that reads the Content-Disposition response header. If attachment and filename are present in the header's value, the body handler downloads the response body and saves the contents in a file specified in the filename parameter. You specify the directory where the downloaded file is saved. If the response does not contain a Content-Disposition header with the values as mentioned, the body handler returned from ofFileDownload() method will not work.

I did not find a URL on Internet for this example that will return Content-Disposition as a response header with a file to download. You will use the `http://httpbin.org/response-headers` URL, which returns response headers specified in this URL as a query string. For this example, you will need to specify `Content-Disposition` with the expected values in a query string with this URL. The server will return a response with a JSON document and a `Content-Disposition` response header as you specify in the query string of the request URL. The query string needs to be URL encoded. Without URL encoding, the URL looks like

```
http://httpbin.org/response-headers?Content-Disposition=attachment;
filename=test.json
```

After encoding the value for the `Content-Disposition` query string parameter, the URL looks like

```
http://httpbin.org/response-headers?Content-Disposition=attachment%3B+filen
ame%3Dtest.json
```

Listing 3-5 contains a complete program to show how to download a file. The discussion of the important parts in the program follows the output. You may get a different output.

Listing 3-5. Downloading an Attachment in a Response Body

```java
// DownloadFile.java
package com.jdojo.http.client;

import java.io.IOException;
import java.net.URI;
import java.net.URLEncoder;
import java.net.http.HttpClient;
import java.net.http.HttpRequest;
import java.net.http.HttpResponse;
import java.net.http.HttpResponse.BodyHandlers;
import static java.nio.charset.StandardCharsets.UTF_8;
import java.nio.file.Path;
import java.nio.file.Paths;
import static java.nio.file.StandardOpenOption.CREATE;
import static java.nio.file.StandardOpenOption.WRITE;
```

```java
public class DownloadFile {
    public static void main(String[] args) {
        // Create an HttpClient with default configurations
        HttpClient client = HttpClient.newHttpClient();

        try {
            // Prepare a query string by encoding the parameter value
            String paramName = "Content-Disposition";
            String paramValue = "attachment; filename=test.json";
            String encodedParamValue
                    = URLEncoder.encode(paramValue, UTF_8);

            // Prepare the URI with a query string
            String uriStr = "http://httpbin.org/response-headers"
                    + "?" + paramName + "=" + encodedParamValue;

            // Create an HttpRequest
            HttpRequest request = HttpRequest.newBuilder()
                    .uri(URI.create(uriStr))
                    .header("Accept", "application/json")
                    .build();

            // Create a Path for the download directory, which would be
            // the current directory in this case
            Path dirPath = Paths.get(".");

            // Send the request to the server
            HttpResponse<Path> response = client.send(request,
                    BodyHandlers.ofFileDownload(dirPath, CREATE, WRITE));

            // Get the response status and body.
            // Response body is a Path to the downloaded file.
            int statusCode = response.statusCode();
            Path filePath = response.body();

            // Print the response status and body
            System.out.println("Response Status: " + statusCode);
```

```
            System.out.println("File downloaded at "
                    + filePath.toAbsolutePath().normalize());
        } catch (IOException | InterruptedException e) {
            e.printStackTrace();
        }
    }
}
```

```
Response Status: 200
File downloaded at D:\Java13Revealed\test.json
```

The ofFileDownload() method accepts two parameters – the first parameter is a Path pointing to the directory where the file will be downloaded. The filename parameter in the Content-Disposition header may specify a file path instead of a file name. The file path specified in the filename parameter is not used for security reasons. Only the last part of the file path is used as a file name. The following statement creates a Path representing the current directory:

```
Path dirPath = Paths.get(".");
```

When you create a body handler, you need to specify the options as a var-args parameter of the OpenOption type as the second parameter to the ofFileDownload() method. In this example, you have specified CREATE and WRITE as these options. They will allow the body handler to create a file – if it does not exist – to store the downloaded content and the file will be opened in write mode. The following statement in the program achieves this:

```
HttpResponse<Path> response = client.send(request,
        BodyHandlers.ofFileDownload(dirPath, CREATE, WRITE));
```

The Path returned from the response body is not normalized. For example, it contains the file path as C:\Java13Revealed\.\test.json. Note the dot in the file path. The path is valid, but not normalized. Before printing the file path, the program gets its absolute path and normalizes it to print a file path like C:\Java13Revealed\test.json. The following snippet of code in the program performs this task:

```
System.out.println("File downloaded at "
        + filePath.toAbsolutePath().normalize());
```

Following Server Redirects

When you send a request to a server, it is common to get redirected to another URL. Redirection is indicated in the response status code. A status code of 3xx indicates redirection. For example, if you receive a status code of 301, it means the URL has permanently moved. In this case, the response will contain a header named `Location` whose value contains the new URL where the resource has moved. For example, when you request the page at `http://google.com`, you receive response with status code of 301 and the `Location` in the response header set to `www.google.com`.

A URL may redirect you to another URL, the new URL may redirect you to another, and so on. Sometimes, a URL on a badly designed server may put you into infinite loop of redirections. Most browsers set a default limit of 20 redirections to follow.

Sometimes, a server may redirect you to another URL just to force you to use secure protocol. For example, `www.abc.com` may redirect you to `www.abc.com`. However, redirecting from HTTPS to HTTP is not a normal practice.

Browsers take care of redirection for you automatically. The HTTP Client API does not follow redirection by default. The redirection policy is set in the `HttpClient`, and it is specified as one of the following values in the `HttpClient.Redirect` enum:

- ALWAYS

- NEVER

- NORMAL

ALWAYS allows redirection in all cases. NEVER, which is the default redirection policy, does not allow redirection. NORMAL behaves the same as ALWAYS, except it denies redirection from HTTPS to HTTP.

Tip   You can set the redirection policy of an `HttpClient` using the `followRedirects()` method of the `HttpClient.Builder` interface.

Listing 3-6 contains a complete program to demonstrate the use of the redirection policy. A discussion follows the program's output. You may get a different output.

Listing 3-6. Following Server Redirects by Setting Redirection Policy in HttpClient

```
// FollowRedirection.java
package com.jdojo.http.client;

import java.io.IOException;
import java.net.URI;
import java.net.URLEncoder;
import java.net.http.HttpClient;
import static java.net.http.HttpClient.Redirect.NORMAL;
import java.net.http.HttpRequest;
import java.net.http.HttpResponse;
import java.net.http.HttpResponse.BodyHandlers;
import static java.nio.charset.StandardCharsets.UTF_8;

public class FollowRedirection {
    public static void main(String[] args) {
        // Create an HttpClient with default configurations
        HttpClient client = HttpClient.newHttpClient();

        // Location of the new URL
        String location = "http://httpbin.org/ip";

        // Prepare the URL that will redirect the request to a new location
        String uriStr = "http://httpbin.org/redirect-to?"
                + "url=" + URLEncoder.encode(location, UTF_8)
                + "&status_code=301";

        HttpRequest request = HttpRequest.newBuilder()
                .uri(URI.create(uriStr))
                .build();

        // Send the request with the default redirection policy of NEVER.
        // Expecting a response with a status code 301.
        printResponse(client, request);

        System.out.println("----------------------------------");

        // Create an HTTPClient with a redirection policy of NORMAL
        client = HttpClient.newBuilder()
```

```java
                .followRedirects(NORMAL)
                .build();

        // Send the request with the redirection policy of NORMAL
        // Expecting a response with a status code 200
        printResponse(client, request);
    }

    public static void printResponse(HttpClient client,
            HttpRequest request) {
        try {
            HttpResponse<String> response
                    = client.send(request, BodyHandlers.ofString());

            // Get the response status and body
            int statusCode = response.statusCode();
            String body = response.body();
            String locationHeader = response.headers()
                    .firstValue("Location")
                    .orElse("");

            System.out.println("Statuc code: " + statusCode);
            System.out.println("Location Header: " + locationHeader);
            System.out.println("Response body:\n" + body);
        } catch (IOException | InterruptedException e) {
            e.printStackTrace();
        }
    }
}
```

```
Status code: 301
Location Header: http://httpbin.org/ip
Response body:

----------------------------------
Status code: 200
Location Header:
Response body:
```

```
{
   "origin": "23.131.128.26, 23.131.128.26"
}
```

The program uses the `http://httpbin.org/redirect-to` URL. The URL redirects to a new URL as specified in the `uri` query string parameter. It returns a response status code as specified in the `status_code` query string parameter. You used `http://httpbin.org/ip` as the redirect URL and 301 as the status code. The same request is sent twice. First time, you send the request with `NEVER` as the redirect policy, which is the default for an `HttpClient`. You receive an expected response with status code of 301 and with a `Location` header set to the redirect URL we set in the request. Second time, you set the redirect policy for the `HttpClient` to `NORMAL`, which allows the `HttpClient` to follow the redirects. After the redirect, you receive a response from the `http://httpbin.org/ip` URL, which sends back the IP address of the client making the request.

Making Asynchronous Requests

When you use the `send()` method of the `HttpClient`, the call is blocked until a response is received. There could be several reasons you do not want to do this. Asynchronous process of HTTP requests gives you a lot of benefits such as improved performance and responsiveness. Your program can do something else while it is waiting for a response. You might send the same request to many servers and want to resume processing when you get a response from all or some servers. This is possible very easily using asynchronous processing of HTTP requests.

Use the `sendAsync()` method of the `HttpClient` class to send a request to a server asynchronously. The method returns a `CompletableFuture<HttpResponse<T>>` where T is the response body type. For example, if you use a body handler to process the response body as a `String`, the method returns a `CompletableFuture<HttpResponse<String>>`. The following snippet of code prints the response body to the standard output asynchronously:

```
// Create an HttpClient with default configurations
HttpClient client = HttpClient.newHttpClient();

// Use the HTTP GET method
HttpRequest request = HttpRequest.newBuilder()
        .uri(URI.create("http://httpbin.org/ip"))
        .build();
```

```
// Print the response body
client.sendAsync(request, BodyHandlers.ofString())
    .thenApply(HttpResponse::body)
    .thenAccept(System.out::println);
```

There is nothing extraordinary in this snippet of code, except calls to `thenApply()` and `thenAccept()` methods. Refer to the documentation of `java.util.concurrent.CompletableFuture<T>` class for more details on these methods. The `thenApply()` method takes a `Function<T,R>` as a parameter, which accepts the response object of type `HttpResponse<String>` as a parameter and returns the response body as a `String`. The `thenAccept()` method prints the response body, which was passed to this from the previous completion stage. The `sendAsync()` method uses separate threads provided by an `Executor` to process the request. You can also use your own `Executor` by configuring the `HttpClient` using the `executor()` method of the `HttpClient.Builder` interface.

The `sendAsync()` method returns immediately, and the request and response are processed later in separate threads. If you have the previous statement as the last statement in your `main()` method, your program may not see any output. By the time your request is sent and a response processed in other daemon threads, the "main" non-daemon thread terminates, which in turn terminates your program. You can fix it by calling the `get()` or `join()` method, which returns the result of the last completion stage. The difference between the two is that the `get()` method throws checked exceptions, whereas the `join()` method throws unchecked exception. The following snippet of code fixes the issue of the program printing no outputs:

```
// Print the response body
client.sendAsync(request, BodyHandlers.ofString())
    .thenApply(HttpResponse::body)
    .thenAccept(System.out::println)
    .join();
```

Listing 3-7 contains a complete program to process a request and its response asynchronously. You may get a different output.

Listing 3-7. Processing HTTP Request and Response Asynchronously

```java
// AsynchronousRequest.java
package com.jdojo.http.client;

import java.net.URI;
import java.net.http.HttpClient;
import java.net.http.HttpRequest;
import java.net.http.HttpResponse;
import java.net.http.HttpResponse.BodyHandlers;

public class AsynchronousRequest {
    public static void main(String[] args) {
        // Create an HttpClient with default configurations
        HttpClient client = HttpClient.newHttpClient();

        // Use the HTTP GET method
        HttpRequest request = HttpRequest.newBuilder()
                .uri(URI.create("http://httpbin.org/ip"))
                .build();

        // Send the request asynchronously and print the response body
        client.sendAsync(request, BodyHandlers.ofString())
                .thenApply(HttpResponse::body)
                .thenAccept(System.out::println)
                .join();
    }
}
```

```
{
  "origin": "23.131.128.26, 23.131.128.26"
}
```

If you know how to use `CompletableFuture<T>` class, asynchronous processing of requests gives you a high degree of flexibility in how you handle the processing. Suppose you want to process a request asynchronously and when the response is available, you want to work with the HttpResponse object. The following snippet of code shows how to achieve this:

```
// Process the request asynchronously and wait for the response
HttpResponse<String> response
        = client.sendAsync(request, BodyHandlers.ofString())
                .join();

/* Access the response details here using the response variable */
```

You can also process multiple concurrent requests asynchronously. Suppose you want to download three images from the http://httpbin.org using the following three URLs:

- http://httpbin.org/image/jpeg

- http://httpbin.org/image/png

- http://httpbin.org/image/svg

Start with storing the three URLs and their corresponding HTTP requests in a list as follows:

```
// Collect all URIs in a List
List<URI> uriList = List.of(
        URI.create("http://httpbin.org/image/jpeg"),
        URI.create("http://httpbin.org/image/png"),
        URI.create("http://httpbin.org/image/svg"));

// Build requests for each URI and store them in a List
List<HttpRequest> requestList = uriList.stream()
        .map(HttpRequest::newBuilder)
        .map(reqBuilder -> reqBuilder.build())
        .collect(toList());
```

The following snippet of code sends all requests asynchronously and saves the downloaded files in the current directory:

```
// Send all requests asynchronously and wait for them to finish
CompletableFuture.allOf(
        requestList.stream()
```

```
            .map(req -> {
                String[] elems = req.uri().getPath().split("/");
                String fileName = "image." + elems[elems.length - 1];
                return client.sendAsync(req,
                    BodyHandlers.ofFile(Paths.get(fileName)));
            }).toArray(CompletableFuture<?>[]::new)
).thenRun(() -> System.out.println("All downloads completed."))
 .join();
```

This is a one statement, but looks intimidating at first. Let us break it down into its logical parts. The `allOf()` method of the `CompletableFuture<T>` class accepts a varargs of the `CompletableFuture<?>` type and returns a `CompletableFuture<Void>`. The returned `CompletableFuture<Void>` completes when all given `CompletableFutures` complete. Your first goal is to create an array of `CompletableFuture<HttpResponse<Path>>` that holds all the asynchronous requests sent to the server. The following part in the previous code snippet does this:

```
requestList.stream()
        .map(req -> {
            String[] elems = req.uri().getPath().split("/");
            String fileName = "image." + elems[elems.length - 1];
            return client.sendAsync(req,
                BodyHandlers.ofFile(Paths.get(fileName)));
        }).toArray(CompletableFuture<?>[]::new)
```

The code obtains a `BodyHandler<Path>` by calling the `ofFile()` method of the `HttpResponse.BodyHandlers` class. You need to pass a unique file name for each downloaded image. I extracted the last part of the URL such as jpeg, png, and svg and used it as the extension to a file named image. Therefore, the jpeg file will be stored in `image.jpeg` in your current directory, the png file will be stored in `image.png`, and so on.

The `allOf()` method returns a `CompletableFuture<Void>`, which completes when all the submitted job completes. The code calls the `thenRun()` method on it to print a message that all downloads are complete. Finally, you need to call the `join()` method to make sure all responses are processed before your program exits. Listing 3-8 contains the complete program.

Listing 3-8. Processing Multiple HTTP Requests and Responses Asynchronously

```java
// MultipleRequests.java
package com.jdojo.http.client;

import java.net.URI;
import java.net.http.HttpClient;
import java.net.http.HttpRequest;
import java.net.http.HttpResponse.BodyHandlers;
import java.nio.file.Paths;
import java.util.List;
import java.util.concurrent.CompletableFuture;
import static java.util.stream.Collectors.toList;

public class MultipleRequests {
    public static void main(String[] args) {
        // Create an HttpClient with default configurations
        HttpClient client = HttpClient.newHttpClient();

        // Collect all URIs in a List
        List<URI> uriList = List.of(
                URI.create("http://httpbin.org/image/jpeg"),
                URI.create("http://httpbin.org/image/png"),
                URI.create("http://httpbin.org/image/svg"));

        // Build requests for each URI and store them in a List
        List<HttpRequest> requestList = uriList.stream()
                .map(HttpRequest::newBuilder)
                .map(reqBuilder -> reqBuilder.build())
                .collect(toList());

        // Send all requests asynchronously and wait for them to finish
        CompletableFuture.allOf(
                requestList.stream()
                        .map(req -> {
                            String[] elems =
                                    req.uri().getPath().split("/");
                            String fileName =
```

```
                                "image." + elems[elems.length - 1];
                    return client.sendAsync(req,
                        BodyHandlers.ofFile(Paths.get(fileName)));
                }).toArray(CompletableFuture<?>[]::new)
        ).thenRun(() -> System.out.println("All downloads completed."))
        .join();
    }
}
```

```
All downloads completed.
```

Server Push

Server push is a feature supported by HTTP/2 in which a server sends additional resources to a client proactively. The client sends a request. By inspecting the client initial request, the server determines that the client will need additional resources along with the response to the initial request. The server responds with a response to the initial request and with additional responses. Typical use case for server push is in displaying the web pages in a browser. A web page is composed of several resources such as stylesheets, JavaScript code, images, embedded fonts, and so on. If you request a web page, the HTTP/2-compliant server may send you the HTML page for the web page and all other resources needed for the web page. This way, you get several resources in making just one request. Without server push, typically, a browser makes several round trips to fetch all resources for a web page. There were several workarounds used to avoid these round trips before HTTP/2.

The HTTP Client API in Java supports server push. When you make a request using an HttpClient, the server may send you additional responses in the form of push promises. You have options to accept or reject push promises. The server synthesizes an HttpRequest and an HttpResponse for each push promise. You have to provide a push promise handler, which will be invoked every time a push promise is received by the HttpClient.

Server push involves server pushing the contents and the client consuming them. Browsers handle the server push for you. In a Java program, you need to write the logic to handle the server push – most importantly, you need to know in advance what kind of resources the server will push to your client, so you know what to do with them in your code.

You need to have a server that sends server push to the client. For this example, I will work with a web page whose URL is www.angular.io. You can find a list of domain names that uses server push at https://http2.netray.io/data.php.

To process server push, you need to send your request using the sendAsync() version of the HttpClient class that accepts an HttpResponse.PushPromiseHandler<T>. The method's declaration is

```
<T> CompletableFuture<HttpResponse<T>> sendAsync(HttpRequest request,
HttpResponse.BodyHandler<T> responseBodyHandler, HttpResponse.
PushPromiseHandler<T> pushPromiseHandler)
```

Tip   Server push is the action of the server pushing resources to the client proactively. The HTTP Client API uses the term *push promise* for one server push. That is, if in response to a request the server pushes five additional resources, you will have five push promises.

The push promise handler is an instance of the HttpResponse.PushPromiseHandler<T> interface. You need to provide an implementation for the applyPushPromise() method of this interface. The method is declared as follows:

```
applyPushPromise(HttpRequest initiatingRequest,
                HttpRequest pushPromiseRequest,
Function<HttpResponse.BodyHandler<T>,CompletableFuture<HttpResponse<T>>>
acceptor)
```

The applyPushPromise() method of the push promise handler is called once for each push promise received from the server. The method accepts three parameters – the first one is the initial request that you sent to the server and the second one is the synthesized request for the server push received. The third parameter is a function<T,R> called acceptor. If you want to accept the push promise, you need to call the apply() method on the acceptor by passing it a HttpReponse.BodyHandler<T>, which will be used to process the response body for that push promise. The apply() method returns a CompletableFuture<HttpResponse<T>> and, when it completes, makes the push promise available as an HttpResponse<T> object.

Listing 3-9 contains a simple implementation of a push promise handler to handle the body of the pushed promise as a `String`. You will use this in your next example. When the client receives a push promise, its `applyPushPromise()` method will be called. I kept the method very simple, which prints the URI of the synthesized request of the push promise. It accepts the push promise by calling the `apply()` method of the acceptor function. Note that the response in the push promise will be processed some time later. The `CompletableFuture` returned from the `apply()` method is complete when the response body is available. The code calls the `thenAccept()` method on the `CompletableFuture` to print the push promise request URI and the response status code. In a real-world application, the code inside the `apply()` method will process the response in a more sophisticated manner.

Listing 3-9. An Implementation of a PushPromiseHandler

```
// ServerPushPromiseHandler.java
package com.jdojo.http.client;

import java.net.http.HttpRequest;
import java.net.http.HttpResponse;
import java.util.concurrent.CompletableFuture;
import java.util.function.Function;
import static java.lang.System.out;

public class ServerPushPromiseHandler implements
        HttpResponse.PushPromiseHandler<String> {
    @Override
    public void applyPushPromise(HttpRequest initiatingRequest,
            HttpRequest pushPromiseRequest,
            Function<HttpResponse.BodyHandler<String>,
                    CompletableFuture<HttpResponse<String>>> acceptor) {

        // Print URIs of the push promise request and
        // its initiating request
        out.printf("Received push promise request URI: %s%n"
                + "Push promise initiating request URI: %s%n%n",
                pushPromiseRequest.uri(),
                initiatingRequest.uri());
```

```
            // Accept the push promise by calling the apply() method
            // on the function passed in to this method
            acceptor.apply(HttpResponse.BodyHandlers.ofString())
                    .thenAccept(response -> {
                        // Print the push promise response details
                        out.printf("%nProcessed push promise request URI: %s%n"
                                + "Pushed response status code: %d%n",
                                pushPromiseRequest.uri(),
                                response.statusCode());
                    });
        }
}
```

Listing 3-10 contains a program to test server push. I am using the www.angular.io URL to send an HTTP GET request and expecting server push. If this URL does not work for you, replace it with another URL, which offers the server push feature. You may get a different output.

Listing 3-10. A Program to Test Server Push

```
// ServerPush.java
package com.jdojo.http.client;

import java.net.URI;
import java.net.http.HttpClient;
import java.net.http.HttpRequest;
import java.net.http.HttpResponse;
import java.net.http.HttpResponse.BodyHandlers;
import static java.net.http.HttpClient.Redirect.ALWAYS;

public class ServerPush {
    public static void main(String[] args) {
        // Create an HttpClient to allow redirects
        HttpClient client = HttpClient.newBuilder()
                .followRedirects(ALWAYS)
                .build();
```

```
        // Build a request
        HttpRequest request = HttpRequest.newBuilder()
                .uri(URI.create("http://www.angular.io"))
                .build();

        // Send the request asynchronously allowing server push
        HttpResponse<String> response = client.sendAsync(request,
                BodyHandlers.ofString(),
                new ServerPushPromiseHandler()
        ).join();

        // Print the response details
        System.out.printf("Initiating request URI: %s%n"
                + "Response's request URI: %s%n"
                + "Response status code: %d%n",
                request.uri(),
                response.request().uri(),
                response.statusCode());

    try {
        // Wait for five seconds to let the push promises finish
        // If you do not see output related to push promises
        // responses, increase the wait time, maybe to 10 seconds.
        Thread.sleep(5000);
    } catch (InterruptedException e) {
        e.printStackTrace();
    }
    }
}
```

```
Received push promise request URI: https://angular.io/generated/navigation.json
Push promise initiating request URI: http://www.angular.io

Received push promise request URI: https://angular.io/generated/docs/index.
json
Push promise initiating request URI: http://www.angular.io

Initiating request URI: http://www.angular.io
```

```
Response's request URI: https://angular.io/
Response status code: 200

Processed push promise request URI: https://angular.io/generated/docs/index.json
Pushed response status code: 200

Processed push promise request URI: https://angular.io/generated/navigation.json
Pushed response status code: 200
```

There are a few interesting points to note in the output:

- The HttpClient is configured to always follow redirects issued by the server.

- You created an HttpRequest with a URI as www.angular.io. This is your initiating URI.

- The server redirects the initiating request to https://angular.io/. The host for the two resources pushed by the server is https://angular.io. Two things changed during the server redirection – the protocol from HTTP to HTTPS and the host from www.angular.io to angular.io. The port change from 80 (HTTP) to 443 (HTTPS) is implied by the protocol change.

- Our host and port for the initiating request and the push promise request are different. We still decided to accept the push promises unconditionally.

- I will use these observations in the next example in which I improve the logic to handle server push.

You are familiar with most of the code in this program, except two new parts. The first part is how you send the request to the server, and the second part is to make the main thread wait for 5 seconds. The relevant code is as follows:

```
// Send the request asynchronously allowing server push
HttpResponse<String> response = client.sendAsync(request,
        BodyHandlers.ofString(),
        new ServerPushPromiseHandler()
).join();
```

Note that you are using the version of the sendAsync() method of the HttpClient class, which accepts a PushPromiseHandler as a third argument. You are passing an instance of the ServerPushPromiseHandler class as a push promise handler. When the join() method returns, the response body for the initial request is available. By this time, you have received the push promise requests, but not necessarily their responses. The responses and their bodies for the push promises will be available some time later. In our program, we do not have the logic to wait until responses for push promises are available. I arbitrarily chose to make the main thread wait for 5 seconds at the end of the main() method using the following statement:

```
Thread.sleep(5000);
```

If you see the first four lines of the output, but not the last four lines, you need to increase this wait time.

Tip   The push promise handler is called to accept or reject a push promise until the response body of the request, which initiated the server push, has been fully received. Any push promise received from the server after the response body is fully received is rejected.

Let us improve the previous server push example. I do not like using Thread.sleep() method to allow push promises to complete. We had to resort to this because we did not save the CompletableFuture returned from the apply() method inside the applyPushPromise() method of our push promise handler in Listing 3-9. The flaw was in the way we implemented our push promise handler. There is a good news! The HttpResponse.PushPromiseHandler<T> interface contains a static of() method that lets you create a push promise handler, which will store all push promise requests and CompletableFuture for the push promise responses in a concurrent map. It is declared as follows:

```
<T> HttpResponse.PushPromiseHandler<T> of(Function<HttpRequest,
HttpResponse.BodyHandler<T>> pushPromiseHandler,
ConcurrentMap<HttpRequest,CompletableFuture<HttpResponse<T>>> pushPromisesMap)
```

Do not be intimidated by the big declaration of this method. It is very simple to use. The first argument is a function, which accepts the push promise request and returns a response body handler. This function will be called once for each push promise received.

The second argument is a concurrent map, which is used to accumulate all push promises. Its keys are the push promise requests and values the `CompletableFuture` representing the push promise responses. Once you receive the response body of the initiating request, you can wait for all values in this concurrent map to complete and, after that, you can be assured that you have fully received the response body of all push promises. The following snippet of code creates a concurrent map:

```
// Create a concurrent map to accumulate all push promises
ConcurrentMap<HttpRequest,CompletableFuture<HttpResponse<String>>>
        pushPromisesMap = new ConcurrentHashMap<>();
```

The following snippet of code creates a push promise handler:

```
// Create a push promise handler
PushPromiseHandler<String> pushPromiseHandler
        = PushPromiseHandler.of(pushPromiseRequest -> {
            out.printf("Received push promise request URI: %s%n"
                    + "Push promise initiating request URI: %s%n%n",
                    pushPromiseRequest.uri(),
                    request.uri());
            return BodyHandlers.ofString();
        }, pushPromisesMap);
```

The first argument to the `of()` method is a function that prints the push promise details and returns a response body handler of `String` type. The second argument is the concurrent map in which you want to accumulate all push promises.

You do not have control over accepting and rejecting push promises when you create a push promise handler this way. The push promise handler will use the following rules to accept and reject push promises:

- A push request is rejected/cancelled if there is already an entry in the concurrent map whose key is equal to the received push promise request.

- A push request is rejected/cancelled if it does not have the same origin as its initiating request.

- Otherwise, a push request is accepted.

The second rule needs little explanation. If your initiating request URI is http://host/path, the push request must be from http://host. The push promise handler compares the host and port of the initiating request and the push request. If both do not match, the push promise is rejected.

Let us revisit the previous server push example in Listing 3-10. The initiating request URI was www.angular.io and the push promise request URI was like https://angular.io/<path>. Both the requests' port (http vs. https) and the host (www.angular.io vs. angular.io) do not match. If you use the push promise handler created by the static of() method of the HttpResponse.PushPromiseHandler<T> interface, push promises will be rejected. In the next example, you will use the initiating request URI as https://angular.io to avoid the issue of your push promises being rejected automatically.

Listing 3-11 contains the complete code to demonstrate the use of the push promise handler created by the static of() method of the HttpResponse.PushPromiseHandler<T> interface. There are ample comments in the code to explain each step. Notice that there is no Thread.sleep() call at the end of the main() method in this example!

Listing 3-11. The Improved Version of the Program to Test Server Push

```java
// ImprovedServerPush.java
package com.jdojo.http.client;

import java.net.URI;
import java.net.http.HttpClient;
import java.net.http.HttpRequest;
import java.net.http.HttpResponse;
import java.net.http.HttpResponse.BodyHandlers;
import java.net.http.HttpResponse.PushPromiseHandler;
import java.util.concurrent.CompletableFuture;
import java.util.concurrent.ConcurrentHashMap;
import java.util.concurrent.ConcurrentMap;
import static java.lang.System.out;

public class ImprovedServerPush {
    public static void main(String[] args) throws InterruptedException {
        // Create an HttpClient with default configurations
        HttpClient client = HttpClient.newHttpClient();
```

```
// Build a request
HttpRequest request = HttpRequest.newBuilder()
        .uri(URI.create("https://angular.io"))
        .build();

// Create a concurrent map to accumulate all push promises
ConcurrentMap<HttpRequest,CompletableFuture<HttpResponse<String>>>
        pushPromisesMap  = new ConcurrentHashMap<>();

// Create a push promise handler
PushPromiseHandler<String> pushPromiseHandler
        = PushPromiseHandler.of(pushPromiseRequest -> {
            out.printf("Received push promise request URI: %s%n"
                    + "Push promise initiating request URI: %s%n%n",
                     pushPromiseRequest.uri(),
                     request.uri());
            return BodyHandlers.ofString();
        }, pushPromisesMap);

// Send the request asynchronously allowing server push
HttpResponse<String> response = client.sendAsync(request,
        BodyHandlers.ofString(),
        pushPromiseHandler
).join();

// Print the response details
out.printf("Initiating request URI: %s%n"
        + "Response's request URI: %s%n"
        + "Response status code: %d%n",
        request.uri(),
        response.request().uri(),
        response.statusCode());

// By this time all push promises are in the pushPromisesMap.
// Their responses might not have been available by now.
CompletableFuture<?>[] allPushPromises
        = pushPromisesMap.values()
                .toArray(CompletableFuture<?>[]::new);
```

```
        // Wait for all push promise response bodies be available
        CompletableFuture.allOf(allPushPromises)
                         .join();

        // Print the push promise response details
        pushPromisesMap.values()
                .stream()
                .map(CompletableFuture::join)
                .forEach(pushResponse -> {
                    out.printf("%nProcessed push promise request URI: %s%n"
                            + "Pushed response status code: %d%n",
                            pushResponse.request().uri(),
                            pushResponse.statusCode());
                });
    }
}
```

```
Received push promise request URI: https://angular.io/generated/
navigation.json
Push promise initiating request URI: https://angular.io

Received push promise request URI: https://angular.io/generated/docs/index.
json
Push promise initiating request URI: https://angular.io

Initiating request URI: https://angular.io
Response's request URI: https://angular.io
Response status code: 200

Processed push promise request URI: https://angular.io/generated/docs/index.json
Pushed response status code: 200

Processed push promise request URI: https://angular.io/generated/
navigation.json
Pushed response status code: 200
```

Using HTTP Basic Authentication

A server may require authentication to allow access to a requested resource. HTTP provides challenge-response type of authentication framework. A client requests a resource from a server. The server challenges the client requesting a specific type of authentication. The client provides the authentication information to the server. The server allows or denies access to the requested resource after validating the authentication information. There are several types of authentications such as Basic, Bearer, Digest, and so on.

The HTTP Client API provides built-in support for basic authentication in which the server responds to the client with a 401 (Unauthorized) HTTP status code and a response header named WWW-Authenticate, which contains at least one challenge. Typically, the client responds with a base64-encoded username and password in the request header named Authorization, which may look like

Authorization: Basic a2lzaG9yaTpzaGFyYW4=

Let us have an example of basic authentication. You will use the following URL that challenges the client for basic authentication:

https://httpbin.org/basic-auth/[username]/[password]

Here, [username] is the username and [password] is the password required for authentication. When challenged by the server, you will need to provide the same username and password for the authentication to succeed. In the example, I use

https://httpbin.org/basic-auth/kishori/sharan

If you enter this URL in a browser, you will be prompted for a username and a password. You need to enter kishori as the username and sharan as the password. To use different username/password, change this URL accordingly.

An instance of the java.net.Authenticator class is used to provide basic authentication using username/password. You need to subclass Authenticator and override the getPasswordAuthentication() method. The method returns an instance of the PasswordAuthentication class, which is simply a holder for the username and password. You will set an instance of this authenticator to the HttpClient object using the authenticator() method of the HttpClient.Builder interface. When the HttpClient needs to authenticate a request, it will call the getPasswordAuthentication() method of your authenticator and send the username/password returned in a PasswordAuthentication to the server.

Listing 3-12 contains the code for a class named BasicAuthenticator. You create its instance by providing a username and a password. Its getPasswordAuthentication() method prints a message when an authentication is required and returns the username and password in a PasswordAuthentication. Typically, you would inspect the request for authentication such as the web site name before providing the username/password. If the user needs to provide this information, you may want to prompt the user with a dialog box where username/password can be entered. I kept the example simple to return the provided username/password.

Listing 3-12. A Basic HTTP Authenticator

```java
// BasicAuthenticator.java
package com.jdojo.http.client;

import java.net.Authenticator;
import java.net.PasswordAuthentication;

public class BasicAuthenticator extends Authenticator {
    private final String userName;
    private final char[] password;

    public BasicAuthenticator(String userName, char[] password) {
        this.userName = userName;
        this.password = password;
    }

    @Override
    protected PasswordAuthentication getPasswordAuthentication() {
        System.out.println(this.getRequestingURL()
                + " is asking for authentication: "
                + this.getRequestingPrompt());

        return new PasswordAuthentication(userName, password);
    }
}
```

Listing 3-13 contains a complete program to demonstrate the basic authentication. You may get a different output. A discussion of the important parts in the program follows the output.

Listing 3-13. Testing Basic HTTP Authentication

```java
// BasicAuthenticationTest.java
package com.jdojo.http.client;

import java.net.Authenticator;
import java.net.URI;
import java.net.http.HttpClient;
import java.net.http.HttpRequest;
import java.net.http.HttpResponse;
import java.net.http.HttpResponse.BodyHandlers;

public class BasicAuthenticationTest {
    public static void main(String[] args) {
        // Set a default authenticator
        String username = "kishori";
        char[] password = new char[]{'s', 'h', 'a', 'r', 'a', 'n'};
        Authenticator.setDefault(
                new BasicAuthenticator(username, password));

        // Create an HttpClient with an authenticator
        HttpClient client = HttpClient.newBuilder()
                .authenticator(Authenticator.getDefault())
                .build();

        // Use the Get HTTP method
        HttpRequest request = HttpRequest.newBuilder()
                .uri(URI.create("https://httpbin.org/basic-auth/"
                        + username + "/" + new String(password)))
                .build();

        // Send the request to the server asynchronously
        HttpResponse<String> response
                = client.sendAsync(request, BodyHandlers.ofString())
                    .join();
```

```java
        // Print the response status and body
        System.out.println("Response Status: " + response.statusCode());
        System.out.println("Response body:\n" + response.body());

        // Print the previous response details
        response.previousResponse()
                .ifPresent(previousResopnse -> {
                    System.out.println("Previous response Status: "
                            + previousResopnse.statusCode());
                    System.out.println("Previous response body:\n"
                            + previousResopnse.body());

                    System.out.println("Previous response headers:");
                    previousResopnse.headers()
                            .map()
                            .entrySet()
                            .forEach(System.out::println);
                });
    }
}
```

```
https://httpbin.org/basic-auth/kishori/sharan is asking for authentication:
Fake Realm
Response Status: 200
Response body:
{
  "authenticated": true,
  "user": "kishori"
}

Previous response Status: 401
Previous response body:
null
Previous response headers:
access-control-allow-credentials=[true]
access-control-allow-origin=[*]
connection=[keep-alive]
```

```
content-length=[0]
date=[Sun, 28 Jul 2019 00:05:49 GMT]
referrer-policy=[no-referrer-when-downgrade]
server=[nginx]
www-authenticate=[Basic realm="Fake Realm"]
x-content-type-options=[nosniff]
x-frame-options=[DENY]
x-xss-protection=[1; mode=block]
```

The program creates an instance of the BasicAuthenticator class by passing it kishori/sharan as username/password. You set a default authenticator in the Authenticator class by calling its setDefault() method and get it by calling its getDefault() method. You set the authenticator in the HttpClient instance. This logic is used in the program

```
// Set a default authenticator
String username = "kishori";
char[] password = new char[]{'s', 'h', 'a', 'r', 'a', 'n'};
Authenticator.setDefault(new BasicAuthenticator(username, password));

// Create an HttpClient with an authenticator
HttpClient client = HttpClient.newBuilder()
                              .authenticator(Authenticator.getDefault())
                              .build();
```

The first line of output indicates that the authenticator was used. The program prints the response status code and the body. In case of basic authentication, the first request receives a response with a 401 status code, no body, and a WWW-Authenticate header. If there are multiple responses involved in fulfilling a request, you can get the reference to the previous response using the previousResponse() method of the HttpResponse<T> interface, which returns an Optional<HttpResponse<T>>. The last part of the output shows the server had responded with a 401 status code and a WWW-Authenticate header.

You can also use Bearer HTTP authentication using the HTTP Client API. If you receive a 401 status code and a `WWW-Authenticate` header with a `Bearer` value, you can simply resend the request with an `Authorization` header with the bearer token. The following snippet of code creates a request with a bearer token of `my-secret-token`:

```
// Prepare a request with the bearer token in the Authorization header
HttpRequest request = HttpRequest.newBuilder()
        .uri(URI.create("https://httpbin.org/bearer"))
        .header("Authorization", "Bearer my-secret-token")
        .build();
```

You can write a program to send this request to the server and print the response details as an exercise.

Using WebSockets

The WebSocket protocol provides a two-way communication between two endpoints – a client endpoint and a server endpoint. The term *endpoint* means any of the two sides of the connection that use the WebSocket protocol. The client endpoint initiates a connection, and the server endpoint accepts the connection. The connection is bi-directional, which means the server endpoint can push messages to the client endpoint on its own. You will also come across another term in this context, which is called *a peer*. A peer is simply the other end of the connection. For example, for a client endpoint, the server endpoint is a peer, and, for a server endpoint, the client endpoint is a peer. A WebSocket *session* represents a sequence of interactions between an endpoint and a single peer.

The WebSocket protocol can be broken into three parts:

- Opening handshake

- Data exchanges

- Closing handshake

The client initiates an opening handshake with the server. The handshake occurs using HTTP protocol with an upgrade request to the WebSocket protocol. The server responds to the opening handshake with an upgrade response. Once the handshake is successful, the client and the server exchange messages. The message exchanges may be initiated by either the client or the server. In the end, either endpoint can send a closing handshake; the peer responds with the closing handshake. Once the closing handshake is successful, the WebSocket is closed.

The HTTP Client API supports creating WebSocket client endpoints. To have a complete example of using the WebSocket protocol, you will need to have both a server endpoint and a client endpoint. The following sections will explain WebSocket details on how to create a client endpoint to interact with a server endpoint. You will use an already built server endpoint, which is available online, as described in the next section.

WebSocket Server Endpoint

The HTTP Client API provides support for creating WebSocket clients, not the server. It is beyond the scope of this book to show you how to create a WebSocket server endpoint. I will use a freely available server endpoint for our examples. The WebSocket server endpoint I will use is `ws://demos.kaazing.com/echo`. Visit `www.websocket.org/echo.html` for more details on this endpoint. You can also test this endpoint using this web page. This endpoint acts as an echo server. When you send a message, it echoes back the message to you.

Creating a Client Endpoint

Developing a WebSocket client endpoint involves using the `HttpClient` class and the `WebSocket` interface, which are part of the HTTP Client API. The `WebSocket` interface contains the following two nested `static` interfaces:

- `WebSocket.Builder`
- `WebSocket.Listener`

An instance of the `WebSocket` interface represents a WebSocket client endpoint. A builder, which is an instance of the `WebSocket.Builder` interface, is used to create a `WebSocket` instance. The `newWebSocketBuilder()` method of the `HttpClient` class returns a `WebSocket.Builder`.

When events occur on a client endpoint, for example, the completion of the opening handshake, a message arrival, closing handshake, and so on, notifications are sent to a listener, which is an instance of the `WebSocket.Listener` interface. The interface contains a `default` method for each type of notification. You will need to create a class that implements this interface providing an implementation for only those methods that correspond to the events of which you are interested in receiving notifications. You need to specify a listener when you create a `WebSocket` instance.

97

When you send a close message to a peer, you may specify a close status code. The WebSocket interface contains a NORMAL_CLOSURE constant of type int. It represents a WebSocket Close message status code (1000), which means that the connection was closed normally. This means that the purpose for which the connection was established was fulfilled.

Recall that a WebSocket provides a two-way communication between a client and a server. The API provides two types of methods – one type to send messages to the server and another to receive messages from the server. You use sendXxx() method of a WebSocket instance to send messages to the server. One of the onXxx() methods of the WebSocket.Listener instance is invoked when a message is received from the server. The following sections describe all steps in setting up a client endpoint in detail.

Creating a Listener

A listener is an instance of the WebSocket.Listener interface. Creating a listener involves creating a class that implements this interface. All methods in the interface are default methods. All methods of the listener are passed the reference of the WebSocket to which the listener is associated. You can break the methods in a listener into the following two categories:

- Connection opening and error reporting methods

- Message receiving methods

The following two methods fall into the first category:

- void onOpen(WebSocket webSocket)

- void onError(WebSocket, Throwable error)

When a WebSocket is connected, the onOpen() method of its listener is called. It is the first method of the listener to be called. It is called only once. Typically, you print an informational message that a connection has been established and request to receive more messages. The default implementation of this message requests to receive one more message. A request for messages is made using the request(long n) method of the WebSocket interface.

```
// Allow one more message to be received
webSocket.request(1);
```

Note that messages can be received in parts. A request(n) call on the WebSocket means that the method that receives messages can be called n times. Suppose a text message is delivered in three parts. Calling request(1) will allow calling the onText() method only once. Typically, you call request(1) in the onOpen() method and when you receive a message such as in onBinary() and onText() methods.

Tip   If the server sends more messages than requested, messages are queued on the TCP connection and may eventually force the sender to stop sending more messages through TCP flow control. It is important that you call the request(long n) method at the appropriate time with an appropriate argument value, so your listener keeps receiving messages from the server. It is a common mistake to override the onOpen() method in your listener and not call the webSocket.request(1) method, which prevents you from receiving messages from the server.

When an error occurs, the onError() method is called. No other methods on the listener are called after the onError() method is called. The second error argument contains the error details. If an exception is thrown from this method, the behavior is undefined.

The following methods fall into the second category – message receiving methods. They are called when a specific type of message is received from the server:

- `CompletionStage<?> onBinary(WebSocket webSocket, ByteBuffer data, boolean last)`

- `CompletionStage<?> onText(WebSocket webSocket, CharSequence data, boolean last)`

- `CompletionStage<?> onPing(WebSocket webSocket, ByteBuffer message)`

- `CompletionStage<?> onPong(WebSocket webSocket, ByteBuffer message)`

- `CompletionStage<?> onClose(WebSocket webSocket, int statusCode, String reason)`

The onClose() method is called when the endpoint receives a close message from the peer. It is the last notification to the listener. An exception thrown from this method is ignored.

The default implementation does not do anything. Typically, you need to send a close message to the peer to complete the closing handshake.

The onPing() method is called when this endpoint receives a Ping message from the peer. A Ping message can be sent by both client and server endpoints. The default implementation of the WebSocket interface sends a Pong message to the peer in response to a Ping message with the same message contents. Therefore, when you create a listener, typically, you do not need to provide an implementation for the onPing() method.

The onPong() method is called when the endpoint receives a Pong message from the peer. A Pong message is typically received as a response to a previously sent Ping message. An endpoint may also receive an unsolicited Pong message. The default implementation of the onPong() method requests one more message on the listener and performs no other actions.

The onBinary() and onText() methods are called when a binary message and a text message are received from the peer, respectively. Binary and text messages can be sent in parts. The third boolean argument to these methods indicates whether it is the last part of a message. A value of false means that it is not the last part and more parts of the message will be received later. A value of true means that it is the last part of the message. Inside these methods, you accumulate the message parts when the last argument is false and process the message when all parts are received as indicated by a value of true in the last argument.

Note that the methods that are called when a message is received return a CompletionStage<?>. The completion of the returned CompletionStage indicates to the WebSocket that the message has been processed, and it may reclaim resources tied up in delivering the message. Returning null from these methods indicates that the message processing is complete.

Let us build a WebSocket listener, which you will use in the subsequent sections to create a WebSocket. Listing 3-14 contains the complete code for our WebSocket listener. The descriptions of its components follow the code.

Listing 3-14. An Implementation of the WebSocket.Listener Interface

```
// WebSocketEchoListener.java
package com.jdojo.http.client;

import java.net.http.WebSocket;
import java.nio.ByteBuffer;
import java.util.ArrayList;
```

```java
import java.util.List;
import java.util.concurrent.CompletableFuture;
import java.util.concurrent.CompletionStage;
import static java.util.stream.Collectors.joining;

public final class WebSocketEchoListener implements WebSocket.Listener {
    // Partial text messages are accumulated in this list
    private final List<String> textMessages = new ArrayList();

    // This CompletableFuture is complete when an error occurs or the
    // WebSocket is closed. See the onError() and onClose() methods.
    CompletableFuture<String> closeStatus = new CompletableFuture<>();

    @Override
    public void onOpen(WebSocket webSocket) {
        System.out.println("Connected...");

        // Request one more message
        webSocket.request(1);
    }

    @Override
    public CompletionStage<?> onText(WebSocket webSocket,
            CharSequence data, boolean last) {
        // Request one more message
        webSocket.request(1);

        // Accumulate the message
        textMessages.add(data.toString());

        if (last) {
            // Received the last part of the message. Let us print it.
            String wholeMessage = textMessages.stream()
                                            .collect(joining(""));
            System.out.println("Received: " + wholeMessage);

            // Clear the accumulated messages, so we can accumulate
            // partial messages received in future
            textMessages.clear();
        }
```

```java
        // Return null to indicate that message proccessing is complete
        return null;
    }

    @Override
    public CompletionStage<?> onPong(WebSocket webSocket,
            ByteBuffer message) {
        // Request one more message
        webSocket.request(1);

        // Decode the message and print it
        String data = new String(message.array());
        System.out.println("Received a Pong: " + data);

        // Return null to indicate that message proccessing is complete
        return null;
    }

    @Override
    public void onError(WebSocket webSocket, Throwable error) {
        // Complete the CompletableFuture exceptionally to indicate that
        // the WebSocket connection is closed with error
        closeStatus.completeExceptionally(error);
    }

    @Override
    public CompletionStage<?> onClose(WebSocket webSocket,
            int statusCode, String reason) {

        // Prepare the close description
        String closeDescription = "Closed with status " + statusCode
                + " and reason: " + reason;

        // Complete the CompletableFuture to indiate that the WebSocket
        // connection is closed.
        closeStatus.complete(closeDescription);

        return null;
    }
```

```
    public CompletableFuture<String> closeStatus() {
        return this.closeStatus;
    }
}
```

Our listener listens for text messages, which can be received in parts. The textMessages instance variable is used to accumulate partial messages. It is used inside the onText() method. When the onText() method receives the last part of a message, it joins all partial messages in the textMessages instance variable, prints it, and clears the list to accumulate parts of a new message in future.

The listener declares another instance variable named closeStatus:

```
CompletableFuture<String> closeStatus = new CompletableFuture<>();
```

When I will create a WebSocket client program, I would like to know when this listener receives the last message. The last message is received by a listener when its onError() or onClose() method is called. The onError() and onClose() methods complete the closeStatus CompletableFuture exceptionally or normally, respectively. The closeStatus() method simply returns this CompletableFuture. The intended usage of this is in a client program to wait for the WebSocket to close:

```
// Create a listner for our WebSocket
WebSocketEchoListener listener = new WebSocketEchoListener();

/* Create a WebSocket with this listener and exchange messages
   with the server here...
*/

// Wait for the WebSocket to close
listener.closeStatus()
        .thenAccept(System.out::println)
        .exceptionally(e -> {
            e.printStackTrace();
            return null;
        })
        .join();
```

The onOpen() method prints an informational message and requests one more message. Note that if you remove the call to webSocket.request(1) method, you will not be able to receive any messages at all.

The onText() method requests for one more message and accumulates the message. If this is the last part of a message, it prints the whole message to the standard output and clears the textMessages instance variable, which will be used to accumulate next text message when the onText() method is called in future. It returns null to indicate that the message processing is complete.

The onPong() method requests one more message to receive, prints the message, and returns null to indicate that the message processing is complete.

The onError() method completes the closeStatus CompletableFuture exceptionally.

The onClose() method completes the closeStatus CompletableFuture normally with a description containing the status code and reason for closing the connection. A status code of 1000 indicates normal closure.

Building a Client Endpoint

You need to build an instance of the WebSocket interface that acts as a client endpoint. The instance is used to connect and exchange messages with the server endpoint. A WebSocket instance is built using a WebSocket.Builder. You need to use the newWebSocketBuilder() method of the HttpClient class to get a builder.

Once you have a builder, you can call one of the following methods of the WebSocket.Builder to configure and build the WebSocket:

- WebSocket.Builder connectTimeout(Duration timeout)

- WebSocket.Builder header(String name, String value)

- WebSocket.Builder subprotocols(String mostPreferred, String... lesserPreferred)

- CompletableFuture<WebSocket> buildAsync(URI uri, WebSocket. Listener listener)

The connectTimeout() method lets you specify a timeout for the opening handshake. If the opening handshake does not complete within the specified duration, the CompletableFuture returned from the buildAsync() method of the WebSocket. Builder completes exceptionally with an HttpTimeoutException.

You can add any custom headers for the opening handshake using the header() method.

You can specify a request for given subprotocols during the opening handshake using the subprotocols() method – only one of them will be selected by the server. The subprotocols are defined by the application. The client and the server need to agree to work on specific subprotocols and their details.

Finally, call the buildAsync() method of the WebSocket.Builder interface to build the endpoint. The first argument is the URI of the server endpoint. The second argument is a WebSocket listener. It returns a CompletableFuture<WebSocket>, which completes normally when this endpoint is connected to the server endpoint; it completes exceptionally when there was an error.

The following snippet of code shows how to build and connect a client endpoint. Notice that the URI for the server starts with ws, which indicates the WebSocket protocol.

```
// Create an HttpClient with default configurations
HttpClient client = HttpClient.newHttpClient();

// Create a listener for our WebSocket
WebSocketEchoListener listener = new WebSocketEchoListener();

// Create a WebSocket
WebSocket webSocket = client.newWebSocketBuilder()
        .buildAsync(URI.create("ws://demos.kaazing.com/echo"), listener)
        .join();
```

Sending Messages to a Peer

Once a client endpoint is connected to a peer, both exchange messages. An instance of the WebSocket interface represents a client endpoint, and the interface contains the following methods to send messages to the peer:

- CompletableFuture<WebSocket> sendBinary(ByteBuffer data, boolean last)

- CompletableFuture<WebSocket> sendText(CharSequence data, boolean last)

- CompletableFuture<WebSocket> sendPing(ByteBuffer message)

- CompletableFuture<WebSocket> sendPong(ByteBuffer message)

- CompletableFuture<WebSocket> sendClose(int statusCode, String reason)

The sendText() method is used to send a text message to the peer. If the second argument is false, it indicates part of the partial message. If the second argument is true, it indicates the last part of a partial message. If there were no partial messages sent before, a true in the second argument indicates a whole message.

The sendBinary() method sends a binary message to the peer.

The sendPing() and sendPong() methods send a Ping and a Pong message to the peer, respectively.

The sendClose() method sends a Close message to the peer. You can send a Close message as part of a closing handshake initiated by a peer, or you can send it to initiate a closing handshake with the peer.

Tip   If you want to close the WebSocket abruptly, use the abort() method of the WebSocket interface.

Running the WebSocket Program

It is time to see a WebSocket client and server exchanging messages. Listing 3-15 contains a complete program. It creates a WebSocket, sends/receives messages with a server at ws://demos.kaazing.com/echo, and closes the WebSocket. The output shows the interactions. The program contains ample comment to explain the logic.

Listing 3-15. A Program to Demonstate a WebSocket Client/Server Interactions

```
// WebSocketClient.java
package com.jdojo.http.client;

import static java.lang.System.out;
import java.net.URI;
import java.net.http.HttpClient;
import java.net.http.WebSocket;
import static java.net.http.WebSocket.NORMAL_CLOSURE;
import java.nio.ByteBuffer;

public class WebSocketClient {
    public static void main(String[] args) throws InterruptedException {
        // Create an HttpClient with default configurations
```

```
HttpClient client = HttpClient.newHttpClient();

// Create a listener for our WebSocket
WebSocketEchoListener listener = new WebSocketEchoListener();

// Create a WebSocket
WebSocket webSocket = client.newWebSocketBuilder()
        .buildAsync(URI.create("ws://demos.kaazing.com/echo"),
                listener)
        .join();

// Send a message to the server. The second argument of true
// in the sendText() indicates that the message is whole.
String helloMessage = "Hello, there.";
webSocket.sendText(helloMessage, true)
        .thenRun(() -> out.println("Sent: " + helloMessage))
        .join();

// Send a Ping message to the server
String pingMessage = "Just checking...";
webSocket.sendPing(ByteBuffer.wrap(pingMessage.getBytes()))
        .thenRun(() -> out.println("Sent Ping: " + pingMessage))
        .join();

// Send a Close message to the server. After this, you cannot
// send any more messages to the server. The server will send
// you back a Close message.
webSocket.sendClose(NORMAL_CLOSURE, "Done")
        .thenRun(() -> out.println("Sent Close"))
        .join();

// Wait for the WebSocket listener to close. Recall that the
// CompletableFuture<String> returned from the closeStatus()
// method completes when the onClose() or onError() method of
// the listener is called.
listener.closeStatus()
        .thenAccept(System.out::println)
        .exceptionally(e -> {
```

```
                        e.printStackTrace();
                        return null;
                })
                .join();
    }
}
```

```
Connected...
Sent: Hello, there.
Sent Ping: Just checking...
Sent Close
Received: Hello, there.
Received a Pong: Just checking...
Closed with status 1000 and reason: Done
```

The program in Listing 3-15 sends one text message to the server using the following snippet of code:

```
// Send a message to the server. The second argument of true
// in the sendText() indicates that the message is whole.
String helloMessage = "Hello, there.";
webSocket.sendText(helloMessage, true)
        .thenRun(() -> out.println("Sent: " + helloMessage))
        .join();
```

I want you to change the code to pass false as the second argument to the sendText() method. The changed code would look like

```
String helloMessage = "Hello, there.";
webSocket.sendText(helloMessage, false)
        .thenRun(() -> out.println("Sent: " + helloMessage))
        .join();
```

Now run the program in Listing 3-15 again. What do you observe? You should find that the hello message was sent to the server, but you do not see any output about receiving the same message back. Your output should look like

```
Connected...
Sent: Hello, there.
Sent Ping: Just checking...
Sent Close
Received a Pong: Just checking...
Closed with status 1000 and reason: Done
```

Our server is an echo server. Whatever you send to the server, you receive the same message back. The `false` in the second argument to the `sendText()` method means that it is a partial message. So, the server sent this message back as a partial message too. The `onText()` method of our WebSocket listener was called with the third argument set to `false`. Recall that our `onText()` method (refer to Listing 3-14) prints the message only when the third argument is set to `true` indicating that it is the final part of the message. The hello message was received back by the listener, but never got printed because it was marked as a partial message. Unless you send another text message to the server marking it as the final part of the message, you will not see the hello message in the output. You can verify that the message was received by printing a message from the `onText()` method of the listener. You can fix this problem by adding the following statement after you send the hello message as a partial message:

```
// Send an empty string marking it as the final part of the message
webSocket.sendText("", true)
        .join();
```

Alternatively, you can send the hello message in two parts – the first part being partial and the second part being final as follows:

```
webSocket.sendText("Hello, ", false)
        .join();

webSocket.sendText("there.", true)
        .thenRun(() -> out.println("Sent: Hello, there."))
        .join();
```

Summary

Java 11 added an HTTP Client API as standard feature that lets you work with HTTP requests and responses in Java applications. The API provides classes and interfaces to develop WebSocket client endpoints with authentication. The API is in the `java.net.http` package, which is in the `java.net.http` module.

The `HttpClient` and `HttpRequest` classes and `HttpResponse<T>` and `WebSocket` interfaces are central to the HTTP Client API. Instances of these types are created using builders. The `HttpClient` class is immutable. An instance of the `HttpClient` class stores HTTP connection configurations that can be reused for multiple HTTP requests. An instance of the `HttpRequest` class represents an HTTP request. An instance of the `HttpResponse` interface represents an HTTP response received from a server. You can send and receive HTTP requests and responses synchronously or asynchronously.

An instance of the `WebSocket` interface represents a WebSocket client endpoint. Communication with the WebSocket server endpoint is accomplished asynchronously. The WebSocket API is event-based. You need to specify a listener, which is an instance of the `WebSocket.Listener` static interface, for a WebSocket client endpoint. The listener is notified – by invoking its appropriate methods – when an event occurs on the endpoint, for example, the listener is notified when the opening handshake with a peer is completed successfully by calling the `onOpen()` method of the listener. The API supports exchanging text as well as binary messages with peers. Messages may be exchanged in parts.

CHAPTER 4

Launching Single File Source Code Programs

In this chapter, you will learn

- What the Java launcher is

- The different modes you can use to run the `java` command

- What the source-file mode for the `java` command is

- How to run source code written in a single file using the `java` command

- How the `java` command selects the class to run in the source-file mode

- About the class loading mechanism in the source-file mode

- How and when to use the `--source` option with the `java` command

- How to create utility programs written in Java on UNIX-like operating systems using a shebang

What Is the Java Launcher?

When you develop a Java application, you need to use at least two tools: a Java compiler and a Java launcher. A Java compiler compiles your source code into class files, and a Java launcher launches (or runs) your application from the class files. When you install the JDK, both tools are copied to the `JDK_HOME\bin` directory. The Java compiler is the

© Kishori Sharan 2019
K. Sharan, *Java 13 Revealed*, https://doi.org/10.1007/978-1-4842-5407-3_4

javac tool, and the Java launcher is the java tool. The java tool is the topic of discussion in this chapter. Sometimes, you will come across the following phrases to refer to the java tool:

- The Java launcher or the java launcher
- The Java application launcher
- The java command

They all refer to the same java tool found in the JDK_HOME\bin or JRE_HOME\bin directory, which is used to run a Java application. In my books, I refer to this as *the java command* and I will continue to do so in this chapter.

Up to Java 8, you had to compile the source code and then run the compiled code. Compiling the source code to run a "HelloWorld" program was just added a bit to the learning curve to the beginners. Every time you make a small change to your program, you had to compile it before running it again. Java 9 added the JShell command-line tool, which lets you run source code by entering directly into the jshell command line. The JShell tool is an interactive tool. It is not meant to run Java program from source files. Rather, it is meant for those who want to explore the Java language interactively.

Until Java 11, if you wanted to run a program, you must compile it before running it. In Java 11, the java command was modified to support running Java programs directly from source code – no need to compile your source code. Starting from Java 11, the java command can be used in one of the following four modes:

- Launching a class file
- Launching the main class of a JAR file
- Launching the main class of a module (added in JDK9)
- Launching a class in a source file (added in JDK11)

In this chapter, I explain the fourth mode, which is the source-file mode. In this mode, you supply a source file to the java command, and it compiles the source code in memory and runs it. If you have source code in a file named HelloWorld.java, you would run it using the source-file mode as follows:

```
java HelloWorld.java
```

The java command looks at the supplied file extension, which is .java and uses the source-file mode to run the program. I will explain rules and restrictions of the source-file mode later. For now, think that it is as simple as running the java command with a source file.

Who should use the source-file mode? It is not intended to be used by everyone. It is intended for those

- Who are learning Java and trying to run small programs written in a single file

- Who want to write utility programs/scripts using Java and run them as if they were OS-level commands/scripts

If your Java program does not fall into one of these two categories, the business is as usual for you. That is, write your source code, compile them into class files, and use the java command in one of the other three modes to run your application.

The java command runs a class with a method that must have the following declaration:

```
public static void main(String[] args)
```

The source-file mode does not change this requirement.

Setting Up Examples

The source-file mode for the java command works in classpath mode, not module mode. That is, you cannot declare your source code in a module. All examples for this chapter are in the src\sourcecode.apps directory in the supplied source code for this book.

Let us have a quick example. Listing 4-1 contains the code for a class named HelloSourceMode. The class is in the com.jdojo.sourcecode.mode package. There is nothing special going on inside this class. It simply prints a message to the standard output.

Listing 4-1. A HelloSourceMode Class

```
// HelloSourceMode.java
package com.jdojo.sourcecode.mode;

public class HelloSourceMode {
    public static void main(String[] args) {
        System.out.println("Hello, Java source-file launcher!");
    }
}
```

Use the following command to run the HelloSourceMode class:

```
C:\Java13Revealed\src\sourcecode.apps>java HelloSourceMode.java
```

```
Hello, Java source-file launcher!
```

The java command was run from inside the src\sourcecode.app directory where the HelloSourceMode.java file is stored.

The HelloSourceMode class is in the com.jdojo.sourcecode.mode package. The source-file mode did not force you to store the source file to conform to the class' package. If you were to run this class using any of the other three modes, you were required to store the class file in a com\jdojo\sourcecode\mode directory. The source-file mode cares only about the existence of the source file. If it can find the file, it will run it. If your current directory is src, you would use the following command to run this file:

```
C:\Java13Revealed\src>java sourcecode.apps\HelloSourceMode.java
```

```
Hello, Java source-file launcher!
```

Source-File Mode Selection

Table 4-1 lists the syntax for the java command to run a program in all four modes.

Table 4-1. *Syntax for Running the java Command in Four Modes*

Mode	Syntax
Class-file mode	java [options] mainclass [args...]
JAR-file mode	java [options] -jar jarfile [args...]
Module mode	java [options] --module module[/mainclass] [args...]
Source-file mode	java [options] source-file [args...]

Compare the syntax for the class-file mode and source-file mode. They are very similar. Consider the following command:

```
C:\Java13Revealed\src\sourcecode.apps>java Unexpected.java
```

Will this command run in the class-file mode or source-file mode? In class-file mode, it will try to run a class whose fully qualified name is Unexpected.java. That is, the class is in java.class file under the Unexpected directory. In the source-file mode, it will try to run the class declared in the Unexpected.java source file. In this case, the source-file mode wins and the Unexpected.java source file is run. I have included the Unexpected.java and Unexpected\java.class file in the source code for this chapter. You can try this example yourself to see the results.

This discussion brings us to the question "How does the java command choose the source-file mode?" It uses two criteria in selecting the source-file mode:

- The first item on the command line that is not an option or part of an option. If this item is the name of an existing file with .java extension, the source-file mode is used.

- Using the --source option on the command line forces the java command to use the source-file mode. If the source-file name does not contain the .java extension, you must use the --source option to use the source-file mode.

Let us go back to running the Unexpected.java source file. Because our file name ends with the .java extension, the java command uses the source-file mode to run the class inside this file.

In subsequent sections, I will explain how the source file is compiled before running it and other rules of the source-file mode.

Must Be a Single Source File

The source-file mode allows your program to be stored in one and only one source file. It compiles only the source file specified on the command line. If the code in your source file refers to code in other source files, the source-file mode will not run your program.

Listing 4-2 contains the code for a class named MultiFileTest. It attempts to create an object of the HelloSourceMode class, which is stored in HelloSourceMode.java file (see Listing 4-1).

Listing 4-2. A MultiFileTest Class That Uses a Class from Another Source File

```
// MultiFileTest.java
package com.jdojo.sourcecode.mode;

public class MultiFileTest {
    public static void main(String[] args) {
        // Create an object of the HelloSourceMode class
        HelloSourceMode hsm = new HelloSourceMode();

        System.out.println("A HelloSourceMode object created.");
    }
}
```

The following command attempts to run the `MultiFileTest.java` source file:

```
C:\Java13Revealed\src\sourcecode.apps>java MultiFileTest.java
```

```
MultiFileTest.java:7: error: cannot find symbol
        HelloSourceMode hsm = new HelloSourceMode();
        ^
  symbol:   class HelloSourceMode
  location: class MultiFileTest
MultiFileTest.java:7: error: cannot find symbol
        HelloSourceMode hsm = new HelloSourceMode();
                                  ^
  symbol:   class HelloSourceMode
  location: class MultiFileTest
2 errors
error: compilation failed
```

The source-file mode fails to run the `MultiFileTest.java` file because it does not find the `HelloSourceMode` class definition during compilation. In source-file mode, it is allowed for a type to refer to other types (classes/interfaces). However, the referred types must be present on the application class path or inside the source file itself. The referred types cannot be in other source files. You can fix the previous error in two ways:

- You can have a HelloSourceMode class in compiled form on the class path.

- You can include the declaration of the HelloSourceMode class in the MultiFileTest.java file.

Listing 4-3 contains the code in a source file named Laptop.java. The file contains two classes named Laptop and Configuration.

Listing 4-3. A Source File with Two Class Declarations – Laptop and Configuration

```
// Laptop.java
package com.jdojo.sourcecode.mode;

public class Laptop {
    private Configuration config;
    public Laptop(Configuration config) {
        this.config = config;
    }

    public static void main(String[] args) {
        Configuration config = new Configuration();
        Laptop laptop = new Laptop(config);
        System.out.println("Created a laptop...");
    }
}

public class Configuration {
    public Configuration() {
        System.out.println("Creating a default configuration...");
    }
}
```

The Laptop class refers to the Configuration class. The following command successfully runs the Laptop.java file in source-file mode:

```
C:\Java13Revealed\src\sourcecode.apps>java Laptop.java
```

```
Creating a default configuration...
Created a laptop...
```

The First Top-Level Class Is Run

In source-file mode, the java command scans the specified source file and attempts to run the first type definition found. This rule implies that if you want to run class C in the source file, C must be defined as the first top-level class in the file. For example, if you have two classes in the file and both have a main() method, the first class is always run. If you want to run the second class, you must move it to the top in the source file. If the first type in the source file is not a class or does not have a main() method, the source-file mode generates an error. Let us have a few examples.

Tip Before addition of the source-file mode, you specified the name of the class to run. The source-file mode works with the file name. It automatically runs the first class declared in the file. Also, the source file name and the class name to run, which is declared inside the source file, do not have to match.

Listings 4-4, 4-5, and 4-6 contain the contents for files named HelloBye.java, ByeHello.java, and EmptyHello.java, respectively. Each file contains two classes. The file name indicates the names of the classes in it. The HelloBye.java file contains Hello and Bye classes. The ByeHello.java file contains Bye and Hello classes. The EmptyHello.java file contains Empty and Hello classes. Hello and Bye classes contain a main() method. The Empty class does not contain a main() method.

Listing 4-4. Contents of a HelloBye.java Source File

```
// HelloBye.java
package com.jdojo.sourcecode.mode;

public class Hello {
    public static void main(String[] args) {
        System.out.println("Hello");
    }
}

public class Bye {
    public static void main(String[] args) {
        System.out.println("Bye");
    }
}
```

Listing 4-5. Contents of a ByeHello.java Source File

```
// ByeHello.java
package com.jdojo.sourcecode.mode;

public class Bye {
    public static void main(String[] args) {
        System.out.println("Bye");
    }
}

public class Hello {
    public static void main(String[] args) {
        System.out.println("Hello");
    }
}
```

Listing 4-6. Contents of an EmptyHello.java Source File

```
// EmptyHello.java
package com.jdojo.sourcecode.mode;

public class Empty {
}

public class Hello {
    public static void main(String[] args) {
        System.out.println("Hello");
    }
}
```

Let us run the three source files in source-file mode one by one:

```
C:\Java13Revealed\src\sourcecode.apps>java HelloBye.java
```

```
Hello
```

```
C:\Java13Revealed\src\sourcecode.apps>java ByeHello.java
```

```
Bye
```

```
C:\Java13Revealed\src\sourcecode.apps>java EmptyHello.java
```

```
error: can't find main(String[]) method in class: com.jdojo.sourcecode.
mode.Empty
```

In the first two cases, the first class found in the source file (Hello or Bye) was run. In the third case, the first class found was Empty, which does not have a main() method. This is why the third case results in an error. If you change the type of Empty to be an interface, enum, or annotation, you will get the same error.

Passing Arguments to the Program

In source-file mode, all arguments specified after the file name on the command line are passed to the main() method of the class that is run. Listing 4-7 contains the code for a class named Stats. It computes and prints statistics such as count, sum, min, max, and average of the numbers specified on the command line. If you do not specify any arguments, it prints the usage information. If you specify any non-numeric arguments, it throws a NumberFormatException.

Listing 4-7. A Stats Class That Computes and Prints Statistics on Numbers Specified on the Command Line

```java
// Stats.java
package com.jdojo.sourcecode.mode;

import static java.lang.System.out;
import java.util.Arrays;
import java.util.DoubleSummaryStatistics;
import static java.util.stream.Collectors.summarizingDouble;

public class Stats {
    public static void main(String[] args) {
        if (args.length == 0) {
            out.println("No numbers were specified.");
            out.println("Usage: Prints stats of the specified numbers "
                    + "such as sum, average, min, and max.");
            out.println("Syntax: java Stats.java [numbers]");
            out.println("Example: java Stats.java 10 20 25 34");
            return;
        }

        // Compute and print the stats on the agruments
        DoubleSummaryStatistics stats = Arrays.asList(args)
                .stream()
                .map(s -> Double.valueOf(s))
                .collect(summarizingDouble(Double::doubleValue));

        out.println(stats);
    }
}
```

Here are a few invocations of the Stats.java file in source-file mode:

```
C:\Java13Revealed\src\sourcecode.apps>java Stats.java
```

```
No numbers were specified.
Usage: Prints stats of the specified numbers such as sum, average, min, and max.
Syntax: java Stats.java [numbers]
Example: java Stats.java 10 20 25 34
```

```
C:\Java13Revealed\src\sourcecode.apps>java Stats.java 6 8 9 4 1 4.9 -6
```

```
DoubleSummaryStatistics{count=7, sum=26.900000, min=-6.000000,
average=3.842857, max=9.000000}
```

```
C:\Java13Revealed\src\sourcecode.apps>java Stats.java 6 x 9
```

```
Exception in thread "main" java.lang.NumberFormatException: For input
string: "x"
        at java.base/jdk.internal.math.FloatingDecimal.readJavaFormatString
        (FloatingDecimal.java:2054)
...
```

Passing Options to the Compiler

In source-file mode, the java command needs to compile the source file before it can run it. It scans the options specified on the command line that are relevant to the compiler and passes them to the compiler. The options, if specified, that are passed to the compiler are as follows:

- --class-path

- --module-path

- --add-exports

- --add-modules

- --limit-modules

- `--patch-module`

- `--upgrade-module-path`

- `--enable-preview`

You cannot pass any additional options to the compiler other than those in this list. If the list of options is big, you can pass them using command-line argument files (@-files).

In source-file mode, annotation processing is disabled during compilation. It is as if you used the `-proc:none` option to compile the source code.

If a version is specified using the `--source` option, the value is used as the argument for an implicit `--release` option for the compilation.

The compiler does not enforce the file name restriction that a type in a named package should exist in a file whose name is composed from the type name followed by the `.java` extension. You have already seen examples of this kind. For example, you had public `Hello` and `Bye` classes in a `HelloBye.java` file. If you compile the `HelloBye.java` file yourself, the compiler will refuse to compile it. The compiler will insist that the public classes must be declared in two separate files named `Hello.java` and `Bye.java`. However, the compiler did not enforce this when you used the source-file mode to run the file.

In source-file mode, the source file is compiled as part of an *unnamed* module. Your code has access to all observable modules. It is as if you have compiled and run your code using the `--add-modules=ALL-DEFAULT` option. If you want your code to have access to other modules, you can do so using additional `--add-modules` options.

Running the `java` command in source-file mode requires the `jdk.compiler` module. It is needed to compile the source file in memory.

Class Loading Mechanism

All types defined in the source file are loaded by a custom class loader known as memory class loader, which delegates to the application class loader. The delegation behavior has changed between Java 11 and Java 12. Here is how it worked in Java 11:

- The memory class loader delegates to the application class loader. If the application class loader is unable to load the class, the memory class loader attempts to load the class from the source file. This has two implications. First, the application class loader cannot see classes in the source file. Second, the classes on the class path, which are loaded by the application class loader, are given precedence over the classes in the source file.

- If the class being run from the source file also exists on the class path, the `java` command gives you an error.

The goal of the `java` command in source-file mode was to provide beginners a way to run a source file with fewer surprises. The previous two rules made it complicated. Suppose you are learning Java and you want to run a class from source file. When you run the file, you get an error "class found on application class path." As a beginner, you will have a hard time understanding this error. As another example, suppose you have a source file, which contains two classes. The class being run uses the second class. When you run the source file, the second class being used is not from your source file. Rather it is picked up from the class path if the second class also happened to be on the class path. Both scenarios were possible in Java 11. As a beginner running a source file, you did not get what you intended to get from the code in your source file. Java 12 fixed this class loading mechanism to keep it simple. This change was tracked by an enhancement request at `https://bugs.openjdk.java.net/browse/JDK-8210839`.

Here is the simplified class loading behavior of the memory class loader in Java 12 and later:

- The memory class loader still delegates to the application class loader as it did in Java 11. This implies that the classes on the class path cannot use classes in the source file.

- The memory class loader looks up a class in the source file first before delegating to the application class loader. This implies that the classes in the source file are given precedence over classes on the class path.

- If the class being run from a source file also exists on the class path, the `java` command does not give you an error. It simply runs the class in the source file.

This new class loading behavior can be thought of as if the classes in the source file are prepended to the class path. Java always allowed duplicate classes on the class path, and it always used the first class found in the class path. This old first-found-on-class-path-used rule still applies from Java 12 when using the source-file mode.

Let us have a few examples to demonstrate the effects of these rules. The `src\sourcecode.apps\examples` directory contains two classes named `Fruits` and `FruitsPrinter`. Both are in the `com.jdojo.sourcecode.mode` package. I have packaged these classes in the `fruits.jar` file and stored the JAR file in the `src\sourcecode.apps` directory.

Listings 4-8 and 4-9 contain the code for the `Fruits` and `FruitsPrinter` classes. Both classes print their class loaders inside a static initializer. The `FruitsPrinter` class references the `Fruits` class. I have kept the logic simple in both classes, so you can focus on the class loading rules. Note that you will be using these classes on the class path. They are not meant to be run from source files.

Listing 4-8. A Fruits Class Meant to Be Placed on the Class Path

```java
// Fruits.java
package com.jdojo.sourcecode.mode;

public class Fruits {
    static {
        // Print the class loader for this class
        var cl = Fruits.class.getClassLoader();
        System.out.println("Fruits class on class path" +
                " was loaded by " + cl);
    }

    public static void print() {
        System.out.println("Fruits on class path: "
                + "Oranges, Papayas, Apples");
    }
}
```

Listing 4-9. A FruitsPrinter Class That References the Fruits Class and Meant to Be Placed on the Class Path

```java
// FruitsPrinter.java
package com.jdojo.sourcecode.mode;

public class FruitsPrinter {
    static {
```

```
        // Print the class loader for this class
        var cl = FruitsPrinter.class.getClassLoader();
        System.out.println("FruitsPrinter class on class path" +
                " was loaded by " + cl);
    }

    public static void print() {
        System.out.println("FruitsPrinter.print() on class path called.");
        Fruits.print();
    }
}
```

Listing 4-10 contains the code of a `Fruits` class. It is saved in the `src\sourcecode.apps` directory in the `Fruits.java` file.

Listing 4-10. A Fruits Class Meant to Be Run from the Source File

```
// Fruits.java
package com.jdojo.sourcecode.mode;

public class Fruits {
    static {
        // Print the class loader for this class
        var cl = Fruits.class.getClassLoader();
        System.out.println("Fruits class in source file"
                + " was loaded by " + cl);
    }

    public static void main(String[] args) {
        Fruits.print();
    }

    public static void print() {
        System.out.println("Fruits in source file: Watermelons");
    }
}
```

Let us run the `Fruits.java` file using Java 11 – once just the source file and once including the `fruits.jar` file on the class path:

```
C:\Java13Revealed\src\sourcecode.apps>SET PATH=C:\java11\bin

C:\Java13Revealed\src\sourcecode.apps>java Fruits.java
```

```
Fruits class in source file was loaded by com.sun.tools.javac.launcher.Ma
in$MemoryClassLoader@3f197a46
Fruits in source file: Watermelons
```

```
C:\Java13Revealed\src\sourcecode.apps>java --class-path fruits.jar Fruits.java
```

```
Fruits class on class path was loaded by jdk.internal.loader.ClassLoaders
$AppClassLoader@2aae9190
error: class found on application class path: com.jdojo.sourcecode.mode.Fruits
```

The first time, the `Fruits` class was run successfully. The second time, the `Fruits` class was found on the class path as is evident by the class loader being used to load it. Recall that in Java 11, if the class being run from a source file is also found on the class path, you would receive an error. The output confirms this.

Let us run the same source file using Java 13 – once just the source file and once including the `fruits.jar` file on the class path:

```
C:\Java13Revealed\src\sourcecode.apps>SET PATH=C:\java13\bin

C:\Java13Revealed\src\sourcecode.apps>java Fruits.java
```

```
Fruits class in source file was loaded by com.sun.tools.javac.launcher.Ma
in$MemoryClassLoader@58a90037
Fruits in source file: Watermelons
```

```
C:\Java13Revealed\src\sourcecode.apps>java --class-path fruits.jar Fruits.java
```

```
Fruits class in source file was loaded by com.sun.tools.javac.launcher.Ma
in$MemoryClassLoader@6c3f5566
Fruits in source file: Watermelons
```

In Java 13, the output confirms that the Fruits class was loaded by the memory class loader and the Fruits class on the class path was not used.

Let us consider the code for the CLTest1 class in Listing 4-11. The file is saved as ClTest1.java. What do you expect when you run this file?

Listing 4-11. Contents of a CLTest1.java File

```
// CLTest1.java
package com.jdojo.sourcecode.mode;

public class CLTest1 {
    public static void main(String[] args) {
        Fruits.print();
    }
}
```

The following command runs the CLTest1.java file without any options. You will get the same output whether you run it in Java 11 or later.

```
C:\Java13Revealed\src\sourcecode.apps>java CLTest1.java
```

```
CLTest1.java:6: error: cannot find symbol
        Fruits.print();
        ^
  symbol:   variable Fruits
  location: class CLTest1
1 error
error: compilation failed
```

This output was expected. The CLTest1 class references a class named Fruits, which is not found in the source file. By default, the class path is set to the current directory. You do not have a Fruits class in the current directory either. Let us run this file by adding the fruits.jar file to the class path as follows:

C:\Java13Revealed\src\sourcecode.apps>java --class-path fruits.jar CLTest1.
java

Fruits class on class path was loaded by jdk.internal.loader.ClassLoaders
$AppClassLoader@2626b418
Fruits on class path: Oranges, Papayas, Apples

Note that you do have a Fruits.java file in the sourcecode.apps directory, which
was not used. This is so because the source-file mode compiles only one source file and
it does not touch any other source files. The Fruits class referenced by the CLTest1 class
was found on the class path (in the fruits.jar file), and it was loaded by the application
class loader.

Let us consider another case where the class in the source file references a class on
the class path, which in turn references another class. Listing 4-12 contains the code
for a CLTest2 class, and it is stored in a CLTest2.java file. The class references the
FruitsPrinter class in the fruits.jar file, so you need to run it with the fruits.jar
file on the class path.

Listing 4-12. Contents of a CLTest2.java File

```
// CLTest2.java
package com.jdojo.sourcecode.mode;

public class CLTest2 {
    public static void main(String[] args) {
        FruitsPrinter.print();
    }
}
```

The following command runs the CLTest2.java source file. You will get the same
output in Java 11 and later.

C:\Java13Revealed\src\sourcecode.apps>java --class-path fruits.jar CLTest2.
java

FruitsPrinter class on class path was loaded by jdk.internal.loader.Class
Loaders$AppClassLoader@2626b418
FruitsPrinter.print() on class path called.
Fruits class on class path was loaded by jdk.internal.loader.ClassLoaders$A
ppClassLoader@2626b418
Fruits on class path: Oranges, Papayas, Apples

There are no surprises in the output. Both FruitsPrinter and Fruits classes were
loaded by the application class loader from the class path. I presented this example as a
background for the next one, which might have a few surprises for you. Are you ready?

Listing 4-13 contains the code for two classes CLTest3 and Fruits. The code is stored
in a CLTest3.java file. The CLTest3 class references the FruitsPrinter class, which in
turn references the Fruits class. The trick here is that the FruitsPrinter class is in the
fruits.jar whereas the Fruits class is at two places – in the fruits.jar and the source
file CLTest3.java. Can you guess which Fruits class will be used when you run the
CLTest3.java file?

Listing 4-13. Contents of a CLTest3.java File

```
// CLTest3.java
package com.jdojo.sourcecode.mode;

public class CLTest3 {
    public static void main(String[] args) {
        FruitsPrinter.print();
    }
}

public class Fruits {
    static {
        // Print the class loader for this class
        var cl = Fruits.class.getClassLoader();
        System.out.println("Fruits class in source file"
                + " was loaded by " + cl);
    }
```

```
    public static void main(String[] args) {
        Fruits.print();
    }

    public static void print() {
        System.out.println("Fruits in source file: Watermelons");
    }
}
```

The following command runs the CLTest3.java file. You will get the same output in Java 11 and later.

```
C:\Java13Revealed\src\sourcecode.apps>java --class-path fruits.jar CLTest3.
java
```

```
FruitsPrinter class on class path was loaded by jdk.internal.loader.Class
Loaders$AppClassLoader@2626b418
FruitsPrinter.print() on class path called.
Fruits class on class path was loaded by jdk.internal.loader.ClassLoaders$A
ppClassLoader@2626b418
Fruits on class path: Oranges, Papayas, Apples
```

Are you surprised that the Fruits class on the class path from the fruits.jar file was used instead of the Fruits class included in the source file? Didn't I say that the classes in the source file take precedence? Yes. I did. Here is a catch. It is true that classes in the source file are given precedence. However, the application class loader does not see the classes in the source file. I stated this rule as the classes on the class path cannot reference classes in the source file. Because the FruitsPrinter class was loaded by the application class loader, the Fruits class, which is referenced by the FruitsPrinter class, must be also loaded by the application class loader. As a result, the Fruits class in the source file was not even considered to be used.

Here is the last example in this section. Listing 4-14 contains the code for three classes CLTest4, FruitsPrinter, and Fruits. It is stored in a CLTest4.java file. What do you expect when you run this class? If your answers are different in Java 11 and Java 12 or later, you are on right track.

Listing 4-14. Contents of a CLTest4.java File

```java
// CLTest4.java
package com.jdojo.sourcecode.mode;

public class CLTest4 {
    public static void main(String[] args) {
        FruitsPrinter.print();
    }
}

public class FruitsPrinter {
    static {
        // Print the class loader for this class
        var cl = FruitsPrinter.class.getClassLoader();
        System.out.println("FruitsPrinter class in source file" +
                " was loaded by " + cl);
    }

    public static void print() {
        System.out.println("FruitsPrinter.print() in source file called.");
        Fruits.print();
    }
}

public class Fruits {
    static {
        // Print the class loader for this class
        var cl = Fruits.class.getClassLoader();
        System.out.println("Fruits class in source file"
                + " was loaded by " + cl);
    }

    public static void main(String[] args) {
        Fruits.print();
    }
```

```
    public static void print() {
        System.out.println("Fruits in source file: Watermelons");
    }
}
```

You will get different outputs in Java 11 and Java 12 (and later) when you run the
CLTest4.java file. The following command runs it in Java 11:

C:\Java13Revealed\src\sourcecode.apps>SET PATH=C:\java11\bin

C:\Java13Revealed\src\sourcecode.apps>java --class-path fruits.jar CLTest4.java

---

```
FruitsPrinter class on class path was loaded by jdk.internal.loader.Class
Loaders$AppClassLoader@2aae9190
FruitsPrinter.print() on class path called.
Fruits class on class path was loaded by jdk.internal.loader.ClassLoaders$A
ppClassLoader@2aae9190
Fruits on class path: Oranges, Papayas, Apples
```

The output shows that both FruitsPrinter and Fruits classes were loaded by the
application class loader from the class path. This is so because, in Java 11, the memory
class loader delegates all class loading to the application class loader without searching
the source file first. In Java 11, the same two classes in the CLTest4.java file were
ignored.

Let us run the same command in Java 13 as follows:

C:\Java13Revealed\src\sourcecode.apps>SET PATH=C:\java13\bin

C:\Java13Revealed\src\sourcecode.apps>java --class-path fruits.jar CLTest4.java

---

```
FruitsPrinter class in source file was loaded by com.sun.tools.javac.
launcher.Main$MemoryClassLoader@4d49af10
FruitsPrinter.print() in source file called.
Fruits class in source file was loaded by com.sun.tools.javac.launcher.Main
$MemoryClassLoader@4d49af10
Fruits in source file: Watermelons
```

You can see the difference now. In Java 12 and later, the memory class loader searches the source file first before delegating to the application class loader. In this case, the memory class loader found both `FruitsPrinter` and `Fruits` classes in the source file and used them.

Non-standard Source File Names

It is common to write small Java utility programs. You may not want to use the `.java` file extension for the source file. Listing 4-15 contains the code for a class named `PrintFullPath`. The class prints the full path of the current directory. The source code is stored in `pfp.txt`. Note that you are not using the standard `.java` extension for the source file. Instead, you are using the `.txt` extension.

Listing 4-15. Contents of a pfp.txt File

```
// pfp.txt
package com.jdojo.sourcecode.mode;

import java.nio.file.Paths;

public class PrintFullPath {
    public static void main(String[] args) {
        // Print the full path of the current directory
        System.out.println(Paths.get(".")
                                .toAbsolutePath()
                                .normalize()
                                .toString());
    }
}
```

Let us run the `pfp.txt` file using the `java` command

```
C:\Java13Revealed\src\sourcecode.apps>java pfp.txt
```

```
Error: Could not find or load main class pfp.txt
Caused by: java.lang.ClassNotFoundException: pfp.txt
```

You did not get the expected output. Let us look at the error message. The java command did not use the source-file mode. Rather, it used the class-file mode, and it started looking for a class name whose fully qualified name is pfp.txt. That is, it looked for a class named txt in the pfp package. It did not use the source-file mode because the file name was not having the .java extension.

If your file extension is not .java, you must use the --source option to use the source-file mode. Let us run it again using the --source option as follows:

```
C:\Java13Revealed\src\sourcecode.apps>java --source 13 pfp.txt
```

```
C:\Java13Revealed\src\sourcecode.apps
```

You received the expected output. The command used the value for the source version as 13. The value of the --source option specifies the JDK version for which the Java language features and APIs are allowed in the source file. What are the valid values for the version? It keeps changing with every release of the JDK. For JDK 13, I get an error when I use 6, but a deprecation warning for 7. Values of 8 to 13 are fine. When you use JDK 14, you may get an error when you use 7 as the source version.

Supporting Shebang Files

UNIX-like operating systems such as Linux and macOS support shebang files. A shebang file is an executable script file with a special first line (a shebang) that specifies the interpreter to be used to execute the script. The first line is called "shebang" or "hash bang". A shebang starts with a hash sign (#) followed with an exclamation mark (!), which is followed with the full path of the interpreter to be used. Consider the following contents on Linux saved in a hello file:

```
#!/bin/bash
echo Hello world!
```

Here, the hello file contains a script. You need to give it the execute permission (chmod +x hello). It is also a shebang file. Its shebang specifies that the interpreter to execute the script – in this case, you have only one echo command in the script – is /bin/bash.

The java command in source code mode supports shebang file. The shebang you need to use in the source file is

```
#![path-to-java] --source [version]
```

Here, [path-to-java] is the full path to the java command and [version] is the source version.

Tip   Shebang files are supported natively only on UNIX-like operating systems such as Linux and macOS. Windows does have support for shebang files.

Listing 4-16 contains the code for a pfp file. I installed JDK13 in the /home/ksharan/java13 directory on my Linux machine, so I have specified the following shebang in my pfp file:

```
#!/home/ksharan/java13/bin/java --source 13
```

Listing 4-16. Contents of a pfp Executable File

```
#!/home/ksharan/java13/bin/java --source 13
package com.jdojo.sourcecode.mode;

import java.nio.file.Paths;

public class PrintFullPath {
    public static void main(String[] args) {
        // Print the full path of the current directory
        System.out.println(Paths.get(".")
                                .toAbsolutePath()
                                .normalize()
                                .toString());
    }
}
```

You will need to modify the shebang in this file to point the path to the java command on your machine. You can find the path to java using the whereis command on Linux. On my machine, it prints the following:

```
$ whereis java
```

```
java: /usr/bin/java /usr/lib/java /etc/java /usr/share/java /home/ksharan/
java9.sh /home/ksharan/java10.sh /home/ksharan/java13/bin/java /usr/share/
man/man1/java.1.gz
```

Before you can execute the pfp file, you need to make it executable using the chmod command. You can execute the pfp file using its full path, relative path, or just the file name. Java is not playing any role in what kind of path you use. It is all about your operating system. If you include the directory in which the pfp is stored in the PATH environment variable, you can just use the file name to execute it. I have stored the pfp file in the /home/ksharan directory on my machine, which is also my current directory. The following sequence of commands shows you how I executed this file in different ways:

```
$ ls -l pfp
-rw-rw-r--. 1 ksharan ksharan 341 Aug  3 09:20 pfp
$ ./pfp
bash: ./pfp: Permission denied
$ chmod +x ./pfp
$ ls -l pfp
-rwxrwxr-x. 1 ksharan ksharan 341 Aug  3 09:20 pfp
$ ./pfp
/home/ksharan
$ pfp
bash: pfp: command not found...
$ export PATH=.:$PATH
$ pfp
/home/ksharan
$ pwd
/home/ksharan
$
```

Note that your pfp command on Linux does the same thing as the pwd Linux command does. The pwd command prints the working directory, so does the pfp command. Aren't you happy that you were able to implement a Linux command in Java?

Shebang support to run Java source file comes with a few rules. Let us first look at the rules and then a few examples:

- You can also run a shebang file in source-file mode using the `java` command using the `--source` option.

- You cannot have the `.java` extension for a shebang file.

The first rule states that you can use the `--source` option to run a shebang file. Consider the following commands:

```
$ java pfp
Error: Could not find or load main class pfp
Caused by: java.lang.ClassNotFoundException: pfp
$ java --source 13 pfp
/home/ksharan
$
```

The first command attempts to run the `pfp` file and generates an error message that `pfp` class is not found. Recall that the `java` command chooses the source-file mode when the file name contains the `.java` extension or you use the `--source` option. This command did not fulfil either condition, so the `java` command chose class-file mode and tried to run a class named `pfp`. You do not have any class named pfp in the current directory, which resulted in this error.

The second command used `--source` option, and it was able to run the pfp source file successfully. Wait a minute! The first line in the `pfp` file is a shebang, which is not a valid Java code:

```
#!/home/ksharan/java13/bin/java --source 13
```

How did the Java compiler compile this shebang line? When you use the --source option, the `java` command examines the first line in the file. If the first line is a shebang, it removes the contents on the first line, except the last character – the newline character – before passing the source code to the compiler. Therefore, the compiler never sees the shebang; it sees all valid Java code. Now you may realize that there was no changes to the compiler to support shebang in a Java source file.

There is one more question to be answered. Why did the `java` command not remove the entire shebang line? Your shebang file contains Java source code, which may contain errors. Suppose in a shebang file the sixth line contains an error. When the compiler reports this error, you would have seen this error reported at fifth line if the java command had removed the entire shebang line. To keep the line numbers in error reporting the same, the java command removes the contents of the shebang, except the last newline character, so the number of lines in the source file remains the same and the compiler will report the correct line numbers in errors.

Let us discuss the second rule. This rule states that either you have a shebang file with no extension or an extension other than .java or you have a valid Java source in a file with the .java extension. If your file contains the .java extension, the contents in the file are interpreted as Java source file without any modification. A shebang file with a .java extension will result in an error on the first line, which specifies the shebang. You can think of this rule another way. The source files with the .java extension are meant for programmers learning Java languages, whereas shebang files are meant for developing utility programs. It is not a common practice to give an extension to your utility programs. The following command copies the pfp file to pfp.java file and runs the pfp.java file using the java command:

```
$ cp pfp pfp.java
$ java pfp.java
pfp.java:1: error: illegal character: '#'
#!/home/ksharan/java13/bin/java --source 13
^

pfp.java:1: error: class, interface, or enum expected
#!/home/ksharan/java13/bin/java --source 13
   ^

2 errors
error: compilation failed
$
```

The error message indicates that the compiler is trying to compile the shebang as Java code and fails.

You can also pass arguments to the main() method in a shebang file. You can convert the program in Listing 4-7 to a shebang file as an exercise. Save this file as stats, add a shebang to the file, and make it executable. You should be able to run the stats file as follows:

```
$ stats 1 2 3 4 5
DoubleSummaryStatistics{count=5, sum=15.000000, min=1.000000,
average=3.000000, max=5.000000}
$
```

Summary

The `java` command to run a Java application is called the `java` launcher or the `java` tool. It can be used in the following four modes:

- Class-file mode

- JAR-file mode

- Module mode

- Source-file mode

The class-file and JAR-file modes existed since the beginning of the JDK release. The module mode was added to JDK9. The source-file mode was added to JDK11. In the source-file mode, the `java` command runs a Java program from a source file without requiring you to compile the source file. In source-file mode, the entire source code must be contained in a single file. The code may reference other code on the class path.

The `java` command uses two criteria in selecting the source-file mode:

- The first item on the command line that is not an option or part of an option. If this item is the name of an existing file with `.java` extension, the source-file mode is used.

- Using the `--source` option on the command line forces the `java` command to use the source-file mode. If your source file does not contain the `.java` extension, you must use the `--source` option to use the source-file mode.

In source-file mode, the `java` command compiles the source code in memory using the `jdk.compiler` module before it runs the code. The first type in the source file must be a class with a `main()` method. The `java` command automatically selects the first top-level class to run.

In source-file mode, arguments specified after the source file name are passed to the `main()` method of the class that is run.

You can specify selected number of compiler options to the `java` command, which will be passed to the compiler to compile the source file. Annotation processing is disabled in the source-file mode. The compiler does not enforce the file name restriction that a type in a named package should exist in a file whose name is composed from the type name followed by the `.java` extension. You can have any number of `public` classes in a source file.

The `java` command uses a custom class loader, called memory class loader, to load the classes in the source file.

In Java 11, you get an error if the class being run from the source file also exists in the class path. The memory class loader delegates to the application class loader. That is, classes on the class path are loaded before classes from the source file.

The behavior of the memory class loader changed in Java 12. In Java 12, it searches the source file for classes before delegating to the application class loader. If the class being run from the source file is also present on the class path, the class from the source file is run in Java 12 without giving you an error as it did in Java 11.

If your source file does not have the standard `.java` file extension, you must use the `--source` option with the `java` command to run such a source file. You can also include a shebang in your source file and use the UNIX-like operating system's support for shebang files to run the source file. The `java` command strips the shebang, except the last newline character, before passing the source file contents to the compiler.

A source file with the `.java` extension and a shebang will not run because the compiler will try to interpret the shebang as Java source code and will fail.

CHAPTER 5

Enhanced Switch

In this chapter, you will learn

- What a preview feature is

- What a `switch` statement and a `switch` expression are

- Enhancements to the traditional `switch`

- About the new syntax for `switch`

- About the rules of using new `switch`

- About the `yield` statement

What Is a Preview Feature?

A preview feature of the Java SE Platform is a fully specified and fully implemented language or virtual machine feature, which is available in a JDK feature release, but is not a permanent feature of the JDK yet. A preview feature is provided to solicit developer feedback. Developers are expected to experiment with the features in real-world use cases. Based on the feedback, a preview feature may become permanent (standard feature) in a future release with or without modifications or it may be removed altogether. A preview feature is not meant to be used in production. Refer to JEP 12 at `https://openjdk.java.net/jeps/12` for more details on preview features.

A preview feature is not backward compatible. You cannot run class files that contain preview features from Java 12 using Java 13 runtime.

Since a preview feature is not meant to be used in production, it is not enabled in the compiler and runtime by default. You must use the `--enable-preview` option with the compiler and runtime to use a preview feature. You will need to use the `--release` or

143

© Kishori Sharan 2019
K. Sharan, *Java 13 Revealed*, https://doi.org/10.1007/978-1-4842-5407-3_5

-source option when you use the --enable-preview option to compile the source code. To compile source code with preview features in JDK 13, you would use

```
javac --enable-preview --release 13 <other-options-and-arguments>
```

If you do not use the --enable-preview option to compile the source code with preview features, you receive compile-time errors similar to the following:

```
C:\Java13Revealed\src\jdojo.enhancedswitch\classes\com\jdojo\
enhancedswitch\Test.java:9: error: switch rules are a preview feature and
are disabled by default.
        case 10->str =  "ten";
  (use --enable-preview to enable switch rules)
1 error
```

If you enable preview features at compile time, the compiler prints notes suggesting you to compile with a -Xlint:preview option, so you can see the warnings.

```
Note: C:\Java13Revealed\src\jdojo.enhancedswitch\classes\com\jdojo\
enhancedswitch\Test.java uses preview language features.
Note: Recompile with -Xlint:preview for details.
```

Here is what you get when you use both --enable-preview and -Xlint:preview options with the compiler, which prints a warning for each usage of the preview feature.

```
C:\Java13Revealed\src\jdojo.enhancedswitch\classes\com\jdojo\
enhancedswitch\Test.java:9: warning: [preview] switch rules are a preview
feature and may be removed in a future release.
        case 10->str =  "ten";
...
4 warnings
```

To run compiled classes with preview features, you specify the --enable-preview option with the java command

```
java --enable-preview <other-options-and-arguments>
```

If you want to use JShell to explore preview features, you need to start it with the `--enable-preview` option

```
C:\Java13Revealed>jshell --enable-preview
|  Welcome to JShell -- Version 13
|  For an introduction type: /help intro

jshell>
```

Example Programs

All examples in this chapter are in the `jdojo.enhancedswitch` module as shown in Listing 5-1.

Listing 5-1. A Module Named jdojo.enhancedswitch

```
// module-info.java
module jdojo.enhancedswitch {
    exports com.jdojo.enhancedswitch;
}
```

The Background

The Java language has the `switch` statement since its inception. It is used as a control flow statement. Syntax and semantics for the `switch` statement were copied from C/C++, which have the following features that were simply irritating to use and were also error-prone:

- The `switch` labels used fall-through semantics. In most cases, you want to execute statements associated with only the matching label and no other labels. Because of the fall-through semantics, you ended up using a `break` statement in each label, which is irritating as well as error-prone.

- If you want to execute the same set of statements for multiple `switch` labels, you must define multiple case labels using the fall-through semantics. In other words, specifying multiple constants in a case label was not permitted – one case label must have one and only one constant.

145

- All switch labels occur in one scope, which means you cannot declare the same variables for different labels.

- It was designed to work only as a statement, not as an expression. A statement indicates an action, whereas an expression evaluates to a value.

The switch statement with these issues has been around for 24 years. Why do we need to address them now? Isn't it too late? The answer is yes and no. Developers may live with it until the end of Java life cycle. However, there is a much more important feature, called pattern matching, which prompted addressing these issues. Pattern matching is not part of Java yet; you can track it in JEP 305 at https://openjdk.java.net/jeps/305. For pattern matching to work, switch in Java must be overhauled. With the new Java release cycle every 6 months, the enhanced switch has been delivered as a preview feature in Java 12 and a refined version of it in Java 13, whereas the final goal, which is the pattern matching, is still being worked on.

I assume that you know how to use the traditional switch statement. In the following sections, I walk you through each of these problems one by one with a simple snippet of code before I explain the enhanced switch features.

The Fall-Through Semantics

The following snippet of code contains a simple switch statement:

```
int count = 2;

// More code goes here...

switch (count) {
    case 1:
        System.out.println("One");
        break;
    case 2:
        System.out.println("Two");
        break;
    case 3:
        System.out.println("Three");
        break;
```

```
default:
    System.out.println("Out-of-range");
}
```

You have an int variable named count. The switch statement prints "One", "Two", or "Three" when the value of count is 1, 2, or 3, respectively. Otherwise, it prints "Out-of-range". Notice the use of the break statement for each case label. You needed it because, by default, the switch statement uses fall-through. Without the break statements, for the count value 1, all four switch labels (three case labels and one default label) would have been executed, which you did not intend.

One Constant per Case Label

Suppose that you are given an English letter and you have to print whether it is a vowel or consonant. Here is the code that does this:

```
char c = 'w';

// More code goes here...

switch(Character.toLowerCase(c)) {
    case 'a':
    case 'e':
    case 'i':
    case 'o':
    case 'u':
        System.out.println("Vowel");
        break;
    default:
        System.out.println("Consonant");
}
```

Notice the use of five case labels using the fall-through semantics. You have five case constants for vowels. Because you could use only one constant per case label, you had to use five separate case labels. Wouldn't it be better if you were able to write one case label like "case 'a', 'e', 'i', 'o', 'u':"?

One Scope for the Switch Block

The switch block defines one scope, and all switch labels are executed in that scope. It means that you cannot define a variable with the same name in more than one case label. Consider the following snippet of code:

```
char c = 'Z';

// More code goes here...

switch(Character.toLowerCase(c)) {
    case 'a':
    case 'e':
    case 'i':
    case 'o':
    case 'u':
        char upperChar = Character.toUpperCase(c);
        System.out.println("Vowel: " + upperChar);
        break;
    default:
        char upperChar = Character.toUpperCase(c); // A compile-time error
        System.out.println("Consonant: " + upperChar);
}
```

This code does not compile. Both declarations of the upperChar variable are in one scope, which is the scope for the switch block. The compiler complains about the duplicate declaration of the upperChar variable inside the default label. There is a way to solve this error. A pair of braces ({}) defines a new scope. You can enclose the code for the case label and default label in braces to solve this. Here is the modified code, which compiles

```
char c = 'Z';

// More code goes here...

switch(Character.toLowerCase(c)) {
    case 'a':
    case 'e':
    case 'i':
    case 'o':
```

```
    case 'u': {
        char upperChar = Character.toUpperCase(c);
        System.out.println("Vowel: " + upperChar);
        break;
    }
    default: {
        char upperChar = Character.toUpperCase(c); // Compiles fine
        System.out.println("Consonant: " + upperChar);
    }
}
```

A Switch Was a Statement

You could use switch only as a statement. You used to simulate a switch to be an expression by defining a variable outside the switch statement and assigning it a value in each switch label. Here is an example:

```
int count = 2;

// More code goes here...

// Declare desc here and assign it a value in each switch label later
String desc;

switch (count) {
    case 1:
        desc = "One";
        break;
    case 2:
        desc = "Two";
        break;
    case 3:
        desc = "Three";
        break;
    default:
        desc = "Out-of-range";
}

System.out.println(desc);
```

This approach works, but it is verbose and a workaround, not a direct support for expressions. It would have been nicer if you were able to use switch as an expression like

```
int count = 2;

// More code goes here...

// Declare desc here and use a switch expression to assign it a value
String desc = switch (count) {
    case 1: yield "One";
    case 2: yield "Two";
    case 3: yield "Three";
    default: yield "Out-of-range";
};
```

I will explain the new syntax using the yield statement shortly.

Enhanced Switch

Now you know the shortcomings of the traditional switch, it is time to see the new exciting features of switch, which address these shortcomings. There are two types of changes to switch:

- Enhancements to the traditional switch

- The new switch syntax

The new switch syntax provides features of the traditional switch statement and many more. I will first explain the enhancements to the traditional switch followed with the detailed coverage of the new switch syntax and semantics.

Enhancements to Traditional Switch

Java has always been backward compatible. Adding breaking changes to the traditional switch was not an option to the language designers. The preview feature provides you new ways of using the traditional switch without breaking your old code. Here are the changes to the traditional switch:

- You can have multiple constants in a case label.

- You can use switch as an expression.

Previously, you had to use one case label per constant. The new switch syntax allows you to use a comma-separated list of constants in a case label. The following snippet of code rewrites the previous example of matching a letter against a vowel and consonant:

```
char c = 'w';

// More code goes here...

switch(Character.toLowerCase(c)) {
    case 'a', 'e', 'i', 'o', 'u': /* Five constants in one case label */
        System.out.println("Vowel");
        break;
    default:
        System.out.println("Consonant");
}
```

Notice the difference between this and the previous code using traditional switch. This time, you have collapsed five case labels into one. You still need to use a break statement because the traditional switch statement still uses default fall-through semantics.

The preview feature allows you to use the traditional switch as an expression. An expression evaluates to a value (or yields a value). Now you can write code like

```
String str = switch(selector) {
                case label1: ...
                case label2: ...
            }; /* Must end with a semicolon */
```

Notice the use of a semicolon at the end of the switch expression. The switch expression is part of the variable declaration for the str variable, so the entire variable declaration must end with a semicolon. Think of the previous variable declaration as shown:

```
String str = <switch-expression>;
```

The traditional switch allowed you to use only statements for a switch label. The preview feature has introduced a new yield statement. Its syntax is

```
yield expression;
```

The yield statement evaluates its expression and transfers control to the enclosing switch expression. The value of the expression becomes the value of the switch expression.

Tip   The yield statement can only be used inside a switch expression. You cannot use the break statement inside a switch expression.

You can rewrite the previous example of computing the description from an integer as follows – this time, using a switch expression:

```
int count = 2;

// More code goes here...

// Declare desc here and use a switch expression to assign it a value
String desc = switch (count) {
    case 1: yield "One";
    case 2: yield "Two";
    case 3: yield "Three";
    default: yield "Out-of-range";
};
```

This is a simple example where each switch label contains only one yield statement. You can have multiple statements in a switch label. However, each switch label must contain one yield statement that will represent the value of the switch expression using normal path of execution. Typically, you will not print something from an expression. Let us do it just for the demonstration purpose to show that you can have multiple statements in a switch label for a switch expression. The following snippet of code prints a message when "case 1:" is executed:

```
String desc = switch (count) {
    case 1:
       System.out.println("Executing case 1:");
       yield "One";
    case 2: yield "Two";
    case 3: yield "Three";
    default: yield "Out-of-range";
};
```

Recall that you cannot use the break statement inside a switch expression. The yield statement completes a switch expression. In this statement, when count is 1, a message is printed, and the yield statement completes the switch expression by yielding "One" and other case labels below "case 1:" are not executed.

Here is a challenge for you. Let me switch the two statements in the previous snippet of code as follows. Now, the yield statement is first and the System.out.println() is second. Will the following snippet of code compile?

```
int count = 2;

// More code goes here...

String desc = switch (count) {
    case 1:
        yield "One";
        System.out.println("Executing case 1:");
    case 2: yield "Two";
    case 3: yield "Three";
    default: yield "Out-of-range";
};
```

If your answer is no, you are correct. The yield statement completes the switch expression making the System.out.println() statement unreachable. Java does not allow unreachable statements. This snippet of code generates the following compile-time error:

```
error: unreachable statement
        System.out.println("Executing case 1:");
1 error
```

Listing 5-2 contains a complete program to demonstrate the use of enhanced traditional switch.

Listing 5-2. A Program to Demonstrate the Enhancements to the Traditional Switch

```
// TraditionalSwitch.java
package com.jdojo.enhancedswitch;

public class TraditionalSwitch {
    public static void main(String[] args) {
```

```java
        whatLetter('a');
        whatLetter('W');
        whatLetter('5');

        for(int i = 1; i <= 4; i++) {
            String desc = getDesc(i);
            System.out.printf("%d:%s%n", i, desc);
        }
    }

    public static void whatLetter(char c) {
        // Use the traditional switch with multiple constants in a case
        switch(Character.toLowerCase(c)) {
            case 'a', 'e', 'i', 'o', 'u':
                System.out.println("Vowel: " + c);
                break;
            default:
                if (Character.isLetter(c)) {
                    System.out.println("Consonant: " + c);
                } else {
                    System.out.println("Not-a-Letter: " + c);
                }
        }
    }

    public static String getDesc(int count) {
        // Use the traditional switch as an expression
        return switch (count) {
            case 1: yield "One";
            case 2: yield "Two";
            case 3: yield "Three";
          default: yield "Out-of-range";
        };
    }
}
```

```
Vowel: a
Consonant: W
Not-a-Letter: 5
1:One
2:Two
3:Three
4:Out-of-range
```

New Switch Syntax

The new switch retains most of the syntax from the traditional switch, except the character to separate a switch label from its code. It uses an arrow (->) instead of a colon (:). The traditional "case label:" becomes "case label->". This is the only syntactic difference you have for the new switch. There are several semantic (how it works) differences that I will explain in this section.

Often, I need to distinguish which switch I am talking about – the new one or the old new. I refer to the old switch as traditional switch, switch-with-colon, or switch with "case label:". I refer to the new one as new switch, switch-with-arrow, or switch with "case label->". Java Language Specification refers to the switch block associated with the traditional switch as *switch labeled statement groups* and the switch block associated with the new switch as *switch labeled rules*. Whichever name you use to refer to the new switch, here is its syntax:

```
switch(selector-expresion) {
    case label1[, label2, label3...] -> [expression|block|throw-statement]
    case label4[, label5, label6...] -> [expression|block|throw-statement]
    ...
    default -> [expression|block|throw-statement]
}
```

The syntax allows for one or more constants in a case label. The code associated with a switch label is restricted to one of the following: an expression, a block statement, and a throw statement. I will explain the rationale behind this rule shortly.

Let us look at the rules used to process the new switch followed with examples of each rule:

- The default is no fall-through in the new switch. This means, you no longer need to use a break statement to stop executing the switch labels following the matched switch label.

- Only one "thing" can be executed as part of a matched switch label. That "thing" can be an expression, a block statement, or a throw statement. In traditional switch, a group of statements was allowed causing the scoping issue where the entire switch block was executed in one scope. Using these constraints, if you have more than one statement to execute, you are forced to use a block statement that will have a new scope for the switch label. This allows you to have the same functionality as the traditional switch, but code is less error-prone.

- The new switch can be used as a statement or as an expression.

The following snippet of code rewrites the previous example, which used the traditional switch statement, using the new switch statement:

```
int count = 2;

// More code goes here...

switch (count) {
    case 1-> System.out.println("One");
    case 2-> System.out.println("Two");
    case 3-> System.out.println("Three");
    default-> System.out.println("Out-of-range");
}
```

Notice the use of the System.out.println() in each switch label. Didn't I say that each switch label can have an expression, a block statement, or a throw statement? I did say that. In Java, a method call (in this case, System.out.println()) is an expression.

When you add a semicolon after the method call, it becomes an expression statement. Here are the detailed rules about using an expression in a switch label with arrow:

- In a switch statement, the *expression* must be *an expression statement* – an expression, which can be converted to a statement by adding a semicolon to it.

- In a switch expression, the *expression* may be any valid Java expression.

The following snippet of code rewrites the previous example using a switch expression:

```
int count = 2;

// More code goes here...

String desc = switch (count) {
    case 1-> "One";
    case 2-> "Two";
    case 3-> "Three";
    default->"Out-of-range";
};

System.out.println(desc);
```

This time, "One", "Two", and so on are expressions. You cannot convert them to expression statements by adding a semicolon. When the switch expression (count) matches one of the case labels, the corresponding expression ("One", "Two", etc.) becomes the value for the switch expression.

If you have to compute the value in a switch label using some logic, you will need to use the yield statement to return the value as the value for the switch expression. Consider the following snippet of code that uses a switch expression to compute a value:

```
char c = 'W';

// More code goes here

String desc = switch(Character.toLowerCase(c)) {
    case 'a', 'e', 'i', 'o', 'u'-> "Vowel";
    default-> {
```

```
        if (Character.isLetter(c)) {
            yield "Consonant";
        } else {
            yield "Not-a-Letter";
        }
    }
};
```

```
System.out.println(desc);
```

The `case` label uses a simple expression `"Vowel"` when the character is a vowel. The `default` label uses a block statement to use logic to determine whether it is a consonant or not a letter. Note the use of the `yield` statements inside the `if` and `else` blocks. The `default` label does not use very complex logic. You can replace it with an expression as shown:

```
String desc = switch(Character.toLowerCase(c)) {
    case 'a', 'e', 'i', 'o', 'u'-> "Vowel";
    default-> Character.isLetter(c)?"Consonant":"Not-a-Letter";
};
```

Note that the previous switch expression does not use any `yield` statements. Consider the following snippet of code that uses the new `switch` statement:

```
char c = 'W';
```

```
// More code goes here
```

```
switch(Character.toLowerCase(c)) {
    case 'a', 'e', 'i', 'o', 'u'-> {
        char upperChar = Character.toUpperCase(c);
        System.out.println("Vowel: " + upperChar);
    }
    default-> {
        if (Character.isLetter(c)) {
            char upperChar = Character.toUpperCase(c);
            System.out.println("Consonant: " + upperChar);
```

```
    } else {
        System.out.println("Not-a-Letter: " + c);
    }
    }
}
```

The code uses one case label and one default label. Both contain more than one statement, so you are forced to use a block statement ({}) in each label. Notice that you have used the same local variable name upperChar inside the code for both labels. Declaring duplicate variables in a switch block like this was also possible with traditional switch, but you had to remember to use a block statement, whereas the new switch forces you to use a block statement.

Listing 5-3 contains a complete program to demonstrate the use of the new switch and its syntax. I have rewritten the program in Listing 5-2, which uses the traditional switch, using the new switch in Listing 5-3.

Listing 5-3. A Program to Demonstrate the New Switch Syntax

```java
// NewSwitch.java
package com.jdojo.enhancedswitch;

public class NewSwitch {
    public static void main(String[] args) {
        whatLetter('a');
        whatLetter('W');
        whatLetter('5');

        for(int i = 1; i <= 4; i++) {
            String desc = getDesc(i);
            System.out.printf("%d:%s%n", i, desc);
        }
    }

    public static void whatLetter(char c) {
        // Use the new switch with multiple constants in a case
        switch(Character.toLowerCase(c)) {
            case 'a', 'e', 'i', 'o', 'u'->
                System.out.println("Vowel: " + c);
```

```
        default-> {
            if (Character.isLetter(c)) {
                System.out.println("Consonant: " + c);
            } else {
                System.out.println("Not-a-Letter: " + c);
            }
        }
    }
}

public static String getDesc(int count) {
    // Use the new switch as an expression
    return switch (count) {
        case 1-> "One";
        case 2-> "Two";
        case 3-> "Three";
        default-> "Out-of-range";
    };
}
}
```

```
Vowel: a
Consonant: W
Not-a-Letter: 5
1:One
2:Two
3:Three
4:Out-of-range
```

Does New switch Replace the Old One

Once the new switch becomes a standard feature in Java SE (maybe in Java SE 14), you are encouraged to use it in place of the traditional switch when it fits your needs. However, it is not a complete replacement for the traditional switch statement. Remember that the traditional switch offers fall-through by default and you have a way (using the `break` statement) to override the default behavior. Consider the following trivial example that uses fall-through feature of the traditional `switch` statement:

```
int count = 2;

// More code goes here...

switch (count) {
    case 1:
        System.out.print("One ");
    case 2:
        System.out.print("Two ");
    case 3:
        System.out.println("Three.");
        break;
    default: System.out.println("Over-My-Head");
}
```

If the value of `count` is 1, it prints `"One Two Three"`; for 2, it prints `"Two Three"`; for 3, it prints `"Three"`; and for any other values, it prints `"Over-My-Head"`. Implementing this logic is simple because of the fall-through feature of the traditional `switch` statement. There is no straightforward way to implement this logic using the new `switch` syntax because the new `switch` does not provide the fall-through feature. You got the point – use the new syntax whenever possible and use the traditional `switch` when fall-through is needed.

I was curious to get a bit more insight into the new `switch` features and how the compiler handles them. So, I tried to decompile all examples in this chapter, which were written using new `switch` syntax. You can use `www.javadecompilers.com` to decompile your Java code. When I decompiled my code, I did not see any new `switch` syntax. I found out that in all cases the code using new `switch` syntax was translated to the traditional `switch`. Even though the new `switch` uses the old switch behind the scene, as a developer you gain a lot of benefits using the new syntax. You get compact and less error-prone code and a new big feature, which is using `switch` as an expression!

Exhaustiveness of Case Labels

The switch labels for a switch expression, not a switch statement, must be exhaustive. That is, you must have a `switch` label for each possible value for the `selector-expression` in a `switch` expression. Consider the following snippet of code:

```
int count = 2;

String desc = switch(count) {
    case 1-> "One";
    case 2-> "Two";
    case 3-> "Three";
};
```

This snippet of code generates the following compile-time error:

```
error: the switch expression does not cover all possible input values
        String desc = switch(count) {
1 error
```

The reason for this error is that the three `case` labels cover only three possible values for `count`. Here, `count` is an `int` and the possible values for an `int` is in millions. Typically, you would cover other values for `count` using a `default` label – just to make the compiler happy:

```
int count = 2;

String desc = switch(count) {
    case 1-> "One";
    case 2-> "Two";
    case 3-> "Three";
    default-> "Out-of-range";
};
```

Suppose your `switch` expression is based on an enum and the `case` labels cover all enum constants. Later, you add a new enum constant to your enum and compile only the enum definition, not the code that uses the enum in the `switch` expression. What would happen if the `switch` expression is executed with the newly added value of the enum constant? Remember that this discussion is for `switch` expressions, not switch statements. If you had used this enum in a switch statement, using the new enum constant in the switch statement will silently do nothing because the new enum constant is not covered by any of the switch labels. However, using a switch expression is different. Typically, you want to compute a value for each enum constant in a switch expression. Because you do not know all enum constants that may be added in future, you may add a default label to your switch expression, which typically would throw an exception or yield a default value.

The compiler assists you when you use switch as an expression – new switch as well as old switch. When a switch expression is based on an enum and all enum constants are covered by case labels, the compiler adds a default label with the following code:

```
default-> throw new IncompatibleClassChangeError();
```

Let us walk through an example. Listing 5-4 contains the declaration for an enum called TrafficLight. It contains two constants GREEN and RED.

Listing 5-4. A TrafficLight Enum with Two Constants GREEN and RED

```
// TrafficLight.java
package com.jdojo.enhancedswitch;

public enum TrafficLight {GREEN, RED}
```

Listing 5-5 contains the code for a Drive class. Its changeLight() method uses a switch expression covering both constants of the TrafficLight enum. The main() method calls the changeLight() method – once for each enum constant in the TrafficLight enum. The output shows the expected results.

Listing 5-5. A Drive Class That Uses the TrafficLight Enum Constants in a switch Expression

```
// Drive.java
package com.jdojo.enhancedswitch;

public class Drive {
    public static void main(String[] args) {
        for (TrafficLight light : TrafficLight.values()) {
            changeLight(light);
        }
    }
```

```
    public static void changeLight(TrafficLight light) {
        String decision = switch (light) {
            case GREEN-> "GO";
            case RED-> "STOP";
        };

        System.out.println(light + ": " + decision);
    }
}
```

```
GREEN: GO
RED: STOP
```

The compiler silently added a safeguard to your switch expression. It changed your switch expression to the following:

```
String decision = switch (light) {
    case GREEN-> "GO";
    case RED-> "STOP";
    default-> throw new IncompatibleClassChangeError();
};
```

The purpose of this hidden default label that was added by the compiler will be clear shortly. Let us add a new constant AMBER to the TrafficLight enum. Listing 5-6 contains the modified enum declaration.

Listing 5-6. A TrafficLight Enum with Three Constants GREEN, RED, and AMBER

```
// TrafficLight.java
package com.jdojo.enhancedswitch;

public enum TrafficLight {GREEN, RED, AMBER}
```

Recompile the `TrafficLight` enum, but not the `Drive` class. Now, rerun the `Drive` class, which produces the following output:

```
GREEN: GO
RED: STOP
Exception in thread "main" java.lang.IncompatibleClassChangeError
    at jdojo.enhancedswitch/com.jdojo.enhancedswitch.Drive.
    changeLight(Drive.java:12)
    at jdojo.enhancedswitch/com.jdojo.enhancedswitch.Drive.main(Drive.
    java:7)
```

The error message in the output makes it clear that the enum definition changed between compile time and runtime. The developer needs to handle the new enum constant `AMBER` in the switch expression in the `changeLight()` method in the `Drive` class. If you add a `default` label to an enum-based `switch` expression, the compiler does not add a `default` label for you.

If you recompile the `Drive` class without adding a `default` label, you get the following compile-time error:

```
C:\Java13Revealed\src\jdojo.enhancedswitch\classes\com\jdojo\
enhancedswitch\Drive.java:12: error: the switch expression does not cover
all possible input values
        String decision = switch (light) {
1 error
```

You need to handle the new enum constant `AMBER` in the `switch` expression in the `changeLight()` method of the `Drive` class to get rid of this error.

In Java, an expression must evaluate to a value or throw an exception. This rule is also enforced for `switch` expressions for which the compiler checks that each `switch` label yields a value or throws an exception. If a `switch` label may not yield a value, a compile-time error occurs. Consider the code in Listing 5-7. Can you spot the compile-time errors in the `SwitchExpressionCompletion` class?

Listing 5-7. A SwitchExpressionCompletion Class

```java
// SwitchExpressionCompletion.java
package com.jdojo.enhancedswitch;

import java.time.LocalDate;

public class SwitchExpressionCompletion {
    public static void main(String[] args) {
        int count = 2;

        String desc = switch(count) {
            case 1-> "One";
            case 2-> throw new IllegalArgumentException("Don't like two!");
            case 3-> {
                if (LocalDate.now().getYear() == 2019) {
                    yield "Three";
                }
                // A compile-time error
            }
            default-> {
                System.out.println("What are you talking about!");
                // A compile-time error
            }
        };
    }
}
```

Compiling the SwitchExpressionCompletion class generates the following errors:

```
C:\Java13Revealed\src\jdojo.enhancedswitch\classes\com\jdojo\
enhancedswitch\SwitchExpressionCompletion.java:18: error: switch rule
completes without providing a value
            }
  (switch rules in switch expressions must either provide a value or throw)
```

```
C:\Java13Revealed\src\jdojo.enhancedswitch\classes\com\jdojo\
enhancedswitch\SwitchExpressionCompletion.java:22: error: switch rule
completes without providing a value
            }
  (switch rules in switch expressions must either provide a value or throw)
```

The errors are pointing to the end of the "case 3->" and "default->" labels. The compiler concludes that these two labels do not yield a value or throw an exception from all possible execution paths. "case 3->" does not yield a value or throws an exception when the current year is other than 2019. "default->" does not yield a value or throws an exception. The compiler is here to help you when you have these logical mistakes in your switch expressions.

This implies that you cannot use control transfer statements such as break, continue, and return in switch expressions. You can use the break statement to break out of switch statements. Remember the following two rules:

- Switch statements only use the break statement and never the yield statement.

- Switch expressions only use the yield statement and never the break statement.

A Switch Expression Is a Poly Expression

A poly expression in Java is an expression whose type depends on the context. Therefore, the same poly expression can take on different types in different contexts. A switch expression is a poly expression. If its target type is known, its type is the type of its target type. If its target type is unknown, its type is computed by combining the types of each switch labels. Consider the following snippet of code:

```
int count = 2;

double value = switch (count) {
    case 1-> 10;
    case 2-> 20.4;
    default-> 1.5F;
};
```

This `switch` expression has a target type `double`, which is the type of the `value` variable. Therefore, the type of the switch expression is `double`. The compiler also checks that the type of the value yielded from each `switch` label is assignment compatible to the target type of the `switch` expression. In this case, the `switch` labels yield an `int` (10), a `double` (20.4), and a `float` (1.5F). All three types, `int`, `double`, and `float`, are assignment compatible to the target type `double`.

Consider the following snippet of code. Will it compile?

```
int count = 2;

int value = switch (count) {
    case 1-> 10;
    case 2-> 20.4;
    default-> 1.5F;
};
```

This snippet of code does not compile. The target type of the `switch` expression is `int`, which is the declared type of the `value` variable. The `double` and `float` values yielded from the two `switch` labels are not assignment compatible to `int`. This is the reason why this code does not compile.

Consider the following snippet of code. Will it compile?

```
int count = 2;

var value = switch (count) {
    case 1-> 10;
    case 2-> 20.4;
    default-> 1.5F;
};
```

The code compiles fine. Notice the use of `var` to declare the `value` variable. This time, the target type of the `switch` expression is unknown. The compiler has to compute the type of the `switch` expression by looking at each `switch` label. The `switch` labels yield values of `int`, `double`, and `float` type. The compiler uses the type-widening rules and computes `double` as the type of the `switch` expression. Remember that the compiler has to infer the type of the `value` variable because of `var`. The type value will be inferred as `double`, which is the same as the computed type of the `switch` expression.

Consider the following snippet of code. Will it compile?

```
int count = 1;

var value = switch (count) {
    case 1-> 10;
    case 2-> 20.4;
    default-> "what";
};
```

If you guessed that this snippet of code won't compile, you are wrong. It compiles fine. Now you might be curious to know the computed type of the switch expression. The compiler uses the following steps:

- There are three types of values yielded from switch labels: int, double, and String.

- The types are mixed – two primitive types and one reference type.

- The primitive types are promoted to reference types Integer and Double.

- The compiler looks at the common types among Integer, Double, and String. The compiler computes a type that is the union of all common types of these three types. All three types implement four interfaces: Serializable, Comparable, Constable, and ConstantDesc. The computed type of the switch expression is a combination of these four interfaces.

So, what is the type of the switch expression in the previous snippet of code? Here it is:

```
Serializable&Comparable<? extends Serializable&Comparable<?>&Constable&
ConstantDesc>&Constable&ConstantDesc
```

This is a non-denotable type. That is, only compiler can use this type in bytecode. You cannot use (or denote) this type in your source code. To see this for yourself, you can use JShell to run this snippet of code. Make sure to use the --enable-preview option to start JShell and set the feedback mode to verbose as shown:

```
C:\Java13Revealed>jshell --enable-preview
|  Welcome to JShell -- Version 13
|  For an introduction type: /help intro
```

```
jshell> /set feedback verbose
|  Feedback mode: verbose

jshell> int count = 2;
count ==> 2
|  created variable count : int

jshell> var value = switch (count) {
   ...> case 1-> 10;
   ...> case 2-> 20.4;
   ...> default-> "what";
   ...> };
value ==> 20.4
|  created variable value : Serializable&Comparable<? extends
Serializable&Comparable<?>&java.lang.constant.Constable&java.lang.constant.
ConstantDesc>&java.lang.constant.Constable&java.lang.constant.ConstantDesc

jshell> /exit
|  Goodbye

C:\Java13Revealed>
```

The yield Statement

The new switch expression has introduced a new statement called the yield statement. Making yield a statement has some implications on the existing code. It might break existing code if you had a yield() method, which was invoked using unqualified syntax. Let us take an example to understand this rule. Consider the following yield statement:

```
yield(10);
```

Before yield being a statement, this was definitely a method call. That is, it will call a method named yield by passing a value 10.

After the introduction of the switch expressions, this statement will be interpreted as a yield statement that yields a value 10, and it is only permitted to be used in switch expressions. Note that using parenthesis around 10 does not make this a method call because now yield is a statement and (10) is its value. All of the following variants will be treated as a yield statement – whitespaces and parenthesis making no difference:

```
yield 10;
yield (10);
yield(10);
```

If you have unqualified yield() method calls in your existing code, you will need to modify it to make them qualified method calls. That is, if you have yield(x) in your existing code, you will need to change it to xxx.yield(x) where xxx could be this, a class name, or a reference variable name depending on the context.

With the introduction of the switch expressions, yield is a *restricted identifier*. Its use is restricted in certain contexts. You cannot use yield as a type name such as a class name or an interface name. However, you can use yield as a method name and a variable name. Using yield as a method is allowed for backward compatibility because the Thread class in Java contains a yield method and, in rare cases, you might have named your methods as yield.

Listing 5-8 contains a complete program to show how to use yield as method/ variable names and how to call such methods. You must use the NoYieldAsTypeName. yield() syntax to call the yield() method.

Listing 5-8. Using yield as Method and Variable Names

```java
// NoYieldAsTypeName.java
package com.jdojo.enhancedswitch;

public class NoYieldAsTypeName {
    public static void main(String[] args) {
        // Must qualify with the class name to call the yield() methods
        NoYieldAsTypeName.yield();
        NoYieldAsTypeName.yield(100);

        // The following unqualified calls generate compile-time error
        //yield();
        //yield(10);

        int yield = 200;
        System.out.println("Variable name yield is okay: " + yield);
    }
```

```
    public static void yield() {
        System.out.println("Method name yield is okay.");
    }

    public static void yield(int x) {
        System.out.println("Method name yield is okay: " + x);
    }
}
```

```
Method name yield is okay.
Method name yield is okay: 100
Variable name yield is okay: 200
```

Mixing Switch Label Syntax

You have two syntax to declare switch labels – one uses a colon (:) and one uses an arrow (->). In one switch, you cannot mix the two syntax. The following snippet of code does not compile:

```
int count = 1;

int value = switch (count) {
    case 1-> 10;
    case 2: yield 20;
    default-> 30;
};
```

```
error: different case kinds used in the switch
            case 2: yield 20;
1 error
```

Summary

A preview feature of the Java SE Platform is a fully specified and fully implemented language or virtual machine feature, which is available in a JDK feature release, but is not a permanent feature of the JDK yet. A preview feature is provided to solicit developer feedback. You must use the `--enable-preview` option with the compiler and runtime to use a preview feature. You must use the `--release` or `-source` option when you use the `--enable-preview` option to compile the source code. You must start the JShell with `--enable-preview` option to use any preview features in JShell.

Java 12 added enhanced `switch` as a preview feature. The feature stays as a preview feature in Java 13 with one change where the `break` with a value statement in Java 12 is replaced with the `yield` statement in Java 13.

In Java 13, you have two flavors of `switch` – the traditional `switch` and a new `switch`. You use an arrow (`->`) to separate a switch label from the label's code in new `switch` as opposed to a colon (`:`) in old switch. You cannot mix the two `switch` label syntax in the same `switch`. The enhanced `switch` can be used as a statement as well as an expression.

The new `switch` makes developers' life a little easier while writing and debugging code. It does not have the `default` fall-through – only one `switch` label can be executed at a time. The code associated with a `switch` label can be an expression, a block statement, or a `throw` statement.

The enhanced `switch` – both traditional `switch` and new `switch` – allows multiple comma-separated case constants in a `case` label.

To support `switch` expressions, Java 13 added a new statement called the `yield` statement. It can be used only in `switch` expressions to yield a value. The value yielded by a `yield` statement becomes the value of the `switch` expression. A control transfer statement such as `break`, `continue`, and `return` is not allowed in a `switch` expression.

The compile checks that all possible values of the `selector-expression` in a `switch` expression are covered by `switch` labels. Otherwise, a compile-time error occurs. If a `switch` expression is based on an enum type and all enum constants are covered by the `switch` labels and there is no `default` label, the compiler adds a `default` label that throws an `IncompatibleClassChangeError`. This implicit `default` label helps you debug the code when new constants are added to the enum and the switch expression is executed with the new enum constants. The implicit `default` label gives you a better error message that helps you identify the issue quickly.

A `switch` expression is a poly expression whose type depends on the context. If the `switch` expression has a known target type, the type of the `switch` expression is the target type. If the target type is unknown, a stand-alone type is computed by combining the types of values yielded from all `switch` labels.

yield is a *restricted identifier*. You cannot use `yield` as a type name such as a class name or an interface name. However, you can use `yield` as a method name and a variable name. You cannot use unqualified `yield()` as a method call. If your existing code contains unqualified `yield()` method calls, you will need to change them to qualified method calls to avoid the compile-time errors.

CHAPTER 6

Text Blocks

In this chapter, you will learn

- What text blocks are

- How to represent text blocks in your code

- The formatting rules for text blocks

- Changes to the String API to support text blocks

- How to detect inconsistent use of whitespaces in text blocks

The Background

Rarely you write a Java program without dealing with strings. Java supports strings as instances of the String class since version 1.0. It also supports String literals, which are sequences of zero or more characters enclosed in double quotes. String literals are represented in the source code, and they are instances of the String class. The biggest pain points in using String literals are

- If a string literal does not fit into a single line, you need to break them into smaller strings and use string concatenation operator (+) to assemble them back into one string.

- If you have a string that contains line terminators, you need to embed the newlines as escape sequences (\n) in the string and use string concatenation operator (+).

- If your string contains double quotes, you need to represent them using the escape sequence \" in your string.

© Kishori Sharan 2019

K. Sharan, *Java 13 Revealed*, https://doi.org/10.1007/978-1-4842-5407-3_6

These problems in using `String` literals make it cumbersome to write Java code with strings and have a huge readability issue. Suppose you want to represent a list of three cities – each on a separate line. Here is how you achieve it using a `String` literal:

```
String cities = "Panama\nParis\nPatna\n";
```

You may agree that this is not very readable. You lose the visual sense that it contains three lines – each containing a city name. Here is another attempt to achieve the same:

```
String cities = "Panama\n" +
                "Paris\n" +
                "Patna\n";
```

This time, it has little better readability, but still contains visual clutters in the form of escape sequences (\n). Can you guess the string represented by the following `String` literal?

```
String quote = "\"A fool thinks of himself to be wise. " +
               "But a wise man knows himself to be a fool.\"\n" +
               "-William Shakespeare\n";
```

This `String` literal represents the following quote from William Shakespeare:

A fool thinks of himself to be wise. But a wise man knows himself to be a fool.

—William Shakespeare

Wouldn't it be nicer if you were able to represent this quote as follows?

```
String quote = """
"A fool thinks of himself to be wise. But a wise man knows himself to be a
fool."
-William Shakespeare
""";
```

Wouldn't it be nicer if you were able to represent the list of three cities – each in a separate line – as follows?

```
String cities = """
                Panama
                Paris
                Patna
                """;
```

Wouldn't it be neat to write HTML code in a Java program as follows?

```
String html = """
              <html>
                  <body>
                      <h1>Hello, HTML</h1>
                  </body>
              </html>
              """;
```

Using `String` literals to represent complex multiline text is not limited to strings like a list of three cities and a quote as I showed you. Typically, Java programs contain non-Java code such as SQL, JSON, XML, and HTML as `String` literals. Representing these types of code in Java has been simply painful. Some developers go to the extent of putting these types of code in files, packaging them in a JAR, and reading the files into instances of `String` at runtime. This approach frees you from the shackles of the `String` literal limitations at the cost of extra headaches of handling files!

Solving the problems faced by Java developers in using `String` literals to represent complex, multiline text blocks has been the focus of the Java language designers for quite some time. They added support for raw string literals in Java 12 as a language preview feature and later withdrew it, so it never made it to Java 12. You can find details on the proposal for raw string literals in JEP 326 at `https://openjdk.java.net/jeps/326`. JEP 326 has been superseded by JEP 355 (`https://openjdk.java.net/jeps/355`), which proposes text block support in Java 13 as a language preview feature. You have already seen text blocks in previous examples when I used """ to start and close strings such as to represent HTML code as a `String`. Text blocks are the topic of discussion in this chapter.

What Is a Text Block?

A text block is a sequence of zero or more characters enclosed by an opening delimiter and a closing delimiter. The content of a text block can span multiple lines, and you do not need to use most escape sequences. Here is the syntax to use a text block:

```
<opening-delimiter>
<content-of-the-text-block>
<closing-delimiter>
```

The syntax allows to place the closing delimiter on a separate line or on the same line where the content of the text block ends:

```
<opening-delimiter>
<content-of-the-text-block><closing-delimiter>
```

The opening delimiter starts with a sequence of three double quote characters ("""), optionally followed with zero or more space, tab, or form feed characters, and ends with a line terminator.

The closing delimiter consists of a sequence of three double quote characters (""").

The content of a text block is the sequence of characters that starts immediately after the line terminator of the opening delimiter and ends immediately before the first double quote of the closing delimiter.

A text block is an instance of the String class. Anywhere you have been using String literals, you can use text blocks. Here are a few examples of text blocks. Each example prints the text block to show you the resulting string:

```
String cities = """
                Panama
                Paris
                Patna""";
System.out.println(cities);
```

```
Panama
Paris
Patna
```

This text block is the same as the `String` literal `"Panama\nParis\nPatna"`.

If you put the closing delimiter on its own line, a newline (\n) is appended to the content of the text block. The following text block is same as the `String` literal `"Panama\nParis\nPatna\n"`:

```
String cities = """
                Panama
                Paris
                Patna
                """;
System.out.println(cities);
```

```
Panama
Paris
Patna
```

Notice the last line in the output, which is an empty line, because you placed the closing delimiter on a separate line.

Consider the following snippet of code:

```
String cities = """
                Panama
                Paris
                Patna
""";

System.out.println(cities);
```

```
                Panama
                Paris
                Patna
```

Are you surprised by the output? The last line in the output is empty because you placed the closing delimiter on a separate line. The three lines in the content have been indented with 16 spaces to the left. This happened because you have moved the closing delimiter to the beginning of the line. Compare the placement of the closing delimiter in the last two examples. Placement of the close delimiter makes a difference in formatting the text block. You need to master the rules behind it. I will explain all formatting rules for text blocks in subsequent sections.

Tip   A text block is not a raw string – meaning you do not get what you type. The content of a text block is transformed by the compiler using a predefined set of rules.

Let us have a few invalid examples of using the opening delimiter in text blocks. Recall that after the three double quote characters (""") in the opening delimiter, you can have spaces, tabs, and line feeds. You must end it with a line terminator. The allowed characters that may follow """ are invisible characters. You cannot use escape sequences for these invisible characters. You simply type them as invisible characters in your source code. The following are invalid text blocks, which generate compile-time errors:

```
// Missing line terminator in the opening delimiter.
String str = """Hello
            """;
```

```
// Missing line terminator in the opening delimiter. You can enter a tab
// character in the opening delimiter, but not as an escape sequence \t.
String str = """\t
            Hello
            """;
```

```
// Missing line terminator in the opening delimiter.
String str = """Hello""";
```

Tip   The opening delimiter in a text block must be placed on a separate line using a line terminator, and the content of the text block must start on the next line.

Text Blocks Are a Preview Feature

Text blocks are a language preview feature in Java 13. Refer to Chapter 5 for more details on what a preview feature is. Chapter 5 also explains how to compile and run Java programs that use Java preview features.

Text Blocks Are Transformed

Let us start with two questions. Is a text block a raw string? Is a text block a multiline `String` literal? The answers to both questions are yes and no. To some extent, a text block is a raw string and a multiline `String` literal; to some extent, it is neither. To clarify the answer, let us define what a *raw* string and a *multiline* `String` *literal* mean.

A raw string means no processing occurs to the string. The term *raw* means "not changed in any way." This is not what you get from a text block. A text block is transformed before you get a final string from it. Therefore, a text block is not certainly a 100% *raw* string.

How about a text block being a multiline `String` literal? Again, the term *literal* means it is represented unchanged. This is not the case with a text block because it is transformed.

On the other side of the argument, a text block does preserve most, if not all, part of the original string and allows you to span the string in multiple lines. In that sense, it is partly raw and multiline.

A text block is sometimes referred to as a multiline `String` literal. Even JEP 355, which defines the text block features, refers to it as a multiline `String` literal. If you want to refer to it as a multiline `String` literal, I would suggest you call it *a multiline* `String` *literal with transformation*, which gives the reader the true sense of what it is.

The compiler uses a set of predefined rules to transform the content of a text block. The resulting string, after the transformation, is represented as a `String` literal in class files. The runtime does not know anything about a text block. Now you may see the reason why I call it *a multiline String literal with transformation*.

Tip   You have a way to opt out of some transformations in a text block, and you are, by default, opted in for other transformations. Automatic transformations of text blocks are designed to work for you as is in most common cases.

Before I explain the transformation rules for a text block, let us have a quick example with complete code. All programs in this chapter are in the `jdojo.textblock` module as defined in Listing 6-1.

Listing 6-1. The Declaration of a Module Named jdojo.textblock

```
// module-info.java
module jdojo.textblock {
    exports com.jdojo.textblock;
}
```

Listing 6-2 contains a few text blocks entered differently by placing the closing delimiter at different positions. The output shows the resulting strings.

Listing 6-2. A Few Examples of Text Blocks

```
// TextBlocks.java
package com.jdojo.textblock;

public class TextBlocks {
    public static void main(String[] args) {
        String html1 = """
                        <html>
                            <body>
                                <h1>Hello, HTML</h1>
                            </body>
                        </html>
                        """;

        System.out.println("html1:\n" + html1);

        String html2 = """
                        <html>
                            <body>
                                <h1>Hello, HTML</h1>
                            </body>
                        </html>
                    """;

        System.out.println("html2:\n" + html2);

        // An empty String. Same as ""
        String empty1 = """
                    """;
```

```
        System.out.println("empty1: " + empty1);
        System.out.println("empty1.length(): " + empty1.length());

        // An empty String. Same as ""
        String empty2 = """
            """;
        System.out.println("empty2: " + empty2);
        System.out.println("empty2.length(): " + empty2.length());

        // Looks like an empty string, but it is not. Same as "\n"
        String empty3 = """

                """;
        System.out.println("empty3: " + empty3);
        System.out.println("empty3.length(): " + empty3.length());
    }
}
```

```
html1:
<html>
    <body>
        <h1>Hello, HTML</h1>
    </body>
</html>

html2:
  <html>
      <body>
          <h1>Hello, HTML</h1>
      </body>
  </html>

empty1:
empty1.length(): 0
empty2:
empty2.length(): 0
empty3:

empty3.length(): 1
```

By this time, you should be convinced that placement of the closing delimiter in a text block has a significant effect on how the content of the text block is transformed. The transformation happens to whitespaces in the content – some for consistency across platforms and some for covering common use cases. Let us consider the following HTML code:

```
String html = """
            <html>
              <body>
                 <h1>Hello, HTML</h1>
              </body>
            </html>
            """;
```

This HTML code contains a lot of spaces. Spaces are not visible in the source code. To visualize the spaces, I rewrote it to show spaces as dots:

```
String html = """
..............<html>
..................<body>....
......................<h1>Hello, HTML</h1>.
..................</body>...
..............</html>..
............""";
```

The first line contains 14 leading spaces and no trailing spaces, the second line 18 leading spaces and 4 trailing spaces, the third line 22 leading spaces and 1 trailing space, and so on.

It is very likely that the author of this code did not want to use the first 14 leading spaces in any of the lines in the content. These spaces exist as part of the indentation to align the content of the code with other part of the code. It is very likely that the four spaces before the <body> in the second line are part of the intended indentation and the developer wants to keep it. Undoubtedly, the developer did not want any trailing spaces in any line of the content; they exist most likely because they were copied and pasted from another source. If you must read the developer's intent for the string to store in the html variable, you may guess it as follows, which does not contain 14 leading spaces and does not contain any trailing spaces. I show spaces as dots for better visualization:

```
<html>
....<body>
........<h1>Hello, HTML</h1>
....</body>
</html>
```

Didn't you get this as the output for the html1 variable in Listing 6-2? Yes. You did. The rules for transformation of a text block cover such common cases by default. Let us look at the text block for html2 variable in Listing 6-2 using dots for spaces for better visualization:

```
String html2 = """
...............<html>
..................<body>
......................<h1>Hello, HTML</h1>
..................</body>
...............</html>
............""";
```

The first line of the content contains 15 leading spaces, the second 19, the third 23, the fourth 19, the fifth 15, and the sixth 13. The content does not include any trailing spaces in any lines. The resulting string after transformation is the same as you saw in the output for the variable html2 in Listing 6-2. The following is the string represented by the text block. I have shown spaces as dots for better visualization:

```
..<html>
......<body>
..........<h1>Hello, HTML</h1>
......</body>
..</html>
```

In this text block, it is assumed that the developer wanted to left-align the content on each line starting with two spaces on the first line and using four spaces to nest HTML tags. This is the assumption made by the compiler during the transformation.

It is common in Java programs to vertically align the content of a text block with other part of the program such as the variable name, assignment operator, and the first double quote character in the opening delimiter. These whitespaces appear as leading whitespaces in the content on each line. Unintended trailing whitespaces may appear on a line. Leading whitespaces may appear in the content for indentation purpose such as indenting nested tags in HTML code.

The whitespaces that are part of the text block that the developer meant to keep in the content after transformation are known as *essential whitespaces*. Whitespaces in the content that exist as part of the indentation in the source code, but the developer does not mean to keep them in the final string, are known as *incidental whitespaces.*

The compiler removes the incidental whitespaces from all non-blank lines in the content. The starting position of the closing delimiter can be used to control the incidental whitespaces in a text block. Trailing whitespaces are always considered incidental, and the compiler always removes them. In the next few sections, I will explain the rules applied by the compiler to transfer text blocks.

Transformation Rules

The compiler transforms a text block in three stages. Each stage processes different types of characters, and they serve different purposes. Transformation to the following types of characters is applied in order:

- Line terminators
- Incidental whitespaces
- Escape sequences

Let us dive deep into each type of these transformations. These rules may be a little overwhelming at first. Do not worry if you do not understand some rules. After I cover a rule, I present several examples explaining each step in the rule with the strings before and after transformation.

Transforming Line Terminators

Line terminators are different on different platforms. Windows uses a carriage return (CR) and a carriage return with a line feed (CRLF) as line terminators. UNIX-like OS uses a line feed (LF) as a line terminator. A CR is represented by ASCII decimal 13, Unicode escape \u000D, octal escape \015, and the escape sequence \r. An LF is represented by ASCII decimal 10, Unicode \u000A, octal escape \012, and the escape sequence \n. An LF is also called a newline character.

Consider the following text block:

```
"""
Hello
Terminator
"""
```

How many characters are in this text block – 15, 17, 19, or other? It is hard to tell the exact number of characters by just looking at this text block. The answer depends on the platform used to write this text block. You can see 15 visible characters – 5 for Hello and 10 for Terminator. Each of the two lines in the content has a line terminator, which is not visible, but you see the effects. Recall that a line terminator could be one or two characters depending on the platform. If you edited this text block on Windows, the invisible line terminators look as follows:

```
"""
HelloCRLF
TerminatorCRLF
"""
```

If you edited this text block on a UNIX-like OS, the invisible line terminators look as follows:

```
"""
HelloLF
TerminatorLF
"""
```

Counting CR and LF as one character each, the text block contains 19 characters on Windows and 17 characters on UNIX-like OS. Two developers writing the same text block on two different platforms will get different number of characters in the text block. You may agree that this difference is neither intended nor acceptable.

The line terminators in the content of a text block are normalized by the compiler. The compiler replaces a CR and a CRLF with an LF. This transformation ensures that a text block with the same visual content contains the same final string across platforms.

That's all that happens at this stage. The content of the text block after transformation in this stage, irrespective of the platform or the source code encoding, looks as follows:

```
"""
HelloLF
TerminatorLF
"""
```

A text block may contain escape sequences such as CR and LF as escape sequences such as \r and \n, which are left untouched at this stage. All escape sequences are transformed in the last stage.

Transforming Incidental Whitespaces

Before this stage, all line terminators have been normalized to LF. I will refer to line terminator as simply line terminators in this stage, which always means LF. All example text blocks in this section use dots to show spaces in their content.

In this stage, the compiler removes the incidental leading and trailing whitespaces. The number of leading whitespaces to be removed from all non-blank lines in the content is computed as follows:

- The line with the opening delimiter is not considered for this computation.

- Lines that consist of only whitespaces are called blank lines and they are not considered for this computation. Blank lines may contain only a line terminator or whitespaces with a line terminator.

- If the closing delimiter is placed on a separate line by itself with or without whitespaces, this line is considered for this computation. Note that with the definition of a blank line, when you place the closing delimiter on a separate line by itself, this line is a blank line. However, it is a significant line for the purpose of this computation and is not ignored.

- Count the number of leading whitespaces on each non-blank line. Each whitespace is counted as 1. That is, if a line contains two spaces and another contains one space and one tab, this step counts two as leading whitespaces on both lines.

- Compute the minimum of the leading whitespace count for all non-blank lines. Suppose you have five non-blank lines with leading whitespace counts as 15, 19, 23, 19, 15, and 13. The minimum of all counts will be 13.

- Remove the minimum whitespace count, as computed in the previous step, from all non-blank lines.

- Remove all trailing whitespaces from all lines, not just the non-blank lines. This step will remove the trailing whitespaces from the non-blank lines. It will collapse blank lines into empty lines – lines with only line terminators.

Example 1

Consider the follow text block:

```
String html = """
..............<html>
..................<body>....
......................<h1>Hello, HTML</h1>.
..................</body>...
..............</html>..
.............""";
```

The leading whitespace counts for all non-blank lines are 14, 18, 22, 18, 14, and 14. The closing delimiter has been placed on a separate line, and it is treated as a non-blank line to compute the number of whitespaces to be removed from all lines. The minimum whitespace count for all lines is 14. Therefore, the compiler removes 14 whitespaces from all lines. The compiler also removes all trailing whitespaces from four lines. The resulting string is

```
<html>
....<body>
........<h1>Hello, HTML</h1>
....</body>
</html>
```

Example 2

Consider the following text block in which the closing delimiter has been placed in the beginning of the line:

```
String html = """
..............<html>
................<body>....
....................<h1>Hello, HTML</h1>.
................</body>...
..............</html>..
""";
```

What will be the resulting string? Remember that the line with the closing delimiter always participates in the minimum whitespace count. In this case, the whitespace count for the last line is 0. So, the leading whitespace counts for all non-blank lines are 14, 18, 22, 18, 14, and 0. The minimum whitespace count is 0, which will result in the compiler removing no leading whitespaces. As usual, all trailing whitespaces will be removed. The resulting string will be as follows:

```
..............<html>
................<body>
....................<h1>Hello, HTML</h1>
................</body>
..............</html>
```

Tip   If you want to preserve all leading whitespaces on the non-blank lines, place the closing line terminator in the beginning on a separate line.

Example 3

Consider the following text block:

```
String html = """
..............<html>
................<body>....
....................<h1>Hello, HTML</h1>.
```

```
................</body>...
..............</html>..
............""";
```

The leading whitespace counts for all non-blank lines are 14, 18, 22, 18, 14, and 12. The minimum of these counts is 12, so 12 leading whitespaces will be removed from all non-blank lines. Trailing whitespaces are removed as usual. The resulting string is as follows:

```
..<html>
....<body>
........<h1>Hello, HTML</h1>
....</body>
..</html>
```

Example 4

Consider the following text block in which I have placed the closing delimiter 18 spaces to the right:

```
String html = """
..............<html>
................<body>....
....................<h1>Hello, HTML</h1>.
................</body>...
..............</html>..
................""";
```

The leading whitespace counts for all non-blank lines are 14, 18, 22, 18, 14, and 18. The minimum of these counts is 14, so 14 leading whitespaces will be removed from all non-blank lines. Trailing whitespaces are removed as usual. The resulting string is as follows:

```
<html>
....<body>
........<h1>Hello, HTML</h1>
....</body>
</html>
```

Notice that when the closing delimiter is placed on a separate line and if it starts anywhere to the right of a non-whitespace character on any non-blank lines, the placement of the closing delimiter does not play any role in leading whitespace removal.

Example 5

Consider the following text block:

```
String html = """
..............<html>
..................<body>....
......................<h1>Hello, HTML</h1>.
..................</body>...
..............</html>..""";
```

In this case, the placement of the closing delimiter is not playing a role in determining how many leading whitespaces will be removed from all lines. The leading whitespace counts for all non-blank lines are 14, 18, 22, 18, and 14. The minimum of these counts is 14, so 14 leading whitespaces will be removed from all non-blank lines. Trailing whitespaces are removed as usual. The resulting string is as follows:

```
<html>
....<body>
........<h1>Hello, HTML</h1>
....</body>
</html>
```

Compare the last example with other examples in this section. When you place the closing delimiter on a separate line, the last non-blank line contains an LF as the last character. When you place the closing delimiter on the same line as the non-blank content, the last line does not contain an LF as a character. In this example, the last line in the content ends as "</html>..", whereas in other examples the last line in the content ends as "</html>LF".

Example 6

How do you represent an empty string in a text block? The following text blocks represent an empty string:

```
String empty1 = """
""";

String empty2 = """
.............. """;

String empty3 = """
...................."""; 
```

These text blocks contain no non-blank lines. Remember that the line with the closing delimiter is always significant. The number of whitespaces to be removed from non-blank lines is computed, but it is not used because there are no non-blank lines. In the second and third text blocks, the trailing spaces on the lone line are collapsed, resulting in an empty string.

Example 7

How will you use a text block to represent a string "Hello"? All of the following text blocks represent the string "Hello". The indentation of the content line does not affect the final string.

```
String str1 = """
            Hello""";

String str2 = """
Hello""";

String str2 =
"""
Hello""";
```

The following text block does not represent "Hello". Rather, it represents "Hello\n" because the first line of the content is not just Hello. It has a line terminator that is normalized to an LF (\n).

```
String str = """
            Hello
            """;
```

> **Tip**   A text block can represent any string that can be represented using a `String` literal. Use `String` literals to represent simple strings such as empty string, a newline as a string, or a one-line string such as `"Hello, world"`. Using a text block for these strings takes at least two lines and is also not as readable as `String` literals.

Example 8

Consider the following text block, which contains no visible content, but has a blank line:

```
String fakeEmpty = """
......................
....""";
```

This text block contains two lines in its content. The first line contains 22 spaces and an LF. The second line contains four spaces. Both lines are considered blank lines and will not be used to remove the leading whitespaces. The second line contains the closing delimiter with whitespace count as 4, which is also the minimum whitespace count because you have only one line to consider. The text block does not contain any non-blank line, so the minimum leading whitespace count of 4 is not applied to any lines. As part of removing the trailing whitespaces, all 22 spaces are removed from the first line reducing it to an empty line with only one character – the normalized line terminator (LF). The resulting string will be `"\n"`. If you count the number of characters in the `fakeEmpty` variable, it will be 1. Seeing is believing. The following snippet of code shows that the resulting string from the text block is `"\n"`:

```
// Define a text block with one empty line with whitespaces
String fakeEmpty = """

                            """;
String LF = "\n";
System.out.println("fakeEmpty.length(): " + fakeEmpty.length());
System.out.println("LF.length(): " + LF.length());
System.out.println("fakeEmpty.equals(LF): " + fakeEmpty.equals(LF));
System.out.println("fakeEmpty == LF: " + (fakeEmpty == LF));
```

```
fakeEmpty.length(): 1
LF.length(): 1
fakeEmpty.equals(LF): true
fakeEmpty == newline: true
```

The output indicates that the two strings are not only equal using the equals() method, they are also equal using the == operator. The final string from a text block, after all compiler transformations have been applied, is interned as all String literals are. This is the reason why the text block and the String literal "\n" are also equals using the == operator.

Transforming Escape Sequences

Escape sequences in a text block are interpreted in the third and the last stage of transformation. Text blocks support the same set of escape sequences as String literals such as \b, \t, \n, \f, \r, \", \', \\, octal escapes (\nnn), and Unicode escapes (\uxxxx). They are interpreted last to give developer a chance to format the content of text blocks using escape sequences. Consider the following text block that uses the escape sequence \t (a tab character) to format the nested tags in HTML code:

```
String html = """
..............<html>
..............\t<body>
..............\t\t<h1>Hello, HTML</h1>
..............\t</body>
..............</html>
.............."""";
```

All leading spaces shown as dots will be removed as part of the second stage transformation. This stage will interpret the tabs in nested lines, and the resulting string will be as follows:

```
<html>
    <body>
        <h1>Hello, HTML</h1>
    </body>
</html>
```

195

Recall that in the second stage all line terminators (CR, CRLF, and LF) are normalized as LF. Suppose you want to end all your lines with a CRLF (\r\n), not LF (\n). How will you achieve this? You can achieve this by inserting the escape sequence \r to the end of each content line in the text block. Here is the text block:

```
String html = """
..............<html>\r
..................<body>\r
......................<h1>Hello, HTML</h1>\r
..................</body>\r
..............</html>\r
..............""";
```

The resulting string will be as follows. I have shown the transformed line terminator (LF) as \n in each line of the string to help you visualize the transformed string. Spaces are shown as dots as usual.

```
<html>\r\n
....<body>\r\n
........<h1>Hello, HTML</h1>\r\n
....</body>\r\n
</html>\r\n
```

How will you add trailing whitespaces to any lines in a text block? The answer is using escape sequences. The ASCII decimal value for a space is 32, which can be represented as \040 as an octal escape and \u0020 as Unicode escape. Let us take a simple example of representing "Hello " as a text block. Note that you have a trailing space in "Hello ". The number of characters in this string is six – five in Hello and one trailing space. Here is our first attempt:

```
String str = """
            Hello """;

System.out.printf("str: '%s'%n", str);
System.out.printf("str.length(): %d%n", str.length());
System.out.printf("str ends with a space: %b%n", str.endsWith(" "));
```

```
str: 'Hello'
str.length(): 5
str ends with a space: false
```

The output indicates that the resulting string from the text block does not contain a trailing space. This is so because the second stage of transformation removes all trailing whitespaces, which removes the space after Hello.

You need to represent the trailing space in this case as an octal escape \040. Here is the second attempt:

```
String str = """
            Hello\040""";

System.out.printf("str: '%s'%n", str);
System.out.printf("str.length(): %d%n", str.length());
System.out.printf("str ends with a space: %b%n", str.endsWith(" "));
```

```
str: 'Hello '
str.length(): 6
str ends with a space: true
```

Congratulations! The output indicates that you were able to insert a trailing space in a line in a text block. The game is not over yet as you might have thought! Let us try using the Unicode escape \u0020 to have a trailing space:

```
String str = """
            Hello\u0020""";

System.out.printf("str: '%s'%n", str);
System.out.printf("str.length(): %d%n", str.length());
System.out.printf("str ends with a space: %b%n", str.endsWith(" "));
```

```
str: 'Hello'
str.length(): 5
str ends with a space: false
```

You didn't get the desired results? Are you surprised? Unicode escapes are interpreted at a very early stage during compilation, before any other processing happens. The compiler interprets Unicode escapes as it reads the source code. The compiler interprets the Unicode escape \u0020 and converts it into a space while reading the source code. When the compiler starts text block transformation, \u0020 was already converted to a space character ' '. The text block transformer does not see the Unicode escape at all – it sees a space instead. The transformer removes this space when it processes all trailing whitespaces. This is the reason why you do not get a trailing space in this example. To prove this point, let us have another example.

Unicode escape for LF is \u000A. Consider the following snippet of code with a `String` literal, which contains the following sequences of characters: He, \u000A, and llo.

```
String str = "He\u000Allo";
```

Does this code compile? No. It does not. The culprit is the usage of the Unicode escape. Before the compile processes the `String` literal, the Unicode escape \u000A has already been interpreted as an LF, making the source code look like

```
String str = "He
llo";
```

A `String` literal cannot span into multiple lines. This is the reason why this code does not compile. The compile-time error is "unclosed string literal". Let us try this example using a text block as shown:

```
String str = """
            He\u000Allo""";
System.out.printf("str: '%s'%n", str);
System.out.printf("str.length(): %d%n", str.length());
```

```
str: '              He
llo'
str.length(): 19
```

There are two surprises in the output. First, you did not get any compile-time errors. Second, the number of characters is 19. You might have expected the number for characters as 6, not 19. Pause for a moment and try to explain the output.

If you could not explain the output, here is the explanation. Let us represent our original text block with spaces shown as dots:

```
String str = """
............He\u000Allo""";
```

There are 13 leading spaces on the content line. Before the text block transformation occurs, the compiler will interpret \u000A as an LF, which will result in the following text block:

```
String str = """
............He
llo""";
```

Now you might be able to see the final string and be able to interpret the previous output. The content of the text block has been converted from one line to two lines. The first line contains 13 leading spaces and the second line none. The compiler does not remove any leading spaces because the minimum whitespace count for all non-blank lines is zero. The final string is as follows:

```
............He
llo
```

The total number of characters is 19–13 leading spaces, 2 in He, 1 in the LF after He, and 3 in llo.

Tip   You do not need to use escape sequences \" and \n to include a double quote and newline in a text block. You are recommended to use " and a line terminator instead. And, beware of using Unicode escapes in text blocks, which are processed earlier than the text block transformations are applied.

Suppose you want to nest a text block in another text block. Consider the first unsuccessfully attempt as follows:

```
String str = """
            String test = """
                    Text blocks are fun if you understand them!
                    """

            """;
```

This text block does not compile. The three double quotes on the second line "...
`String test = """"` are interpreted as the closing delimiter for the opening delimiter
on the first line. Now the third, fourth, and fifth lines are not valid Java code. If you want
to use three consecutive double quotes inside a text block, you must escape at least
one of the three double quotes to avoid them being interpreted as the closing delimiter.
You can make the previous text block valid as follows. I chose to escape the first double
quote.

```
String str = """
            String test = \"""
                         Text blocks are fun if you understand them!
                         \"""
            """;
```

A Complete Example

In this section, I present a complete example, which includes all types of transformations
to a text block. First, I explain all steps in the transformation. In the end, I include a
complete program. Our example text block is as follows:

```
String html = """
..............<html>\040CRLF
...........CRLF
...................<body>...CRLF
.......................<h1>Hello, HTML</h1>\tCRLF
CRLF
...................</body>CRLF
...........................CRLF
..............</html>CRLF
..............""";
```

Here are the syntax that I used for the text block:

- I am using dots for spaces to show you that there are spaces in the
  text block. In actual text block, you would have spaces, not dots.

- I am writing the code on Windows, so use CRLF to show the line
  terminators. In actual text block, line terminators are not visible.

- \040 is the octal escape for a space (ASCII decimal 32).

- \t is an escape sequence for a tab.

- Everything else in the content of the text block is a character as it appears.

There are nine lines in the content of the text block as follows:

```
..............<html>\040CRLF
..........CRLF
..................<body>...CRLF
......................<h1>Hello, HTML</h1>\tCRLF
CRLF
..................</body>CRLF
........................CRLF
..............</html>CRLF
............
```

Let us start the text block transformation process. In the first step, the line terminators are normalized to LF resulting in the following string:

```
..............<html>\040LF
..........LF
..................<body>...LF
......................<h1>Hello, HTML</h1>\tLF
LF
..................</body>LF
........................LF
..............</html>LF
............
```

Now the compiler computes the number of whitespaces that it must remove from the beginning of each non-blank line. Lines 2, 5, 7, and 9 are blank lines. Line 9 is the last line that contains the closing delimiter, so it is considered a significant line for this computation. So, the compiler ignores lines 2, 5, and 7, but includes line 9, for this computation. The whitespace counts are 14 on line 1, 18 on line 3, 22 on line 4, 18 on line 6, 14 on line 8, and 14 on line 9. The minimum whitespace count from these lines is 14.

The compiler removes 14 leading whitespaces from all non-blank lines 1, 3, 4, 6, and 8. The resulting string is as follows:

```
<html>\040LF
...........LF
....<body>...LF
........<h1>Hello, HTML</h1>\tLF
LF
....</body>LF
........................LF
</html>LF
.............
```

Now trailing whitespaces are removed from all lines resulting in the following string:

```
<html>\040LF
LF
....<body>LF
........<h1>Hello, HTML</h1>\tLF
LF
....</body>LF
LF
</html>LF
```

Note that the blank lines have become empty lines; they contain only LF in the resulting string. The last line had no LF and it is an empty string now, which just disappears from the resulting string.

As a final transformation, the escape sequences are interpreted resulting in the following string:

```
<html> LF
LF
....<body>LF
........<h1>Hello, HTML</h1>   LF
LF
....</body>LF
LF
</html>LF
```

Listing 6-3 contains a complete program to show this transformation. The program uses the lines() method of the String class, which returns a stream of lines from the text block. The map() method encloses the content of each line in single quotes. I used single quotes to enclose each line's content, so you can see the trailing whitespaces in the output. The forEach() method prints each line enclosed in single quotes to the standard output.

Listing 6-3. Visualizing Text Block Transformation

```java
// TextBlockTransformation.java
package com.jdojo.textblock;

public class TextBlockTransformation {
    public static void main(String[] args) {
        String html = """
                        <html>\040

                            <body>
                                <h1>Hello, HTML</h1>\t

                            </body>

                        </html>
                        """;

                // let us print each line by enclosing it in single quotes
                html.lines()
                    .map(s -> "'" + s + "'")
                    .forEach(System.out::println);
    }
}
```

```
'<html> '
"
'    <body>'
'        <h1>Hello, HTML</h1>    '
"
'    </body>'
"
'</html>'
```

Concatenating Text Blocks

Text blocks can be used anywhere you have been using `String` literals. You can concatenate them as you concatenate `String` literals. Keep the code readability in mind because concatenated text blocks make it difficult to read the code.

The following snippet of code concatenates a text block and a `String` literal to get a string `"Hello, Text Block"`:

```
String str = """
            Hello""" + ", Text Block";
```

The code is not very readable. Let us replace the `String` literal with a text block:

```
String str = """
             Hello""" + """
            , Text Block""";
```

The readability is further reduced. You must pay attention to the opening and closing delimiters of each text block to understand what is going on.

Suppose the name in the message comes from a variable. To get a `"Hello, <name>"` string, where the `<name>` comes from a variable, you can use the following text block. Notice the use of the octal escape `\040` to insert a space:

```
String name = "Text Block";
String str = """
            Hello,\040""" + name;
```

This is not an optimum solution. If you have placeholders in your text block whose values come from variables, using string format specifiers with the `formatted()` method of the `String` class is a better option. You can rewrite the previous snippet of code as follows:

```
String name = "Text Block";
String str = """
            Hello, %s""".formatted(name);
```

The `formatted()` method has been added to the `String` class in Java 13 as part of supporting text blocks. It is an instance method. It accepts a var-args argument, which are the values for the format specifiers in the text block. If you want to generate text based on a template, you can use a text block with format specifiers as the template and use the `formatted()` method to get desired text into the template.

Addition to the String API

The following instance methods have been added to the String class to support text blocks:

- String formatted(Object... args)
- String stripIndent()
- String translateEscapes()

Tip   The three methods added to the String class to support text blocks are deprecated and marked for removal because text block is a preview feature, which may be removed or refined in a future release. You are not supposed to use text blocks and these methods in production.

The formatted() instance method formats the string using the specified arguments. It works the same as the format(String format, Object...args) static method of the String class. Using the formatted() method, instead of the format() method, gives you cleaner code. Otherwise, there is no difference in the result. The following snippet of code formats the same text block with both methods:

```
String name = "Text Block";

// Use the formatted() instance method
String str = """
            Hello, %s""".formatted(name);
System.out.println(str);

// Use the format() static method
String str2 = String.format("""
                    Hello, %s""", name);
System.out.println(str2);
```

```
Hello, Text Block
Hello, Text Block
```

The stripIndent() method removes the incidental whitespaces from the beginning and end of every line in the string. You can use this method when you receive strings from files or other sources, which may contain incidental whitespaces. You will not need to use this method while working with text blocks because text blocks remove the incidental whitespaces automatically. Java 12 had added an indent(int n) method, which adds n spaces to the beginning of each line and normalizes the line terminators in each line to use LF. If n is less than zero, it removes up to n number of leading whitespaces from each line. Listing 6-4 contains a complete program to show the use of both methods. A discussion on the output follows the output.

Listing 6-4. Using stripIndent() and indent() method of the String Class

```java
// IndentTest.java
package com.jdojo.textblock;

public class IndentTest {
    public static void main(String[] args) {
        String html = " <html>\n"
                + "      <body>\n"
                + "          <h1>Hello, HTML</h1>\n"
                + "      </body>\n"
                + " </html>";

        System.out.println("Original:\n" + html);

        // Remove incidental whitespaces
        String html2 = html.stripIndent();
        System.out.println("\nAfter stringIndent():\n" + html2);

        // Indent the string with one space, which add an LF
        // to the last line in the content
        String html3 = html2.indent(1);
        System.out.println("\nAfter indent():\n" + html3);

        // Print the details
        System.out.println("html.length(): " + html.length());
        System.out.println("html3.length(): " + html3.length());
        System.out.println("html.equals(html3): " + html.equals(html3));
        System.out.println("html.endsWith(\"\\n\"): "
                + html.endsWith("\n"));
        System.out.println("html3.endsWith(\"\\n\"): "
```

```
                + html3.endsWith("\n"));
    }
}
```

```
Original:
 <html>
     <body>
         <h1>Hello, HTML</h1>
     </body>
 </html>

After stringIndent():
<html>
    <body>
        <h1>Hello, HTML</h1>
    </body>
</html>

After indent():
 <html>
     <body>
         <h1>Hello, HTML</h1>
     </body>
 </html>

html.length(): 71
html3.length(): 72
html.equals(html3): false
html.endsWith("\n"): false
html3.endsWith("\n"): true
```

The string in the html variable contains multiple lines, and there is one incidental whitespace in the string. The output shows that the effects of stripIndent() and indent() are not opposite. The html variable contains 71 characters, whereas html3 contains 72. Notice that there is no line terminator (\n) added to the last line after </html> in the string stored in the html variable. The indent() method removes the line terminators (CR, CRLF, and LF) from each line and adds an LF to the end of each line as a line terminator. If a line in the string does not have a line terminator, an LF is appended to that line by the `indent()` method. In our case, the last line `"</html>"` in the `html2` variable became `"  </html>\n"` in `html3`, which explains why you got one character more in `html3` than in `html`.

You can receive a string that may contain escape sequences as characters, and you want to translate those characters as escape sequences. The `translateEscapes()` instance method translates the escape sequences such as \n, \r, \t, and so on and octal escapes. It does not translate Unicode escapes because they are translated by the compiler when the compiler reads the source code.

Consider the following snippet of code in which I have embedded escape sequences by escaping the backslashes, so they are interpreted as a sequence of characters, not as escape sequences. \012 is an octal escape for ASCII decimal 10 (\n) and \t is an escape sequence for a tab. The output shows the string before and after translation.

```
String html = "<html>\\012" +
              "\\t<body>\n" +
              "\\t\\t<h1>Hello, HTML</h1>\n" +
              "\\t</body>\n" +
              "</html>" ;
System.out.println("Original:\n" + html);

// Translate escape sequences in the string
String html2 = html.translateEscapes();
System.out.println("\nAfter html.translateEscapes():\n" + html2);
```

```
Original:
<html>\012\t<body>
\t\t<h1>Hello, HTML</h1>
\t</body>
</html>

After html.translateEscapes():
<html>
    <body>
        <h1>Hello, HTML</h1>
    </body>
</html>
```

Detecting Inconsistent Whitespaces

It is possible to inadvertently mix whitespaces such as spaces and tabs while indenting lines in a text block. This can result in undesirable indentation when the text block removes the incidental whitespaces. Sometimes, you may want to keep the trailing whitespaces in a line inside a text block, but the text block will automatically remove them. Consider the following text block in which the developer wants to indent each planet on a line with four spaces:

```
String planets = """
                Mercury
                    Venus
                        Earth
            """;
```

The string represented by this text block should look like

```
Mercury
    Venus
        Earth
```

When this text block is printed, it looks as follows:

```
Mercury
                Venus
                Earth
```

The problem lies in the inconsistent use of leading whitespaces in three lines. I mixed spaces and tabs to align the planet names, so they look four spaces to the right from the planet name on the previous line. A tab may be displayed differently in different editors. Sometimes, a tab is equal to four spaces and sometimes it is eight spaces.

When a text block removes incidental whitespaces, it counts each whitespace as one irrespective of the character used for the whitespace. For example, two tabs and eight spaces are counted as two whitespaces and eight whitespaces even though they may align the contents on two lines vertically at the same position.

You may have to spend some time to figure out the indentation issue in a text block that mixes up whitespaces for indentation. JDK13 provides a `lint` named `text-blocks`, which you can use to get warnings in such a case. You will need to use `-Xlint:text-blocks` option when you compile the source code. The lint issues two kinds of warnings:

- Warnings for inconsistent use of leading whitespaces to indent lines, which may result in undesirable indentation.

- Warnings for trailing whitespaces, so you know that the trailing whitespaces will be removed. If you need to keep the trailing whitespaces, use escape sequences instead.

Listing 6-5 contains a text block with mixed leading whitespaces and trailing whitespaces. The program does not print an expected output. Your output may be a little different than the one shown here depending on the tab settings for your editor.

Listing 6-5. Using text-blocks lint to Identify Inconsistent Whitespaces in Text Blocks

```java
// TextBlocksLinting.java
package com.jdojo.textblock;

public class TextBlocksLinting {
    public static void main(String[] args) {
        String planets = """
                         Mercury
                            Venus
                              Earth
                """;

        System.out.println("Planets:\n" + planets);
    }
}
```

```
Planets:
Mercury
                Venus
                Earth
```

Compiling the TextBlocksLinting.java file prints the warnings for inconsistent use of whitespaces and trailing whitespaces in the text block:

```
C:\Java13Revealed>javac --enable-preview --release 13 -Xlint:preview
-Xlint:text-blocks -d build\modules\jdojo.textblock src\jdojo.textblock\
classes\com\jdojo\textblock\TextBlocksLinting.java
```

```
C:\Java13Revealed\src\jdojo.textblock\classes\com\jdojo\textblock\
TextBlocksLinting.java:6: warning: [preview] text blocks are a preview
feature and may be removed in a future release.
        String planets = """
C:\Java13Revealed\src\jdojo.textblock\classes\com\jdojo\textblock\
TextBlocksLinting.java:6: warning: [text-blocks] inconsistent white space
indentation
        String planets = """
C:\Java13Revealed\src\jdojo.textblock\classes\com\jdojo\textblock\
TextBlocksLinting.java:6: warning: [text-blocks] trailing white space will
be removed
        String planets = """
warning: [preview] classfile for C:\Java13Revealed\build\modules\jdojo.
textblock\module-info.class uses preview features of Java SE 13.
4 warnings
```

To avoid mixing spaces and tabs for indentation in NetBeans IDE, you can set a preference to expand tabs to X spaces, where X is a number, say, 4. You can access this option in the Apache NetBeans by selecting Tools➤ Options➤ Editor➤ Formatting➤ Expand Tabs to Spaces.

Summary

Java has supported String literals since version 1.0. String literal has a big limitation that it must be represented in one line. Developers often need to represent multiple lines of text in String literals, which forces them to use string concatenation. Using multiple lines of text as String literals has been the pain point for Java developers for about 24 years. The Java language designer knew this problem and finally they are paying attention. They proposed – later withdrew – support for raw strings in Java 12. In Java 13, they included support for text blocks as a language preview feature.

A text block is a sequence of zero or more characters enclosed by an opening delimiter and a closing delimiter. The content of a text block can span multiple lines, and you do not need to use most escape sequences. The opening delimiter starts with a sequence of three double quote characters ("""), optionally followed with zero or more space, tab, or form feed characters, and ends with a line terminator. The closing delimiter consists of a sequence of three double quote characters (""").

A text block is an instance of the String class. You can use a text block anywhere you can use a String literal.

The content of a text block is transformed by the compiler, finally resulting in a String literal. The runtime never sees (or does not know about) text blocks. Runtime only sees String literals that result after transforming text blocks.

Compiler performs the transformation of a text block in three stages. In the first stage, it normalizes line terminators. It replaces all line terminators (CR, CRLF, and LF) with an LF.

In the second stage, the compiler removes the common leading whitespaces from all non-blank lines. A blank line is a line with only LF or whitespaces followed with an LF. Placement of the closing delimiter in a text block plays an important role in computing the number of leading whitespaces to be removed. If you do not want to remove any leading whitespaces, place the closing delimiter in the beginning on a separate line. Escape sequences are not interpreted in this stage. Trailing whitespaces from all lines are removed in this stage.

In the third and the final stage of transformation, the compiler interprets escape sequences.

The String class has received three new instance method to support text blocks: formatted(), stripIndent(), and translateEscapes(). These methods are deprecated because they exist to support text blocks which are a preview feature. The formatted() method is used to format text block using format specifiers. The stripIndent() method removes incidental whitespaces from a text block. The translateEscapes() method interprets escape sequences in the text block.

It is possible to inadvertently mix different types of whitespaces such as spaces and tabs to indent lines in a text block in the source code, which may lead to an undesirable indentation. Sometimes, you may want to preserve trailing whitespaces in lines, which are automatically removed by the compiler. Use the -Xlint:text-blocks option for the compiler to detect such inconsistent use of whitespaces. The compiler will print warnings when it detects inconsistent leading whitespaces or trailing whitespaces in text blocks.

CHAPTER 7

Class Data Sharing

In this chapter, you will learn

- What class data sharing (CDS) is

- What application class data sharing (AppCDS) is

- How to use CDS and AppCDS in your applications

- What the default CDS archive is in JDK12 and how Java applications use it automatically

- What the dynamic CDS archives are in JDK13

- How to generate and use dynamic CDS archives for your applications

When a JVM starts, it typically loads thousands of classes from Java core library. Loading so many classes at startup takes time. If you start multiple JVMs, each JVM performs the same task – loads the same copy of thousands of system classes at the startup. This has two drawbacks:

- JVMs start slower.

- Each JVM loads a copy of the same system classes into memory, thus increasing the runtime footprint.

Class data sharing (CDS) – introduced in JDK5 – is a HotSpot JVM feature that allows pre-processing of system classes and sharing them across JVMs, thus reducing the startup time and runtime footprint. CDS allowed sharing of Java core classes loaded by the bootstrap class loader.

Application class data sharing (AppCDS) – introduced in JDK10 – extends the CDS feature to allow sharing application classes on the class path across JVMs. From JDK10, all types of class loaders (bootstrap, platform, application, and custom) can load classes using AppCDS. JDK13 has introduced dynamic CDS archives that makes using AppCDS a lot simpler.

213

© Kishori Sharan 2019
K. Sharan, *Java 13 Revealed*, https://doi.org/10.1007/978-1-4842-5407-3_7

I will explain CDS and AppCDS in detail in the subsequent sections.

Tip   AppCDS was available in Oracle JDK 8 and 9, which needed commercial licenses. In JDK 10, AppCDS is available in the OpenJDK.

Class Data Sharing

Class data sharing (CDS) was introduced in JDK5. The JRE installer loads the commonly used core Java classes into memory and dumps the loaded classes into a file called *shared archive*. A shared archive contains classes in a pre-processed format to be memory mapped later. The shared archive is a `classes.jsa` file in your JAVA_HOME directory. On UNIX-like platforms, the shared archive is stored in `JAVA_HOME/lib/[arch]/server/classes.jsa`. On Windows platform, the shared archive is stored in `JAVA_HOME\bin\server\classes.jsa`. If you do not find the shared archive on your machine, you can generate it at any time. You sometimes regenerate it after making changes to system classes. I will show you how to generate the shared archive shortly.

When a JVM is launched, it looks for shared archive and memory maps the shared archive. When the JVM needs to load a class, it attempts to load the class from the shared archive in memory first instead from the disk, thus reducing the class loading time. If another JVM is launched, the JVM first checks if the shared archive data is already loaded in memory by another JVM and reuses the same classes from the shared archive in memory, thus reducing the startup time further for the second JVM onward and also significantly reducing the footprint by sharing the same class data in same shared archive in memory.

CDS is supported with the G1, serial, parallel, and parallelOldGC garbage collectors. The shared Java heap object feature (part of CDS) supports only the G1 garbage collector on 64-bit non-Windows platforms.

Creating a Shared Archive

You can create a shared archive using the `java` command with a `-XShare:dump` option as follows:

```
C:\Java13Revealed>java -Xshare:dump
```

The command creates a shared archive (a `classes.jsa` file) in a sub-directory in the JAVA_HOME directory as described in the previous section. The command prints informational messages as it creates the shared archive.

Tip   If you are using JDK12 or later, a default CDS archive is available to you as part of the JDK and you do not need to run this command. Running this command will regenerate the default CDS archive.

Using a Shared Archive

In this section, I will show you how to use a shared archive when you run a Java application. All example programs in this chapter are in the `jdojo.cds` module, which is defined in Listing 7-1.

Listing 7-1. A Module Named jdojo.cds

```
// module-info.java
module jdojo.cds {
    exports com.jdojo.cds;
}
```

Let us create a simple Java class that you will run to test CDS features. Listing 7-2 contains the code for a simple class named HelloCDS. It prints a message to the standard output.

Listing 7-2. A HelloCDS Class

```
// HelloCDS.java
package com.jdojo.cds;

public class HelloCDS {
    public static void main(String[] args) {
        System.out.println("Hello, CDS and AppCDS");
    }
}
```

The source code contains these classes compiled in JDK13 with the --enable-preview option because the source code uses preview features such as `switch` expressions and text blocks. If you want to experiment with other JDKs, you will need to compile and package the code for this chapter yourself. The compiled module code is saved in the `build\modules\jdojo.cds` directory. The module JAR is saved in `dist\jdojo.cds.jar` file. I assume that you are running these commands from the directory where you have downloaded the source code and the `JAVA_HOME\bin` directory is added to the PATH environment variable.

Use the following command to compile the source code:

```
C:\Java13revealed>javac -d build\modules\jdojo.cds src\jdojo.cds\classes\
module-info.java src\jdojo.cds\classes\com\jdojo\cds\HelloCDS.java
```

Use the following command to package the source code into `jdojo.cds.jar` file. Notice the last character in the command, which is a dot (`.`).

```
C:\Java13revealed>jar --verbose --create --file dist\jdojo.cds.jar -C
build\modules\jdojo.cds .
```

Use one of the three options to use the shared archive when you run your application:

- `-Xshare:on`
- `-Xshare:off`
- `-Xshare:auto`

The `-Xshare:on` option requires using shared class data. If it is not possible to use the shared class data, this option fails the launch of the application. This option exists for testing purpose only. It may sometimes fail if the shared archive cannot be shared. The failure may occur if the memory mapping is not possible because the required address space is not available or the class path does not map. Do not use this option in production.

The `-Xshare:off` option does not attempt to use the shared archive.

The `-Xshare:auto` option uses the shared archive, if possible. This option does not fail if it cannot use the shared archive. Prefer using the `-Xshare:auto` option.

> **Tip**   Starting from JDK11, the `-Xshare:auto` option is enabled by default for the server VM.

The following command attempts to run the `HelloCDS` class using JDK10 – once with `-Xshare:off` and once with `-Xshare:on`:

```
C:\Java13Revealed>java -Xshare:off --module-path dist\jdojo.cds.jar
--module jdojo.cds/com.jdojo.cds.HelloCDS
```

```
Hello, CDS and AppCDS
```

```
C:\Java13Revealed>java -Xshare:on --module-path dist\jdojo.cds.jar --module
jdojo.cds/com.jdojo.cds.HelloCDS
```

```
An error has occurred while processing the shared archive file.
Specified shared archive not found.
Error occurred during initialization of VM
Unable to use shared archive.
```

When you used `-Xshare:on`, you received an error indicating that it could not find the shared archive. In OpenJDK10 and OpenJDK11, you will need to generate the shared archive using the `-Xshare:dump` option. From OpenJDK12, a shared archive is generated when the JDK image is built. If you had already generated the shared archive in the previous section, this command would have run successfully. Here is how you can generate the shared archive and rerun the previous command using JDK10:

```
C:\Java13Revealed>java -Xshare:dump
```

```
...
```

```
C:\Java13Revealed>java -Xshare:on --module-path dist\jdojo.cds.jar --module
jdojo.cds/com.jdojo.cds.HelloCDS
```

```
Hello, CDS and AppCDS
```

You did not see any difference in the output when the shared archive was disabled and enabled. However, the second time – when the shared archive was enabled – the JVM started faster. How do you prove this?

On UNIX-like OS, the `time` command measures the time to run a process. On Windows, you need to use the `Measure-Command` PowerShell command. All commands use JDK10. The following are results on Linux:

```
[/home/ksharan/Java13Revealed] $ time java -Xshare:off --module-path dist/
jdojo.cds.jar --module jdojo.cds/com.jdojo.cds.HelloCDS
```

```
Hello, CDS and AppCDS

real 0m0.215s
user 0m0.124s
sys 0m0.034s
```

```
[/home/ksharan/Java13Revealed] $ time java -Xshare:on --module-path dist/
jdojo.cds.jar --module jdojo.cds/com.jdojo.cds.HelloCDS
```

```
Hello, CDS and AppCDS

real 0m0.108s
user 0m0.098s
sys 0m0.023s
```

Here are the results on Windows using PowerShell, not Windows Command Prompt:

```
PS C:\Java13revealed> Measure-Command {java -Xshare:off --module-path dist\
jdojo.cds.jar --module jdojo.cds/com.jdojo.cd
s.HelloCDS | Write-Host}
```

```
Hello, CDS and AppCDS
...
TotalMilliseconds : 281.1476
```

```
PS C:\Java13revealed> Measure-Command {java -Xshare:on --module-path dist\
jdojo.cds.jar --module jdojo.cds/com.jdojo.cds
```

```
.HelloCDS | Write-Host }
```

```
Hello, CDS and AppCDS
...
TotalMilliseconds : 180.3489
```

Notice the time taken to run the program the second time, which was less compared to the first time. On Linux, the application ran approx. 49% faster, and, on Windows, it ran approx. 36% faster. You may get slightly different results.

Knowing the Loaded Class Location

When CDS is enabled, core system classes are loaded from the shared archive. You can print the location of the loaded class using the -Xlog:class+load=info option. The following commands use this option with JDK10 – once when CDS is enabled and once when CDS is disabled:

```
C:\Java13Revealed>java -Xshare:off -Xlog:class+load=info --module-path
dist\jdojo.cds.jar --module jdojo.cds/com.jdojo.cds.HelloCDS
```

```
[0.011s][info][class,load] opened: C:\java10\lib\modules
[0.021s][info][class,load] java.lang.Object source: jrt:/java.base
[0.022s][info][class,load] java.io.Serializable source: jrt:/java.base
[0.022s][info][class,load] java.lang.String source: jrt:/java.base
...
[0.202s][info][class,load] com.jdojo.cds.HelloCDS source: file:/C:/
Java13Revealed/dist/jdojo.cds.jar
...
Hello, CDS and AppCDS
...
```

```
C:\Java13Revealed>java -Xshare:on -Xlog:class+load=info --module-path dist\
jdojo.cds.jar --module jdojo.cds/com.jdojo.cds.HelloCDS
```

```
[0.012s][info][class,load] opened: C:\java10\lib\modules
[0.024s][info][class,load] java.lang.Object source: shared objects file
[0.024s][info][class,load] java.io.Serializable source: shared objects file
[0.024s][info][class,load] java.lang.String source: shared objects file
...
[0.150s][info][class,load] com.jdojo.cds.HelloCDS source: file:/C:/
Java13Revealed/dist/jdojo.cds.jar
...
Hello, CDS and AppCDS
...
```

When CDS is disabled, the sources for system classes such as `Object` and `String` classes are listed as `jrt:/java.base`. This means that these classes are loaded from the disk from `C:\java10\lib\modules` file, which is the JRE runtime image. When CDS is enabled, the sources for the same classes are listed as "shared objects file", which means they are loaded from the shared archive. Note that the application class `HelloCDS` was loaded from the disk in both cases because CDS allows for sharing only system class data. To share application classes, you need to use AppCDS, which is explained in the next section.

Application Class Data Sharing (AppCDS)

Until JDK10, sharing of class data was possible only for core Java classes, which were loaded by the bootstrap class loader. JDK10 extends the CDS feature to share application classes. In JDK10, platform class loader, application class loader, and custom class loaders can also load classes from the shared archive.

In JDK10, you need to use the `-XX:+UseAppCDS` option with the `java` command to use AppCDS. In JDK11 and later, this option is obsolete.

To share application class data, you need to create your own shared archive that will include the application classes as well as core Java classes. When you run your application, you will need to specify your shared archive file path using the `-XX:SharedArchiveFile` option. Your shared archive will contain all classes in the `jdojo.cds.jar` file, which is supplied in the `dist` directory for this source code of this book. The supplied source is compiled using JDK13. If you are using earlier JDK, you will need to recompile and re-create the `jdojo.cds.jar` file.

> **Tip**   Java 10 supports AppCDS only for classes loaded from the class path, not from the module path. The support for module path is available in JDK11 and later.

Using AppCDS involves three steps:

- Creating a class list for the classes to be included in the shared archive
- Generating the shared archive
- Using the shared archive when running the application

The following sections walk you through the steps of using AppCDS. I will show the same steps using JDK10 and JDK11. You can pick any one JDK you want and follow the instructions for that JDK.

Creating a Class List

First, you need to create the list of classes you want to include in your shared archive for AppCDS. You can use the `-XX:DumpLoadedClassList` option to dump the list of loaded system classes into the JVM to a file. The `-XX:DumpLoadedClassList` option includes only the classes loaded by the bootstrap class loader. Make sure to use the `-XX:+UseAppCDS` option to include the classes loaded by the application and platform class loaders. You need to run the `java` command with the `-Xshare:off` option to generate the list of classes.

The following command creates a `jdojoclasses.lst` file, which contains the list of all classes loaded into the JVM. It is a text file. You can open and edit it in a text editor of your choice. Here is the command to use with JDK10:

```
C:\Java13Revealed>java -Xshare:off -XX:+UseAppCDS -XX:DumpLoadedClassList=
jdojoclasses.lst --class-path dist\jdojo.cds.jar com.jdojo.cds.HelloCDS
```

```
Hello, CDS and AppCDS
```

In JDK11 and later, you do not need to include the `-XX:+UseAppCDS` option with the `java` command. You can also use module path to generate the list of classes using the following command:

```
C:\Java13Revealed>java -Xshare:off -XX:DumpLoadedClassList=jdojoclasses.lst
--module-path dist\jdojo.cds.jar --module jdojo.cds/com.jdojo.cds.HelloCDS
```

Hello, CDS and AppCDS

Open the `jdojoclasses.lst` file to look at the classes. You can find a line with the following entry: `com/jdojo/cds/HelloCDS`. This entry indicates that the `HelloCDS` class will be part of the shared archive when you use the `jdojoclasses.lst` file to create a shared archive. You will use this file in the next section.

Generating a Shared Archive for AppCDS

Let us use the `-Xshare:dump` and `-XX:SharedArchiveFile` options with the `java` command to create a shared archive with the list of classes in the `jdojoclasses.lst` file. This step creates a shared archive, which will be a `jdojo.jsa` file on your machine. The command prints informaitonal messages to the standard output, which is not shown. Here is the command to generate the shared archive for AppCDS in JDK10:

```
C:\Java13Revealed>java -Xshare:dump -XX:+UseAppCDS -XX:SharedClassList
File=jdojoclasses.lst -XX:SharedArchiveFile=jdojo.jsa --class-path dist\
jdojo.cds.jar
```

Here is the command to generate the shared archive for AppCDS in JDK11 and later:

```
C:\Java13Revealed>java -Xshare:dump -XX:SharedClassListFile=jdojoclasses.
lst -XX:SharedArchiveFile=jdojo.jsa --module-path dist\jdojo.cds.jar
--module jdojo.cds/com.jdojo.cds.HelloCDS
```

You will use the shared archive – the `jdojo.jsa` file – to run the `HelloCDS` class in the next section.

Running Application Using AppCDS

It is time to see your shared archive with AppCDS in action. Now when you run the HelloCDS class, you will specify the jdojo.jsa shared archive to use. Here is the command to use with JDK10:

```
C:\Java13Revealed>java -Xshare:on -XX:+UseAppCDS -XX:SharedArchiveFile=
jdojo.jsa --class-path dist\jdojo.cds.jar com.jdojo.cds.HelloCDS
```

```
Hello, CDS and AppCDS
```

Here is the command to use with JDK11 and later:

```
C:\Java13Revealed>java -Xshare:on -XX:SharedArchiveFile=jdojo.jsa --module-
path dist\jdojo.cds.jar --module jdojo.cds/com.jdojo.cds.HelloCDS
```

```
Hello, CDS and AppCDS
```

Since JDK 11, -Xshare:auto is the default, so removing the -Xshare:on from the previous command will also work. Recall that -Xshare:auto works the same as -Xshare:on, except that if the CDS cannot be used, the former disables CDS and continues, whereas the latter fails to launch the application.

Note the use of the following three options in the previous commands. The -Xshare:on option enables CDS. The -XX:+UseAppCDS option enables AppCDS indicating that you want to use AppCDS, which is not needed in JDK11 or later. The -XX:SharedArchiveFile=jdojo.jsa option specifies the shared archive to use. There is nothing extraordinary in the output. The startup time was less, and multiple JVMs will also share application classes at runtime.

Use the -Xlog:class+load=info option to verify that your application class, HelloCDS, was loaded from shared archive. Here is the command to use with JDK10:

```
C:\Java13Revealed>java -Xshare:on -XX:+UseAppCDS
-XX:SharedArchiveFile=jdojo.jsa -Xlog:class+load=info --class-path dist\
jdojo.cds.jar com.jdojo.cds.HelloCDS
```

```
[0.011s][info][class,load] opened: C:\java10\lib\modules
[0.037s][info][class,load] java.lang.Object source: shared objects file
[0.038s][info][class,load] java.io.Serializable source: shared objects file
[0.038s][info][class,load] java.lang.String source: shared objects file
...
[0.103s][info][class,load] com.jdojo.cds.HelloCDS source: shared objects
file
...
Hello, CDS and AppCDS
...
```

Here is the command to use with JDK11 and later:

```
C:\Java13Revealed>java -Xshare:on -XX:SharedArchiveFile=jdojo.jsa --module-
path dist\jdojo.cds.jar -Xlog:class+load=info --module jdojo.cds/com.jdojo.
cds.HelloCDS
```

```
[0.012s][info][class,load] opened: C:\java11\lib\modules
[0.042s][info][class,load] java.lang.Object source: shared objects file
[0.042s][info][class,load] java.io.Serializable source: shared objects file
[0.042s][info][class,load] java.lang.String source: shared objects file
...
[0.141s][info][class,load] com.jdojo.cds.HelloCDS source: shared objects
file
...
Hello, CDS and AppCDS
...
```

Notice that, in the output, the source for the com.jdojo.cds.HelloCDS class is "shared objects file", which indicates that the HelloCDS class was loaded from the shared archive.

Class Path and Module Path Rules

Let us rerun the HelloCDS class with AppCDS enabled and using two different class paths with JDK10:

```
C:\Java13Revealed>java -Xshare:on -XX:+UseAppCDS
-XX:SharedArchiveFile=jdojo.jsa --class-path build\modules;dist\jdojo.cds.
jar com.jdojo.cds.HelloCDS
```

```
An error has occurred while processing the shared archive file.
shared class paths mismatch (hint: enable -Xlog:class+path=info to diagnose
the failure)
Error occurred during initialization of VM
Unable to use shared archive.
```

```
C:\Java13Revealed>java -Xshare:on -XX:+UseAppCDS
-XX:SharedArchiveFile=jdojo.jsa --class-path dist\jdojo.cds.jar;build\
modules com.jdojo.cds.HelloCDS
```

```
Hello, CDS and AppCDS
```

Recall that you had created the jdojo.jsa shared archive by specifying the class path as dist\jdojo.cds.jar. When you specified a class path as build\modules;dist\jdojo.cds.jar, you received an error stating that there was a mismatch in the shared class path.

A shared archive makes a note of the class path used at the time it was created. When you enable the shared archive to run the application, one of the following must be true; otherwise, you get an error:

- The class path used to launch the JVM is the same as the class path used to create the shared archive.

- The class path used to launch the JVM contains the class path used to create the shared archive as a prefix.

In this example, the shared archive was created with the class path dist\jdojo.cds.jar. When you use dist\jdojo.cds.jar as the only part or as the first part in the class path, your application runs fine. In the previous example, when you got an error, you had specified dist\jdojo.cds.jar as the last part in the class path. To see the details of what JVM was looking for when you got the error, run the command with a -Xlog:class+path=info option as follows:

```
C:\Java13Revealed>java -Xshare:on -XX:+UseAppCDS
-XX:SharedArchiveFile=jdojo.jsa -Xlog:class+path=info --class-path build\
modules;dist\jdojo.cds.jar com.jdojo.cds.HelloCDS
```

```
[0.010s][info][class,path] bootstrap loader class path=D:\jdk-10\lib\modules
[0.012s][info][class,path] opened: C:\java10\lib\modules
[0.022s][info][class,path] type=BOOT
[0.023s][info][class,path] Expecting BOOT path=C:\java10\lib\modules
[0.024s][info][class,path] ok
[0.025s][info][class,path] type=APP
[0.026s][info][class,path] Expecting -Djava.class.path=dist\jdojo.cds.jar
[0.027s][info][class,path]
[0.027s][info][class,path] [APP classpath mismatch, actual: -Djava.class.
path=build\modules;dist\jdojo.cds.jar
An error has occurred while processing the shared archive file.
shared class paths mismatch (hint: enable -Xlog:class+path=info to diagnose
the failure)
Error occurred during initialization of VM
Unable to use shared archive.
```

JDK11 added support for the following for AppCDS shared archives:

- Any valid combinations of class path and module path are supported.

- A non-empty directory in the module path causes a fatal error. In other words, you can include only modular JARs in the module path.

- Unlike the class path, there is no restriction that the module path at dump time must be equal to or be a prefix of the module path at runtime.

- The archive is invalidated if an existing JAR in the module path is updated after archive generation.

- Removing a JAR from the module path does not invalidate the shared archive. Archived classes from the removed JAR are not used at runtime.

Default CDS Archives

JDK12 added support for default CDS archive for native builds on 64-bit platforms. The JDK image contains a default CDS archive. It is named `classes.jsa`. It is saved in the `JAVA_HOME/lib/server` directory on UNIX-like OS and in the `JAVA_HOME/bin/server` directory on Windows. The `JAVA_HOME/lib/classlist` file contains the list of system classes in the default CDS archive. You can open the `classlist` file in a text editor to see what classes are included in the default shared archive.

To take advantage of the default CDS in JDK12 and later, you do not need to do any additional work. That is, you do not need to run `-Xshare:dump` and run your application with `-Xshare:auto` or `-Xshare:on`. The job of `-Xshare:dump` is performed when the JDK image is built. The CDS archive is used automatically when you run the application because `-Xshare:auto` is the default for the server VM in JDK 11 and later.

Let us run the `HelloCDS` class with JDK12 using the `-Xlog:class+load=info` option, so the output can show from where each class is loaded:

```
C:\Java13Revealed>java --module-path dist\jdojo.cds.jar
-Xlog:class+load=info --module jdojo.cds/com.jdojo.cds.HelloCDS
```

```
[0.012s][info][class,load] opened: C:\java12\lib\modules
[0.023s][info][class,load] java.lang.Object source: shared objects file
[0.023s][info][class,load] java.io.Serializable source: shared objects file
[0.023s][info][class,load] java.lang.String source: shared objects file
...
[0.131s][info][class,load] com.jdojo.cds.HelloCDS source: file:/C:/
Java13Revealed/dist/jdojo.cds.jar
...
Hello, CDS and AppCDS
...
```

The output shows that default CDS archive is used without you specifying any additional options. System classes are loaded from "shared objects file", which is the default CDS archive. Notice the location of the `HelloCDS` class, which is loaded from the `jdojo.cds.jar` file, not from the shared archive. This is so because the default CDS is only for system classes, not for application classes. If you want to load application classes from a shared archive, you need to use AppCDS as described in the previous section. JDK13 introduced a new way of using AppCDS using dynamic CDS archives, which I will explain in the next section.

Dynamic CDS Archives

Using CDS and AppCDS improves the application's startup time significantly. It also greatly reduces runtime footprint. The default CDS archive introduced in JDK12 is made using the CDS archive transparent. However, you still needed to perform a three-step process to use AppCDS in JDK12:

- Create a class list.

- Dump a shared archive.

- Run the application with the shared archive.

The final goal is to make the use of AppCDS transparent in which you do not need to take any action to take advantage of shared archives. However, as of JDK13, we are not there yet. JDK13 has significantly simplified the way you generate a shared archive to use AppCDS making it a simple two-step process:

- Run your application with the `-XX:ArchiveClassesAtExit=<file-name>`, where `<file-name>` is the name of the shared archive file. A shared archive will be generated when the application exits. If the application exits abruptly, no shared archive will be generated.

- Run your application with the `-XX:SharedArchiveFile=<file-name>` option to use the shared archive for AppCDS.

Let us create a shared archive for our `HelloCDS` application using the following command with JDK13. Refer to the following text for troubleshooting if you get an error running this command:

```
C:\Java13Revealed>java -XX:ArchiveClassesAtExit=jdojo.jsa --module-path
dist\jdojo.cds.jar --module jdojo.cds/com.jdojo.cds.HelloCDS
```

```
Hello, CDS and AppCDS
[0.137s][warning][cds] Skipping java/util/stream/FindOps$FindSink$OfRef$$
Lambda$6: Unsafe anonymous class
...
```

In the source code, I have compiled all classes with the --enable-preview option. If you have not re-created the dist\jdojo.cds.jar file by recompiling the source code without the --enable-preview option, you will get the following error message:

```
Error: Unable to load main class com.jdojo.cds.HelloCDS in module jdojo.
cds
        java.lang.UnsupportedClassVersionError: Preview features are not
        enabled for com/jdojo/cds/HelloCDS (class file version 57.65535).
        Try running with '--enable-preview'
...
```

To fix this error, you need to run the HelloCDS class with the --enable-preview option, like so:

```
C:\Java13Revealed>java --enable-preview -XX:ArchiveClassesAtExit=jdojo.jsa
--module-path dist\jdojo.cds.jar --module jdojo.cds/com.jdojo.cds.HelloCDS
```

The dynamic CDS archive (top-layer archive) created by this command is created on top of the default CDS archive (base-layer archive), which is packaged with the JDK. The top-layer archive depends on the base-layer archive. If the top-layer archive cannot be used, it is disabled and only the base-layer archive is used. If the base-layer archive cannot be used, the top-layer archive is disabled.

The top-layer archive (or dynamic CDS archive) contains all loaded application classes and library classes that are not present in the default CDS archive (base-layer archive).

Tip   Classes that exist in a JAR file on the class path or module path but are not loaded during execution are not dynamically archived. Java heap objects created during an application execution are also not dynamically archived.

Let us run the HelloCDS class with the dynamic archive. I use the -Xlog:class+load=info option, so you can see in the output that the HelloCDS class is loaded from the dynamic archive. Use the --enable-preview option with the following command if you are using the dist\jdojo.cds.jar file supplied with the source code for this book:

```
C:\Java13Revealed>java -XX:SharedArchiveFile=jdojo.jsa --module-path dist\
jdojo.cds.jar -Xlog:class+load=info --module jdojo.cds/com.jdojo.cds.HelloCDS
```

```
[0.011s][info][class,load] opened: C:\java13\lib\modules
[0.023s][info][class,load] java.lang.Object source: shared objects file
[0.023s][info][class,load] java.io.Serializable source: shared objects file
[0.023s][info][class,load] java.lang.String source: shared objects file
...
[0.145s][info][class,load] com.jdojo.cds.HelloCDS source: shared objects
file (top)
...
Hello, CDS and AppCDS
...
```

Notice the use of "(top)" in the location "shared objects file (top)" for the HelloCDS class in the output. It indicates that the HelloCDS class is loaded from the top-layer shared archive, which is the dynamic CDS archive. System classes do not contain the word "top" in their location, meaning that they were loaded from the base layer, the default CDS archive.

Stay tuned for more improvements to the dynamic CDS archives in the future JDK releases.

Summary

Class data sharing (CDS), introduced in JDK5, is a JVM featured that allows sharing of classes across JVMs, thus reducing the startup time and runtime footprints. CDS allows sharing of Java core classes loaded by the bootstrap class loader.

Application class data sharing (AppCDS) in JDK10 extends the CDS feature to allow sharing application classes on the class path across JVMs. From JDK10, all types of class loaders (bootstrap, platform, application, and custom) can load classes from AppCDS. AppCDS was available in Oracle JDK 8 and 9, which needed commercial licenses. In JDK 10, AppCDS is available in the OpenJDK. In JDK10, you could create a shared archive for AppCDS only for classes on the class path. JDK11 and later allows including classes from module path as well as class path.

When you use shared archive for AppCDS, the class path used to create the shared archive must be the same or a prefix of the class path that is used to launch the application with AppCDS enabled. Otherwise, a class path mismatch error occurs, and the application fails to start.

JDK12 added support for default CDS archive for native builds on 64-bit platforms. The JDK image contains a default CDS archive. It is named `classes.jsa`. It is stored in `JAVA_HOME/lib/server` directory on UNIX-like OS and in the `JAVA_HOME/bin/server` directory on Windows. The `JAVA_HOME/lib/classlist` file contains the list of system classes in the default CDS archive. To take advantage of the default CDS in JDK12 and later, you do not need to take any action.

JDK13 has significantly simplified the way you generate a shared archive to use AppCDS. First run your application with the `-XX:ArchiveClassesAtExit=<file-name>`, where `<file-name>` is the name of the shared archive file. A shared archive be generated when the application exits. If the application exits abruptly, no shared archive will be generated. Second, run your application with the `-XX:SharedArchiveFile=<file-name>` option to use the shared archive with AppCDS.

The dynamic CDS archive (top-layer archive) is created on top of the default CDS archive (base-layer archive), which is packaged with the JDK. The top-layer archive depends on the base-layer archive. If the top-layer archive cannot be used, it is disabled and only the base-layer archive is used. If the base-layer archive cannot be used, the top-layer archive is disabled.

The top-layer archive contains all loaded application classes and library classes that are not present in the default CDS archive. Classes that exist in a JAR file on the class path or module path but are not loaded during execution are not dynamically archived. Java heap objects created during an application execution are also not dynamically archived.

CHAPTER 8

Tools and APIs Changes

In this chapter, you will learn

- About the deprecated and removed tools and APIs

- About the JVM Constants API

- About the new methods added to the `String` class, the `Optional<T>` class, the `Predicate<T>` interface, `Files` class, and `Filesystems` class

- About changes to the Collection, Buffer, FileSystem, and Stream APIs

- How to format numbers in compact form

- The Java platform support for the Unicode standards

This chapter contains the topics that are not big enough to deserve a chapter on their own, but important enough to deserve a mention in this book. All example programs in this chapter are in the `jdojo.misc` module as shown in Listing 8-1.

Listing 8-1. A Module Named jdojo.misc

```
// module-info.java
module jdojo.misc {
    exports com.jdojo.misc;
}
```

Deprecated Tools

In this section, I list and explain the deprecated tools and APIs in JDK 10 through JDK 13. I list only important tools that you need to know about as a developer. For a comprehensive list of all deprecated tools and APIs, refer to the release notes for a specific JDK.

© Kishori Sharan 2019
K. Sharan, *Java 13 Revealed*, https://doi.org/10.1007/978-1-4842-5407-3_8

The Nashorn JavaScript Engine

The Nashorn JavaScript engine, which was added to JDK8, was a complete implementation of the ECMAScript-262 5.1 standard. The maintainers of the engine found it difficult to keep up with the changes in ECMAScript and finally decided to deprecate it for removal. In JDK11, the Nashorn JavaScript script engine and APIs and the jjs tool were deprecated with the intent to remove them in a future release.

The `javax.script` API that allows using scripting languages in Java is not affected by the Nashorn JavaScript engine deprecation. If you are using other scripting engines in Java applications, they will continue to work.

Oracle has announced support for GraalVM, which can be used to migrate your Nashorn applications. You can read more about the Oracle's announcement at `https://blogs.oracle.com/developers/announcing-graalvm`. You can find more on GraalVM on its official web site `www.graalvm.org`.

The rmic Tool

JDK13 has deprecated the `rmic` tool for removal in a future release. It creates static stubs for Remote Method Invocation (RMI). Since Java 5, stubs can be generated dynamically, which is the recommended way to generate stubs. If you are still using static stubs for RMI, migrate your code to use dynamic stubs. You can refer to my book titled *Java APIs, Extensions and Libraries: With JavaFX, JDBC, Jmod, Jlink, Networking, and the Process API* (ISBN-1484235452) for more details on how to use dynamic stubs with RMI.

The Pack200 Tools and API

JDK11 deprecated the `pack200` and `unpack200` tools and the `Pack200` API in `java.util.jar` package. They will be removed in a future JDK release. Pack200 is a compression scheme for JAR file to reduce the disk and bandwidth needs for the JDK downloads and Java applications.

JDK ships with `pack200` and `unpack200` tools, which are used to compress and uncompress JAR files in the JDK up to JDK8. The Pack200 API is used programmatically for the same purpose. The high-speed Internet and other technological improvements such as removal of applets support in browsers made the Pack200 scheme obsolete. JDK9 also introduced new file formats, JMOD and JImage, for packaging the Java modules, which is more efficient than the JAR file format and does not use Pack200.

The Swing Motif Look and Feel

Java 13 has deprecated Swing Motif Look and Feel. It is unsupported on macOS. Refer to `https://bugs.openjdk.java.net/browse/JDK-8177960` for more details.

Removed Tools

In this section, I list the tools that have been removed with their brief description.

The appletviewer Tool

Java 9 had deprecated the Applet API and the `appletviewer` tool. Java 11 removed the `appletviewer` tool, which was used to launch applets locally without using a browser.

The javah Tool

The JDK used to ship a tool named `javah`. The tool was used to generate C/C++ native header files for all native method declarations in your Java code. The tool was deprecated in JDK 9 for future removal. In JDK 10, the tool has been removed.

JDK 8 had added a `-h` option to the Java compiler (`javac`) to generate the C/C++ header files. The `-h` option accepts the directory name where it will place the generated header files. The following command compiles the `HelloJNI.java` file and places any C/C++ header files in the `jni_headers` directory:

```
javac -h jni_headers HelloJNI.java
```

When the `-h` option is used, the compiler scans the source files for native method declarations and generates the C/C++ header files in the specified directory.

The Runtime Class

The following two methods in the `java.lang.Runtime` class were deprecated in Java 9 for removal in a future release and have been removed in Java 13:

- `void traceInstructions(boolean on)`
- `void traceMethodCalls(boolean on)`

The Thread Class

The destroy() and stop(Throwable) methods in the Thread class have been removed in Java 11. The no-args stop() method is unaffected.

The JVM Constants API

JDK12 introduced the JVM Constants API, which is a low-level API to deal with how entries in a constant pool of class files are described by libraries and tools, which manipulates the bytecodes. As a developer, you will not need to use this API in your applications. The API is in the java.lang.constant package in the java.base module. You will often come across two of the following interfaces in this API:

- Constable

- ConstantDesc

A Constable represents a constant that can be represented in the constant pool of a class file. In other words, a type whose instances represent constant values is Constable. A few of the types that implement the Constable interface are String, Integer, Long, Float, Double, Class, MethodType, and MethodHandle.

A Constable can describe itself nominally as a ConstantDesc. In other words, a ConstantDesc is a nominal descriptor of the constant value represented by a Constable. It is called a "nominal descriptor" because it is not the value itself. Rather, it is a "link" or "recipe" to describe the value or to reconstruct the value in a given class loading context. The nominal descriptor can also be used to store the value in a constant pool in a symbolic form (or a nominal form). There are specialized types of ConstantDesc such as ClassDesc to serve as a nominal descriptor for a Class constant.

Tip   The JVM Constants API is a low-level API meant for libraries and tools that manipulate bytecodes. As an application developer, you will not use them directly.

Both interfaces contain a single method. The Constable interface contains the following method:

```
Optional<? extends ConstantDesc> describeConstable()
```

The `describeConstable()` method returns an `Optional`, which is empty if a nominal descriptor cannot be constructed for this `Constable`.

The `ConstantDesc` interface contains the following method:

```
Object resolveConstantDesc(MethodHandles.Lookup lookup) throws
ReflectiveOperationException;
```

The `resolveConstantDesc()` method returns the resolved constant value using the `MethodHandles.Lookup` argument as the resolution and access control context.

The `String`, `Integer`, `Long`, `Float`, and `Double` classes implement both `Constable` and `ConstantDesc` interfaces, and serve as nominal descriptors for themselves. Listing 8-2 contains a trivial example of using these methods on a `String`.

Listing 8-2. Using the JVM Constants API

```java
// ConstableTest.java
package com.jdojo.misc;

import java.lang.invoke.MethodHandles;
import java.util.Optional;

public class ConstableTest {
    public static void main(String[] args) {
        String str1 = "Hello, JVM Constants API";

        // The Optional in desc contains the string itself (str1)
        Optional<String> desc = str1.describeConstable();
        String str2  = desc.get();

        // str3 contains the string itself (str1)
        String str3 = str1.resolveConstantDesc(MethodHandles.lookup());

        System.out.println("str1: " + str1);
        System.out.println("str2: " + str2);
        System.out.println("str3: " + str3);
        System.out.println("str1 == str2: " + (str1 == str2));
        System.out.println("str2 == str3: " + (str2 == str3));
    }
}
```

```
str1: Hello, JVM Constants API
str2: Hello, JVM Constants API
str3: Hello, JVM Constants API
str1 == str2: true
str2 == str3: true
```

The String Class

The String class has received several new methods in Java 11 through Java 13. I have described the new methods in Java 13 and the indent() method in Java 12 in Chapter 6. The describeConstable() and resolveConstantDesc() methods exist because the String class implements the Constable and ConstantDesc interfaces from the JVM Constants API introduced in Java 12. I do not explain these methods in this section. I have listed all new methods in the String class here for completeness.

Methods Added in Java 11

- String strip()

- String stripLeading()

- String stripTrailing()

- boolean isBlank()

- Stream<String> lines()

- String repeat(int count)

Methods Added in Java 12

- String indent(int n)

- <R> R transform(Function<? super String,? extends R> f)

- Optional<String> describeConstable()

- String resolveConstantDesc(MethodHandles.Lookup lookup)

Methods Added in Java 13

- `String stripIndent()`

- `String translateEscapes()`

- `String formatted(Object... args)`

I will explain these methods with examples in the subsequent sections.

Stripping Whitespaces

Java 11 added three methods to the `String` class that remove leading/trailing, leading, and trailing whitespaces: `strip()`, `stripLeading()`, and `stripTrailing()`. The `strip()` method returns the `String` after removing both leading and trailing whitespaces. The other two methods return the `String` after removing only leading or trailing whitespaces. These methods remove whitespaces. Refer to the `isWhitespace(int codepoint)` method of the `Character` class to see the definition of whitespaces in Java.

The `trim()` method of the `String` class returns the `String` after removing the leading and trailing spaces where a space is defined as any character whose codepoint is equal to or less than Unicode value of 32 (a space character). Compare the `strip()` and `trim()` method. The `trim()` method works on ASCII control characters (or ASCII whitespaces), whereas the `strip()` method works on Unicode whitespaces.

Testing for a Blank String

You can test whether a string contains only whitespaces using the `isBlank()` method of the `String` class. It returns `true` if the string contains only whitespaces. Otherwise, it returns `false`.

Obtaining Stream of Lines

You can use the `lines()` method of the `String` class to obtain a stream of lines in a string. A line in a string is defined as a sequence of zero or more characters followed by a line terminator, which can be `"\n"`, `"\r"`, or `"\r\n"`. A line may not end with a line terminator if it is the end of the string. The following snippet of code uses a text block to create a multiline string for a stanza from the Lucy poems by William Wordsworth. It prints character count in each line followed by the text. It uses the `lines()` method of the `String` class to obtain a stream of each line in the text.

```
String text = """
                Upon the moon I fixed my eye,
                All over the wide lea;
                With quickening pace my horse drew nigh
                Those paths so dear to me.
                """;
text.lines()
    .map(s -> s.length() + ": " + s)
    .forEach(System.out::println);
```

```
29: Upon the moon I fixed my eye,
22: All over the wide lea;
39: With quickening pace my horse drew nigh
26: Those paths so dear to me.
```

Repeating a String

The repeat(int count) method of the String class returns a string whose content is concatenation of the string repeated count times. For example, "hello".repeat(2) returns "hellohello". If it is an empty string or count is zero, an empty string is returned. If count is less than zero, an IllegalArgumentException is thrown. The method comes in handy for creating indentations. The following snippet of code prints five lines of asterisks by indenting them with spaces. The first line is composed of four spaces and one asterisk, the second line three spaces and two asterisks, and so on.

```
IntStream.rangeClosed(1, 5)
        .mapToObj(n -> " ".repeat(5-n) + "*".repeat(n))
        .forEach(System.out::println);
```

```
    *
   **
  ***
 ****
*****
```

Transforming Strings

Java 12 added a transform() method to the String class to transform the string into another object by applying a Function<T,R>. The Function<T,R> accepts a String and returns an object of any type. The method is declared as follows:

```
<R> R transform(Function<? super String,? extends R> f)
```

The use of this method is not obvious. It was added as part of the support for *raw strings* in Java 12. The *raw string* feature was later dropped from Java 12, but the transform() method continued.

The following is a trivial example in which the string "Hello" is transformed to "Hello, World" using the transform() method:

```
String str = "Hello";
String greeting = str.transform(s -> s + ", World");
System.out.println(greeting);
```

```
Hello, World
```

The lambda expression accepts a string as an input and returns the input string by appending ", World" to it. You would agree that you did not gain anything by using the transform() method just to concatenate two strings. It is recommended to write the following instead:

```
String str = "Hello";
String greeting = str + ", World";
System.out.println(greeting);
```

```
Hello, World
```

Let us have another trivial example in which you use a method reference Integer::parseInt or Integer::valueOf with the transform() method to convert a string to an int:

```
String str = "1969";
int year = str.transform(Integer::parseInt);
```

```
//int year = str.transform(Integer::valueOf);
System.out.println(year);
```

1969

You may argue that the previous snippet of code could be written as follows without losing readability:

```
String str = "1969";
int year = Integer.parseInt(str);
System.out.println(year);
```

1969

The point of these two examples is that if a method accepts a string and returns another object by applying some logic to the string, you can always call the method directly, rather than using the `transform()` method and pass the method's reference.

How about applying multiply transformations to a string? Typically, string transformation methods are static methods of a class, which cannot be chained. In this situation, your code may be more readable using the `transform()` method. Assume that there are two transformations you want to apply to a multiline string:

- Sanitize blank lines by removing them.

- Prepend a line number to each line.

Suppose that you create a `Transforms` class with two static methods `sanitizeBlanks(String str)` and `addLineNumber(String str)` to perform these transformations. Both methods return a `String`. You can write the following code to perform this task:

```
String str = "your original string goes here";

// Apply two transformations to str
String newStr = str.transform(Transforms::sanitizeBlanks)
                .transform(Transforms::addLineNumber);
```

You could rewrite this snippet of code that calls static methods of the Transforms class instead of using the transform() method of the String class as follows:

```
String str = "your original string goes here";

// Apply two transformations to str
String str1 = Transforms.sanitizeBlanks(str);
String newStr = Transforms.addLineNumber(str1);
```

Compare the two previous snippets of code. The one using the transform() method of the String class is more readable. Listing 8-3 contains a complete program to demonstrate the two transformations in our discussion.

Listing 8-3. Using the transform() Method of the String Class

```
// Transforms.java
package com.jdojo.misc;

import java.util.concurrent.atomic.AtomicInteger;
import java.util.function.Predicate;
import static java.util.stream.Collectors.joining;

public class Transforms {
    /**
     * Returns the string after removing blank lines, and leading
     * and trailing whitespaces from each line. A line with only whitespaces
     * is considered a blank line.
     * @param str The string to be sanitized
     * @return The string after removing blank lines and leading/trailing
     *         whitespaces from each line.
     */
    public static String sanitizeBlanks(String str) {
        return str.lines()
                .filter(Predicate.not(String::isBlank))
                .map(String::strip)
                .collect(joining("\n"));
    }
```

```
/**
 * Adds a line number to each line in the string.
 * @param str The string to which line numbers are added
 * @return Returns a string by prefixing each line in the string with
 *         the line number.
 */
public static String addLineNumber(String str) {
    AtomicInteger lineNumber = new AtomicInteger();
    return str.lines()
            .map(s-> lineNumber.incrementAndGet() + ":" + s)
            .collect(joining("\n"));
}

public static void main(String[] args) {
    String str = """
            Upon the moon I fixed my eye,

              All over the wide lea;
          With quickening pace my horse drew nigh

            Those paths so dear to me.
            """;
    System.out.println("Original string:\n" + str);

    String newStr = str.transform(Transforms::sanitizeBlanks)
                    .transform(Transforms::addLineNumber);
    System.out.println("The string after transformations:\n" + newStr);

    /* Alternative to using the transform() method of the String class
    String str1 = Transforms.sanitizeBlanks(str);
    String str2 = Transforms.addLineNumber(str1);
    System.out.println("\nThe string after transformations:\n" + str2);
    */
}
}
```

```
Original string:
   Upon the moon I fixed my eye,

      All over the wide lea;
With quickening pace my horse drew nigh

    Those paths so dear to me.

The string after transformations:
1:Upon the moon I fixed my eye,
2:All over the wide lea;
3:With quickening pace my horse drew nigh
4:Those paths so dear to me.
```

Notice the blank lines and extra leading spaces in the lines that make up the original string, which are removed when you apply the first transformation. The second transformation prepends line number in the "#:" form to each line. The original string contains six lines, whereas the transformed string contains only four lines. The code contains ample comments to explain the logic.

Optional and Predicate

The following are two new methods that have been added to the `java.util.Optional<T>` class:

- `T orElseThrow()`
- `boolean isEmpty()`

The no-args `orElseThrow()` method was added to the `Optional<T>` class in Java 10. If the `Optional` contains a value, the method returns the value. Otherwise, it throws a `java.util.NoSuchElementException` runtime exception.

Tip   The two methods `orElseThrow()` and `isEmpty()` have also been added to the `OptionalInt`, `OptionalLong`, and `OptionalDouble` classes.

The `Optional` class already had another version of the `orElseThrow()` method, which is declared as follows:

```
<X extends Throwable> T orElseThrow(Supplier<? extends X>
exceptionSupplier) throws X extends Throwable
```

This method accepts a `Supplier<T>`, which supplies the exception to be thrown when a value is not present. The exception thrown could be checked or unchecked. You could also use a custom message when creating the exception. The no-args `orElseThrow()` method throws an unchecked exception with a message `"No value present"`. The following snippet of code shows how to use both existing and new `orElseThrow()` methods:

```
Optional<String> name = Optional.of("Kishori Sharan");

// More code goes here...

// Supply an exception to be thrown when name is empty
String name1 = name.orElseThrow(
        () -> new NoSuchElementException("No value present"));

// Let the runtime throw a NoSuchElementException if name is empty
String name2 = name.orElseThrow();
```

The `Optional<T>` class had a method named `isPresent()` that returned `true` if a value was present and `false` otherwise. Java 11 added a new method `isEmpty()` that is same as calling `!isPresent()`. The new method makes the code more readable if you are using a logic to check for absence of value. Earlier by using `!isPresent()`, you had to check for "not presence", rather than for "absence". It is also useful in lambda expressions to be used as a method reference.

Listing 8-4 contains a complete program to demonstrate the use of these new methods in the `Optional<T>` class.

Listing 8-4. Testing New Methods in the Optional Class

```
// OptionalTest.java
package com.jdojo.misc;

import java.util.List;
import java.util.NoSuchElementException;
```

```java
import java.util.Optional;

public class OptionalTest {
    public static void main(String[] args) {
        Optional<String> name = Optional.of("Kishori Sharan");
        String fn1 = name.orElseThrow(
            () -> new NoSuchElementException("No value present"));
        String fn2 = name.orElseThrow();

        System.out.println("fn1: " + fn1);
        System.out.println("fn2: " + fn2);

        try {
            Optional<String> phone = Optional.empty();
            String f2 = phone.orElseThrow();
        } catch (NoSuchElementException e) {
            System.out.println("Phone: " + e.getMessage());
        }

        // Have a list of Optional<String>
        List<Optional<String>> list = List.of(Optional.empty(),
                Optional.of("Kishori"),
                Optional.empty(),
                Optional.of("Sharan"),
                Optional.empty());

        // Count the empty Optionals in the list
        long emptyCount = list.stream()
                .filter(Optional::isEmpty)
                .count();
        System.out.println("Empty name count: " + emptyCount);
    }
}
```

```
fn1: Kishori Sharan
fn2: Kishori Sharan
Phone: No value present
Empty name count: 3
```

Note the use of the `Optional::isEmpty` method reference when counting the empty names in the list:

```
long emptyCount = list.stream()
                      .filter(Optional::isEmpty)
                      .count();
```

Before Java 11, you had to use the `isPresent()` method and your code would have been written as follows:

```
long emptyCount = list.stream()
                      .filter(n -> !n.isPresent())
                      .count();
```

Java 11 has added a new `not()` static method to the `Predicate<T>` interface, which returns the negation of the specified predicate. Its declaration is

```
static <T> Predicate<T> not(Predicate<? super T> target)
```

Using the `not()` static method in the `Predicate<T>` interface, you can rewrite the previous statement as follows:

```
long emptyCount = list.stream()
                      .filter(Predicate.not(Optional::isPresent))
                      .count();
```

The `not()` static method comes in handy when you want to negate a method reference as you negated the `Optional::isPresent` method reference in the previous statement.

Compact Number Format

Java 12 added a `CompactNumberFormat` class to the `java.text` package in the `java.base` module. It is a subclass of the `NumberFormat` class. It formats a decimal number in its compact form. A compact form of a number is suitable to be used where space is limited to display the number. For example, instead of displaying one billion as 1000000000, you can display it in a compact form like 1B or 1 billion. The compact number format is defined by Unicode Locale Data Markup Language (LDML) defined as `http://unicode.org/reports/tr35/tr35-numbers.html#Compact_Number_Formats`.

Use the `getCompactNumberInstance()` factory method in the `NumberFormat` class to obtain an instance of the `CompactNumberFormat` class:

- `NumberFormat getCompactNumberInstance()`

- `NumberFormat getCompactNumberInstance(Locale, NumberFormat. Style formatStyle)`

The no-args `getCompactNumberInstance()` method uses the default locale and the short number format.

Listing 8-5 contains a complete program to demonstrate formatting numbers in their compact format. The program formats two integers in English-US, German-Germany, and Hindi-Indian locales. Notice the rounding of numbers in different locales.

Listing 8-5. Formatting Numbers in Their Compact Forms

```java
// CompactNumbers.java
package com.jdojo.misc;

import java.text.NumberFormat;
import java.util.Locale;
import static java.text.NumberFormat.Style.LONG;
import static java.text.NumberFormat.Style.SHORT;

public class CompactNumbers {
    public static void main(String[] args) {
        printCompact(24000, Locale.US);
        printCompact(1969, Locale.US);

        printCompact(24000, Locale.GERMANY);
        printCompact(1969, Locale.GERMANY);

        Locale hindiIndia = new Locale("hi", "IN");
        printCompact(24000, hindiIndia);
        printCompact(1969, hindiIndia);
    }

    public static void printCompact(int num, Locale locale) {
        NumberFormat shortFormatter
                = NumberFormat.getCompactNumberInstance(locale, SHORT);
```

```
        NumberFormat longFormatter
                = NumberFormat.getCompactNumberInstance(locale, LONG);
        String shortStr = shortFormatter.format(num);
        String longStr = longFormatter.format(num);
        System.out.printf("%s: %d, %s, %s%n",
            locale, num, shortStr, longStr);
    }
}
```

```
en_US: 24000, 24K, 24 thousand
en_US: 1969, 2K, 2 thousand
de_DE: 24000, 24.000, 24 Tausend
de_DE: 1969, 1.969, 2 Tausend
hi_IN: 24000, 24 हज़ार, 24 हज़ार
hi_IN: 1969, 2 हज़ार, 2 हज़ार
```

Unicode Support

The Java platform keeps up with the latest Unicode Standards. Here are the Java different versions and the supported Unicode versions:

- Java 10 supports Unicode Standard version 8.0.0.

- Java 11 supports Unicode Standard version 10.0.0.

- Java 12 supports Unicode standard version 11.0, plus the Japanese Era code point, U+32FF, from the first version of the Unicode Standard after 11.0 that assigns the code point.

- Java 13 supports Unicode Standard version 12.1.

The Files Class

The following methods have been added to the Files class:

- String readString(Path path) throws IOException

- String readString(Path path, Charset cs) throws IOException

- Path writeString(Path path, CharSequence csq, OpenOption...
  options) throws IOException

- Path writeString(Path path, CharSequence csq, Charset cs,
  OpenOption... options) throws IOException

- long mismatch(Path path, Path path2) throws IOException

The readString() and writeString() methods were added in Java 11. The readString() method reads content of a file as a String. The writeString() method writes a CharSequence such as String and StringBuilder to a file.

The mismatch() method was added in Java 12. It finds a mismatch in the two specified files by comparing their contents byte by byte. It returns -1L if there is no mismatch in their contents. Otherwise it returns the position of the first mismatched byte. Two files are considered to match if one of the following conditions is true:

- The two specified paths locate the same file.

- Two files are of the same size and have the same contents compared byte to byte.

Listing 8-6 contains a complete program to demonstrate reading and writing string to files and testing two files for a mismatch. You may get a different output.

Listing 8-6. Reading and Writing Strings to Files and Testing Two Files for a Mismatch

```
// FilesTest.java
package com.jdojo.misc;

import java.io.IOException;
import java.nio.file.Files;
import java.nio.file.Path;
import java.nio.file.Paths;

public class FilesTest {
    public static void main(String[] args) throws IOException {
        // Two files and their contents
        String text1 = "Hello, Text1";
        String text2 = "Hello, Text2";
        Path file1 = Paths.get("greeting1.txt");
```

```
        Path file2 = Paths.get("greeting2.txt");

        // Ensure test files exist. If they do not exist, create them.
        createTestFile(file1, text1);
        createTestFile(file2, text2);

        printMismatch(file1, file2);
        printMismatch(file1, file1);
    }

    public static void createTestFile(Path file, String text)
            throws IOException {
        Path absPath = file.toAbsolutePath();
        if (Files.exists(file) && Files.isRegularFile(file)) {
            System.out.printf("Information: %s exists.%n", absPath);
        } else {
            // Write the text to the file
            System.out.printf("Created %s.%n", absPath);
            Files.writeString(file, text);
        }

        // Print the contents of the file
        String str = Files.readString(file);
        System.out.printf("%s contains:%n%s%n", absPath, str);
    }

    public static void printMismatch(Path file1, Path file2)
            throws IOException {
        long pos = Files.mismatch(file1, file2);
        if (pos == -1L) {
            System.out.printf("%s and %s matched.%n",
                    file1.toAbsolutePath(), file2.toAbsolutePath());
        } else {
            System.out.printf("%s and %s mismatched at position %d.%n",
                    file1.toAbsolutePath(), file2.toAbsolutePath(), pos);
        }
    }
}
```

```
Created C:\Java13Revealed\greeting1.txt.
C:\Java13Revealed\greeting1.txt contains:
Hello, Text1
Created C:\Java13Revealed\greeting2.txt.
C:\Java13Revealed\greeting2.txt contains:
Hello, Text2
C:\Java13Revealed\greeting1.txt and C:\Java13Revealed\greeting2.txt
mismatched at position 11.
C:\Java13Revealed\greeting1.txt and C:\Java13Revealed\greeting1.txt matched.
```

The program creates two text files named greeting1.txt and greeting2.txt in the current directory with their contents as "Hello, Text1" and "Hello, Text2", respectively. If these files already exist, the program does not create them. The program prints the informational message such as files' path and their contents. In the end, it compares files for a mismatch and prints the position where the first mismatch is found. The mismatch position is zero-based. That is, if the first bytes in files do not match, the mismatch() method returns zero. The output differs between the first and the subsequent runs.

Collections

There are two changes to the Collection API. Java 10 added a static copyOf() factory method to List, Set, and Map interfaces, which allows you to create an unmodifiable List, Set, and Map from another collection. Java 11 added a new default method named toArray(IntFunction<T[]> generator) to the Collection<E> interface, which can be used to pass in *an array constructor reference* to copy elements of a collection to an array of specific type. I will explain these additions in next sections.

Creating Unmodifiable Copies of Collections

Java 10 added a static copyOf() factory method to List, Set, and Map interfaces. The method returns an unmodifiable List, Set, or Map. It is declared as

- <E> List<E> copyOf(Collection<? extends E> coll)

- <E> Set<E> copyOf(Collection<? extends E> coll)

- <K, V> Map<K,V> copyOf(Map<? extends K,? extends V> map)

The copyOf() method that returns a List is in the List interface, the one that returns a Set is in the Set interface, and the one that returns a Map is in the Map interface. The source collection must not be null, and it must not contain a null element. In the case of a Map, the Map should not contain any null key or value. The elements in the returned List are in the iteration order of the specified collection. The returned collection from the copyOf() method is unchanged even if the source collection is modified.

Listing 8-7 contains a complete program to demonstrate the use of the copy factory method in the List interface. Using this method for a Set or Map would be very similar.

Listing 8-7. Using the copyOf() Method of the List Interface to Create an Unmodifiable List

```java
// UnmodifiableListTest.java
package com.jdojo.misc;

import java.util.List;
import java.util.ArrayList;
import java.util.Comparator;

public class UnmodifiableListTest {
    public static void main(String[] args) {
        // Create a modifiable list
        List<String> names = new ArrayList<>();
        names.add("John");
        names.add("Buddy");
        names.add("Vishwa");
        names.add("Amy");

        // Copy the modifiable list into an unmodifiable list
        List<String> namesCopy = List.copyOf(names);

        // Print both lists
        System.out.println("\nAfter copying the original list:");
        System.out.println("names: " + names);
        System.out.println("namesCopy: " + namesCopy);

        // Let us add a name to the modifiable list
        names.add("Mamta");
```

```
        // Print both lists
        System.out.println("\nAfter adding a name to the original list:");
        System.out.println("names: " + names);
        System.out.println("namesCopy: " + namesCopy);

        // Let us try sorting the unmodifiable list
        try {
            namesCopy.sort(Comparator.naturalOrder());
            System.out.println("\nSorted namesCopy: " + namesCopy);
        } catch (Exception e) {
            System.out.println("\nCannot sort an unmodifiable list");
        }
    }
}
```

```
After copying the original list:
names: [John, Buddy, Vishwa, Amy]
namesCopy: [John, Buddy, Vishwa, Amy]

After adding a name to the original list:
names: [John, Buddy, Vishwa, Amy, Mamta]
namesCopy: [John, Buddy, Vishwa, Amy]

Cannot sort an unmodifiable list
```

Converting Collections to an Array

The Collection<E> interface contains an overloaded toArray() method to convert a collection to an array:

- Object[] toArray()

- <T> T[] toArray(T[] a)

- default <T> T[] toArray(IntFunction<T[]> generator)

If you do not have an array and can deal with Object[], use the toArray() method, which creates an Object[] that contains the elements of the collection. If you want the returned array to be of the same type as the collection, you should not use this method.

255

If you already have an array and want to reuse the array to copy the elements of the collection to the array, use the toArray(T[] a) method. The returned array type is the same as the passed-in array type. If the passed-in array is big enough to hold all elements of the collection, the same array is used to copy the collection. If the passed-in array is bigger than the collection, the first element in the array after the collection elements is set to null. If the collection does not contain null values, the index of the first null in the array will give you the size of the collection from which the elements were copied to the array. If the size of the passed-in array is smaller than the collection, a new array is created.

Java 11 added the default toArray(IntFunction<T[]> generator) method. Use this method when you do not have an array. You can use an array constructor reference as its argument. The method creates an array, copies the collection, and returns the array. The default implementation calls the generator function with zero and passes the returned array to the toArray(T[] a) method. The following snippet uses this version of the toArray() method to copy elements of a list to an array:

```
List<String> namesList = List.of("Buddy", "John", "Lisa");

// Use the toArray(IntFunction<T[]> generator) method passing a
// String[] constructor reference to copy the list to an array
String[] namesArray = namesList.toArray(String[]::new)
```

Listing 8-8 contains a complete program that uses all three versions of the toArray() method to copy a list to an array.

Listing 8-8. Copying the Elements of a Collection to an Array

```java
// CollectionToArray.java
package com.jdojo.misc;

import java.util.Arrays;
import java.util.List;

public class CollectionToArray {
    public static void main(String[] args) {
        // Create a list of strings
        List<String> names = List.of("Buddy", "John", "Lisa");
        System.out.println("List: " + names);
```

```
        // Use the toArray() method to copy list to an Object[]
        Object[] names1 =  names.toArray();
        System.out.println("names1: " + Arrays.toString(names1));

        // Pass a String[] of zero length, so the toArray() method
        // creates a new array of the same size as the list
        String[] names2 = names.toArray(new String[0]);
        System.out.println("names2: " + Arrays.toString(names2));

        // Pass a bigger array to toArray(). The first 3 elements in the
        // array will be overwritten by the elements from the list,
        // the 4th will be set to null, and 5th and 6th will be untouched.
        String[] team = new String[] {"Lu", "Xi", "Ho", "Yo", "To", "Mo"};
        System.out.println("team: " + Arrays.toString(team));

        String[] newTeam = names.toArray(team);
        System.out.println("newTeam: " + Arrays.toString(newTeam));
        System.out.println("team == newTeam: " + (team == newTeam));

        // Use the toArray(IntFunction<T[]> generator) to copy the list
        String[] names3 = names.toArray(String[]::new);
        System.out.println("names3: " + Arrays.toString(names3));
    }
}
```

```
List: [Buddy, John, Lisa]
names1: [Buddy, John, Lisa]
names2: [Buddy, John, Lisa]
team: [Lu, Xi, Ho, Yo, To, Mo]
newTeam: [Buddy, John, Lisa, null, To, Mo]
team == newTeam: true
names3: [Buddy, John, Lisa]
```

New Collectors

Java 10 and 12 added five new collectors, which you can obtain using the new static factory methods added to the `java.util.stream.Collectors` class. I will explain those collectors in the subsequent sections.

Unmodifiable Collectors

Java 10 added four methods to the `java.util.stream.Collectors` class, which return a `Collector` that accumulates elements in an unmodifiable `List`, `Set`, and `Map`:

- `<T> Collector<T,?,List<T>> toUnmodifiableList()`

- `<T> Collector<T,?,Set<T>> toUnmodifiableSet()`

- `<T, K, U> Collector<T,?,Map<K,U>> toUnmodifiableMap (Function<? super T,? extends K> keyMapper, Function<? super T,? extends U> valueMapper)`

- `<T, K, U> Collector<T,?,Map<K,U>> toUnmodifiableMap (Function<? super T,? extends K> keyMapper, Function<? super T,? extends U> valueMapper, BinaryOperator<U> mergeFunction)`

The `Collector` returned from these methods works the same way as returned from the `toList()`, `toSet()` , and `toMap()` methods, except that new methods return unmodifiable `List`, `Set`, and `Map`.

The following snippet of code shows how to filter and collect elements from a modifiable list to an unmodifiable list using the `Collector` returned from the `toUnmodifiableList()` method of the `Collectors` class:

```
import java.util.List;
import java.util.ArrayList;
import static java.util.stream.Collectors.toUnmodifiableList;

// More code goes here...

// Create a modifiable list
List<String> names = new ArrayList<>();
names.add("John");
```

```
names.add("Buddy");
names.add("Vishwa");
names.add("Amy");

// Collect the names, which are less than or equal to four characters
// into an unmodifiable list
List<String> shortNames = names.stream()
                              .filter(name -> name.length() <= 4)
                              .collect(toUnmodifiableList());
// Print both lists
System.out.println("names: " + names);
System.out.println("shortNames: " + shortNames);

// Will throws an UnsupportedOperationException
// shortNames.add("Jaya");
```

```
names: [John, Buddy, Vishwa, Amy]
shortNames: [John, Amy]
```

The Teeing Collector

Sometimes, you want to collect two different types of results from a stream and finally merge the two results into one. Java 12 gives a built-in collector to do just that.

Java 12 added a collector, which uses two collectors to collect distinct types of results and, in the end, uses a BiFunction to merge the results of the two collectors. The merged result is the result of the collector. The new teeing() method in the java.util.stream. Collectors class returns such a collector:

```
<T, R1, R2, R> Collector<T,?,R> teeing(Collector<? super T,?,R1>
downstream1, Collector<? super T,?,R2> downstream2, BiFunction<? super R1,?
super R2,R> merger)
```

Here, downstream1 and downstream2 are two downstream collectors that will process the elements in the stream. R1 and R2 are the result types of the first and the second downstream collectors, respectively. R is the final result type. The merger BiFunction is passed the results of the first and second downstream collectors and its returned value is the result of the collector.

Listing 8-9 contains a complete program to demonstrate the use of the collector that merges results of two other collectors.

Listing 8-9. Using a Collector That Merges Results of Two Other Collectors

```java
// TeeingCollector.java
package com.jdojo.misc;

import java.util.List;
import java.util.Map;
import static java.util.stream.Collectors.averagingDouble;
import static java.util.stream.Collectors.counting;
import static java.util.stream.Collectors.joining;
import static java.util.stream.Collectors.summingDouble;
import static java.util.stream.Collectors.teeing;

public class TeeingCollector {
    public static void main(String[] args) {
        // Concatenate names in the list separating them with a comma and
        // and count the number of names in the final string
        String displayText = List.of("Buddy", "John", "Lisa")
                .stream()
                .collect(teeing(joining(","),
                            counting(),
                            (names, count) -> names + "\nTotal:" + count));

        System.out.println(displayText);

        // Compute sum and average of doubles and collect the two results
        // into a Map.Entry in which key is the sum and value is the average
        Map.Entry<Double, Double> stat = List.of(10.0, 20.0, 30.0, 40.0)
                .stream()
                .collect(teeing(summingDouble(x -> x.doubleValue()),
                            averagingDouble(n -> n),
                            Map::entry));
```

```
        System.out.printf("sum: %f, average: %f%n",
                stat.getKey(), stat.getValue());
    }
}
```

```
Buddy,John,Lisa
Total:3
sum: 100.000000, average: 25.000000
```

The first example uses a list of names. The first argument to the `teeing()` method is a `joining` collector that joins the names with a comma. The second argument is a `counting` collector that counts the number of names. The third argument is a `BiFunction` that accepts the concatenated names and the count and returns a string. The first line in the string contains the concatenated names and the second line contains a string "Total: <count>", where <count> is the name count.

```
String displayText = List.of("Buddy", "John", "Lisa")
    .stream()
    .collect(teeing(joining(","),
                    counting(),
                    (names, count) -> names + "\nTotal:" + count));
```

The second example uses a list of numbers (`Doubles`). The first downstream collector to the `teeing()` method computes the sum of all numbers. The second downstream collector computes the average of all numbers. The third argument is a `BiFunction`, which is a method reference to the `entry()` method of the `Map` interface. The `entry()` method takes a key and a value and returns a `Map.Entry` object. In this case, the key will be the result (the sum) of the first downstream collector. The value will be the result (average) of the second downstream collector.

```
Map.Entry<Double, Double> stat = List.of(10.0, 20.0, 30.0, 40.0)
    .stream()
    .collect(teeing(summingDouble(x -> x.doubleValue()),
                    averagingDouble(n -> n),
                    Map::entry));
```

The Buffer API

Java 13 has added absolute bulk get and put methods to the subclasses of the `java.nio.Buffer` class such as `ByteBuffer`, `CharBuffer`, `IntBuffer`, and so on. The method signatures differ based on the buffer class. The new methods in the `ByteBuffer` class look as follows. For other buffer types, the method signatures differ in the return type and the destination array type.

- `ByteBuffer get(int index, byte[] dst)`
- `ByteBuffer get(int index, byte[] dst, int offset, int length)`
- `ByteBuffer put(int index, byte[] src)`
- `ByteBuffer put(int index, byte[] src, int offset, int length)`

These methods return the `ByteBuffer` itself. The `get()` method lets you copy bytes from the buffer to the specified array without changing the position of the buffer. The `put()` method copies bytes from the specified array to the buffer without changing the position of the buffer.

Java 13 also added a `slice()` method to the `Buffer` class, which lets you specify the absolute range to be sliced. Other buffer classes override this method. The method in the `ByteBuffer` class is declared as follows:

```
ByteBuffer slice(int index, int length)
```

The existing no-args `slice()` method creates a slice of the original buffer starting at the current position, whereas the new method lets you specify the start position and the length. You can think of the new method as providing absolute slicing capability, whereas the old one provides a relative slicing capability.

Java 11 added a `mismatch()` method to the specific type of buffer classes such as `ByteBuffer`, `CharBuffer`, `IntBuffer`, and so on. Its declaration in the `ByteBuffer` class looks as follows:

```
int mismatch(ByteBuffer that)
```

The `mismatch()` method finds and returns the relative index of the first mismatch between this buffer and the specified buffer. The returned value is relative to the position of each buffer, which will be between 0 (inclusive) and smaller of the remaining elements in each buffer. It returns –1 if there is no mismatch.

Refer to the API documentation for specific buffer classes for more details.

Creating File Systems from a Path

Java has been supporting custom file system for quite some time. Creating a new FileSystem instance using a file system provider that lets you treat contents of a file as a file system such as the Zip File System was cumbersome using the existing factory methods in the java.nio.file.FileSystems class. You had to construct a URI to refer to the file. Java 13 has added the following factory methods to the FileSystems class, which lets you use a Path to refer to the file:

- FileSystem newFileSystem(Path path) throws IOException

- FileSystem newFileSystem(Path, Map<String,?> env) throws IOException

- FileSystem newFileSystem(Path, Map<String,?> env, ClassLoader loader) throws IOException

Listing 8-10 contains a complete program to demonstrate the use of the new methods in the FileSystems class. I have used a throws clause in the createFile() and readFile() methods to keep the code simple. The program creates a new file zipfstest.zip file in the current directory, overwriting the file if it already exists.

Listing 8-10. Using New FileSystems API to Create a Zip File System

```java
// ZipFileSystemTest.java
package com.jdojo.misc;

import java.io.IOException;
import java.nio.file.FileSystem;
import java.nio.file.FileSystems;
import java.nio.file.Files;
import java.nio.file.Path;
import java.nio.file.Paths;
import java.util.Map;

public class ZipFileSystemTest {
    public static void main(String[] args) {
        // Path to the zip file that will be used as a file system
        Path path = Paths.get("zipfstest.zip");
        System.out.println("Using Zip File System: "
```

```
                + path.toAbsolutePath());

    // Store the properties of the Zip File System in a Map
    Map<String, String> env = Map.of("create", "true",
                                     "encoding", "UTF-8");

    // Create a Zip File system and use it to write and read a file
    try (FileSystem fs = FileSystems.newFileSystem(path, env)) {
        String fileName = "greeting.txt";

        // Create a file with some text, if the file does not exist.
        createFile(fs, fileName);

        // Read the contents of the file in the zip file
        readFile(fs, fileName);
    } catch (IOException e) {
        e.printStackTrace();
    }
}

public static void createFile(FileSystem fs, String fileName)
        throws IOException {
    Path filePath = fs.getPath(fileName);
    if (Files.exists(filePath)) {
        System.out.printf("The %s file exists in %s.%n", filePath, fs);
        return;
    }

    // Create a file and add a greeting to the file
    Files.writeString(filePath, "Hello, ZIP File System!");
    System.out.printf("Created a %s file in %s.%n", filePath, fs);
}

public static void readFile(FileSystem fs, String fileName)
        throws IOException {
    Path filePath = fs.getPath(fileName);

    // Read the contents of the file
    String text = Files.readString(filePath);
```

```
        System.out.printf("Contents of %s:%n%s%n", fileName, text);
    }
}
```

The main() method creates a Path from the zipfstest.zip file name. It stores the properties for the Zip File system, which it creates later, in a Map. It stores two properties "create" and "encoding". The "create" property is set to "true", meaning that if the zip file does not exist, it will be created. The "encoding" property sets "UTF-8" as the encoding for the file system.

```
Path path = Paths.get("zipfstest.zip");
```

```
// Store the properties of the Zip File System in a Map
Map<String, String> env = Map.of("create", "true",
                                 "encoding", "UTF-8");
```

The program creates a new file system inside a try-with-resources block, so the file system is closed automatically after its use.

```
try (FileSystem fs = FileSystems.newFileSystem(path, env)) {
    // ...
} catch (IOException e) {
    e.printStackTrace();
}
```

The createFile() method checks if a greeting.txt file exists in the file system. If the file exists, it prints a message to this effect. Otherwise, it creates this file in the zipfstest.zip file and writes one line of greeting to the file.

The readFile() method reads the contents of the greeting.txt file in the zip file and prints them to the standard output.

When I run the program for the first time, I get the following output. You may get a different output.

```
Using Zip File System: C:\Java13Revealed\zipfstest.zip
Created a greeting.txt file in zipfstest.zip.
Contents of greeting.txt:
Hello, ZIP File System!
```

When I run the program for the second time, I get the following output. You may get a different output.

```
Using Zip File System: C:\Java13Revealed\zipfstest.zip
The greeting.txt file exists in zipfstest.zip.
Contents of greeting.txt:
Hello, ZIP File System!
```

Other Significant Changes in JDK11

The following are some of the significant changes in JDK11 that may impact you when you migrate your Java applications to use JDK11 or later:

- No JRE and Server JRE downloads are available from Oracle.

- No 32-bit Windows download is available.

- Java Web Start, Java Plugin, and Java Control Panel are not available in JDK.

- JavaFX is no longer included in the JDK. It is now available as a separate download from `https://openjfx.io/`.

- The Java EE and CORBA modules were removed. These modules were deprecated for removal in JDK 9. As a result, JAXB and JAX-WS are no longer bundled with JDK11. Refer to JEP 320 at `http://openjdk.java.net/jeps/320` for more details.

Summary

Several JDK tools and Java APIs have been deprecated and removed in last few versions of the JDK. JDK10 has removed the `javah` tool. JDK11 has deprecated the Nashorn JavaScript engine and the Pack200 tools. JDK11 has removed the `appletviewer` tool. JDK13 has deprecated the `rmic` tool for removal in a future release. Java 13 has deprecated the Swing Motif Look and Feel and does not support it on macOS.

The `traceInstructions()` and `traceMethodCalls()` methods in the `java.lang.Runtime` class were deprecated in Java 9 for removal in a future release and have been removed in Java 13.

The destroy() and stop(Throwable) methods in the Thread class have been removed in Java 11.

JDK12 introduced the JVM Constants API, which is a low-level API to deal with how entries in a constant pool of class files are described by libraries and tools, which manipulates the bytecodes. As a developer, you will not need to use this API in your applications. The API is in the java.lang.constant package in the java.base module.

The String class has received several new methods in Java 11 through Java 13. Many of them deal with multiline strings.

Java 11 added three methods to the String class that removes leading/trailing, leading, and trailing whitespaces: strip(), stripLeading(), and stripTrailing().

Java 11 also added an isBlank() method to the String class, which returns true if the string contains only whitespaces and returns false otherwise.

You can use the lines() method of the String class to obtain a stream of lines in a string. A line in a string is defined as a sequence of zero or more characters followed by a line terminator, which can be "\n", "\r", or "\r\n".

The repeat(int count) method in the String class returns a string whose content is the concatenation of the string repeated count times.

Java 12 added a transform(Function<? super String,? extends R> f) method to the String class, which transforms the string into another object by applying a Function. The Function accepts a String and returns an object of any type.

The no-args orElseThrow() method was added to the Optional<T> class in Java 10. If the Optional contains a value, the method returns the value. Otherwise, it throws a java.util.NoSuchElementException runtime exception. Java 11 added an isEmpty() method that returns true if the Optional is empty and false otherwise.

Java 11 has added a new not() static method to the Predicate<T> interface, which returns the negation of the specified Predicate.

Java 12 added a CompactNumberFormat class to the java.text package in the java.base module. It is a subclass of the NumberFormat class. It formats a decimal number in its compact form. A compact form of a number is suitable to be used where space is limited to display the number. For example, instead of displaying one billion as 1000000000, you can display it in a compact form like 1B or 1 billion. Use the getCompactNumberInstance() factory method in the NumberFormat class to obtain an instance of the CompactNumberFormat class.

Java 10 supports Unicode Standard version 8.0.0. Java 11 supports Unicode Standard version 10.0.0. Java 12 supports Unicode standard version 11.0, plus the Japanese Era code point, U+32FF, from the first version of the Unicode Standard after 11.0 that assigns the code point. Java 13 supports Unicode Standard version 12.1.

The readString() and writeString() methods were added to the Files class in Java 11. The readString() method reads the content of a file as a String. The writeString() method writes a CharSequence such as String and StringBuilder to a file.

The mismatch() method was added to the Files class in Java 12. It finds a mismatch in the two specified files by comparing their contents byte by byte. It returns -1L if there is no mismatch in their contents. Otherwise it returns the position of the first mismatched byte.

There are two changes to the Collection API. Java 10 added a static copyOf() factory method to List, Set, and Map interfaces to create an unmodifiable List, Set, and Map from another collection. Java 11 added a new default method toArray(IntFunction<T[]> generator) to the Collection interface, which can be used to pass in an array constructor reference to copy elements of a collection to an array of specific type.

Java 10 added three methods to the Collectors class, which return a Collector that accumulates elements in an unmodifiable List, Set, and Map: toUnmodifiableList(), toUnmodifiableSet(), and toUnmodifiableMap(). Java 12 added another type of collector, which uses two collectors to collect distinct types of results and finally uses a BiFunction to merge the results of the two collectors. The merged result is the result of the collector. The new teeing() method in the Collectors class returns such a collector.

Java 13 has added the absolute bulk get and put methods to the subclasses of the java.nio.Buffer class such as ByteBuffer, CharBuffer, IntBuffer, and so on. These methods allow reading from and writing to a buffer in bulk without affecting the current position of the buffer. Java 13 also added a new slice() method in the Buffer class, which lets you specify the absolute range to be sliced.

Java 13 added three factory methods in the FileSystems class that allows to use a Path to create a FileSystem using a file system provider that lets you treat contents of a file as a file system such as the Zip File System. Before Java 13, you had to use a URI to refer to the file representing the file system and other factory methods in the FileSystems class that accepted a URI.

Index

T, U

Printed in the United States
By Bookmasters